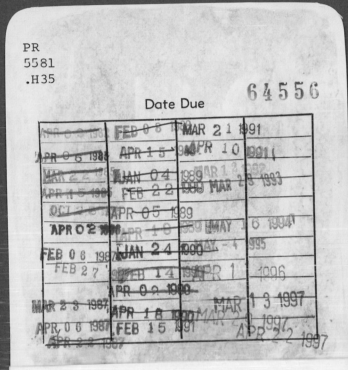

DONALD S. HAIR is a member of the Department of English at the University of Western Ontario and the author of *Browning's Experiments with Genre*.

Tennyson shared the assumptions of his age concerning the value of family life, and treated the domestic as the source of the heroic in both action and character.

This book provides a critical examination of these major Victorian themes as they appear in Tennyson's poetry and demonstrates how the poet's assumptions illuminate his use of elegy, idyl, and epyllion and his treatment of romance.

Professor Hair analyses *In Memoriam*, the *English Idyls*, *The Princess*, and *Idylls of the King*; he examines Tennyson's view of the family as the model of social order, a civilizing influence on the nation, and a place where the greater man, or hero, is nurtured; and he reveals how much of Tennyson's poetry explores the link between domestic and heroic.

He also discusses the patterns into which these pervasive domestic concerns fall, with emphasis on the most significant: separation and reunion. The myth of Demeter and Persephone, the Biblical story of Ruth, and the Sleeping Beauty fairy tale are all versions of Tennyson's treatment of this pattern.

The *English Idyls* and other idyls and epyllia are explored as varying combinations of romance, satire, tragedy, comedy, and irony, with a detailed analysis of *The Princess*, the most complex of these medleys. *Idylls of the King*, wherein the fate of Camelot rests on the marriage of Arthur and Guinevere, is treated as the fullest exploration of the link between domestic and heroic.

Sir Edward Burne-Jones
The Sleeping Beauty 1871
Reproduced with the permission of The City of Manchester Art Galleries

DONALD S. HAIR

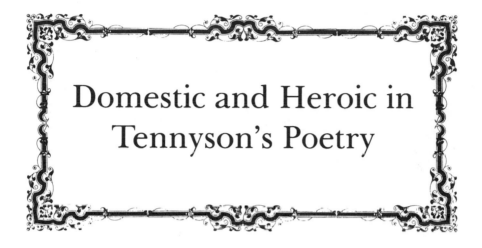

Domestic and Heroic in Tennyson's Poetry

UNIVERSITY OF TORONTO PRESS
Toronto Buffalo London

© University of Toronto Press 1981
Toronto Buffalo London
Printed in Canada
ISBN 0-8020-5530-3

Canadian Cataloguing in Publication Data

Hair, Donald S., 1937–
Domestic and heroic in Tennyson's poetry

Bibliography: p. 239
Includes index.
ISBN 0-8020-5530-3
1. Tennyson, Alfred Tennyson, Baron, 1809–1892 –
Criticism and interpretation. I. Title.
PR5581.H35   821'.8   c80-094853-x

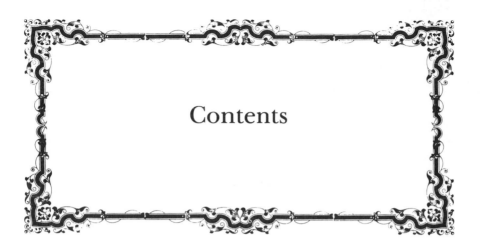

Contents

Contents vi

FOUR: *Idylls of the King* 122

Acknowledgments

In the conclusion to this book, I name scholars to whom I am deeply indebted, for no one writes in isolation about a major poet like Tennyson, and all criticism of him is, I like to think, 'toil cöoperant to an end.' Two teacher-scholars in particular have provided more intellectual stimulus than I can now give an accurate account of; they are F.E.L. Priestley and R.M. Stingle. No critic could ask for better colleagues, nor ones whom he would wish to honour more, than these.

I am grateful to Miss Susan Desmond for typing the manuscript, and to Miss Jean C. Jamieson and Miss Judith Williams of University of Toronto Press for editing it with their customary care. I am grateful, too, to the Faculty of Arts at the University of Western Ontario for funds to cover research expenses over a number of years, and to the Canada Council for two awards: a Research Grant which enabled me to read at libraries in London and at the Tennyson Research Centre in Lincoln, and a Leave Fellowship which gave me the time to write.

The first parts of chapter 4 appeared in a shorter version as 'Tennyson's *Idylls of the King*: Truth "in the fashion of the day,"' in *English Studies in Canada* 2 (Fall 1976) 288–98. The material is used here with the permission of the editor, Professor Lauriat Lane, Jr.

This book has been published with the help of a grant from the Canadian Federation for the Humanities, using funds provided by the Social Sciences and Humanities Research Council of Canada, and a grant from the Publications Fund of University of Toronto Press.

DOMESTIC AND HEROIC IN TENNYSON'S POETRY

Richard Redgrave
Sunday Morning – The Walk from Church (detail) 1846
Reproduced with the kind permission of Mr T.E.V. Craig, London

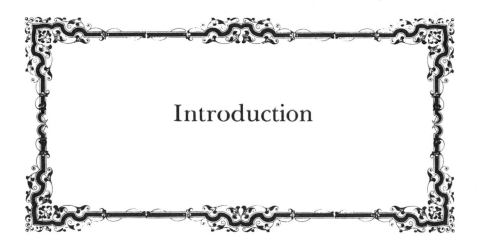

Introduction

The ending of *The Two Voices* has always seemed problematic. Clearly
Tennyson intends the domestic picture to resolve the inconclusive debate,
and clearly it does so by reminding us that the debate is cut off from
ordinary life, and that, in F.E.L. Priestley's words, 'No one decides to live
or not to live, or feels or fails to feel the value of existence, by this sort of
logic or by search for this sort of proof.'[1] If logic and empirical evidence
are inadequate ways by which to affirm the value of life, why is this picture
of a family apparently so effective? Clearly it carries such a weight of
meaning for Tennyson that it could almost be called an icon:

> One walked between his wife and child,
> With measured footfall firm and mild,
> And now and then he gravely smiled.
>
> The prudent partner of his blood
> Leaned on him, faithful, gentle, good,
> Wearing the rose of womanhood.
>
> And in their double love secure,
> The little maiden walked demure,
> Pacing with downward eyelids pure. (412–20)

For the twentieth-century reader this picture seems hopelessly sentimental and archetypally Victorian. But if we were to exercise our historical
imaginations a bit – as indeed we must if we are to respond to this passage
properly – what then would we see?

The patterns are obvious enough: there is a husband and wife united by love above their child; there is a 'little maiden' (note that the child is not a boy) who is enclosed and protected; and there is an observer who approaches this scene and experiences an inner renewal:

> These three made unity so sweet,
> My frozen heart began to beat,
> Remembering its ancient heat.
>
> I blest them, and they wandered on. ...   (421–4)

Even a casual reader of Tennyson must notice that these patterns recur, with variations, in many of his poems. Why does he use these patterns? What is their significance? To what literary styles and kinds do they lend themselves? Why does Tennyson use the idyl(l) so frequently when he is dealing with domestic themes and images? These are the questions that initiated this study, and the analyses that follow are attempts to suggest some of the answers.

Why undertake such a study at all? Because domestic themes and images are a major aspect of Tennyson's poetry, and because the twentieth century has viewed such concerns, for the most part, with little sympathy. I begin with the assumption that Tennyson knew what he was about in using such themes and images; that he was not simply mouthing Victorian platitudes, but was rather making brilliant use of popular ideals; and that he was exploring the implications of these ideals and the various ways in which they could be treated.

It was Ruskin who best defined the popular ideal of the home and the family. In his lecture 'Of Queens' Gardens' in *Sesame and Lilies*, he said:

This is the true nature of home – it is the place of Peace; the shelter, not only from all injury, but from all terror, doubt, and division. In so far as it is not this, it is not home; so far as the anxieties of the outer life penetrate into it, and the inconsistently-minded, unknown, unloved, or hostile society of the outer world is allowed by either husband or wife to cross the threshold, it ceases to be home; it is then only a part of that outer world which you have roofed over and lighted fire in. But so far as it is a sacred place, a vestal temple, a temple of the hearth watched over by Household Gods, before whose faces none may come but those whom they can receive with love, – so far as it is this, and roof and fire are types only of a nobler shade and light, – shade as of the rock in a weary land, and light as of the Pharos in the stormy sea; – so far it vindicates the name, and fulfils the praise, of Home.[2]

Ruskin's description of the home as a place of peace and contentment suggests that it occupied the same place in the Victorian imagination that a pastoral retreat did in the imaginations of earlier ages. Walter Houghton has made the suggestion explicit: 'In the recoil from the City, the home was irradiated by the light of a pastoral imagination. It could seem a country of peace and innocence where life was kind and duty natural.'[3] Given this link between the domestic and the pastoral, one might argue that, in terms of literary conventions, Tennyson replaced the pastoral with the domestic. It is with that idea that I want to begin, by examining a poem which, conventionally, ought to be a pastoral elegy. That poem is *In Memoriam*.[4]

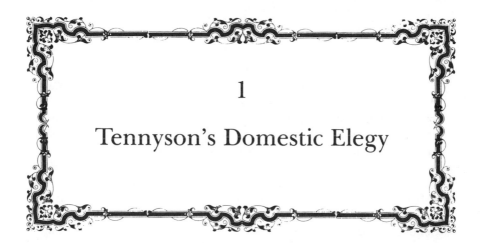

1

Tennyson's Domestic Elegy

The early reviews of *In Memoriam* are instructive, because they record the first reactions to the poem, and because these reactions emphasize one aspect of the poem that has not received much attention from modern critics: the simplicity, truthfulness, and effectiveness with which it portrays the ideals and emotions associated with the home and family life. For modern critics, the domestic references and analogies may seem unfortunate examples of Victorian sentimentality, but for Tennyson's contemporaries, they were one of the most frequently praised aspects of the poem. For in 'the delineation of the domestic affections' and the 'pictures of common landscape and of daily life'[1] the reviewers found a particularly effective combination of the familiar and the ideal. *The Christian Reformer*, for instance, said that 'There need not be a truer proof than this little volume ... that the truest and highest poetry is that of daily human life.'[2] And there is this sentence from the review in *Sharpe's London Journal*: 'The various aspects under which the poet contemplates his bereavement, suggests to him many charming pictures, and ideal resemblances drawn from the beaten path of human life, full of exquisite truth and beauty.'[3] *The Eclectic Review*, too, had much to say about 'the passages of familiar life' and the 'ideal analogies' the poet's sorrow found in them.[4] Tennyson, said the *Westminster and Foreign Quarterly Review*, 'seeks not to adorn the tale he finds. ... He leaves it untouched in its simple perfect beauty, and, from the homely village-hearth, – no home in a picture, but warm with the atmosphere of home, warm with the tenderness of hearts that have loved and mourned, and are now overflowing with grateful pious joy, – he breathes out, rather than utters, the feelings that may well have been experienced by her who "chose the better part." His soul divines, through sympathy with hers, her loss and gain.'[5]

So obvious was the domestic aspect of the poem that one reviewer was apologetic about pointing out 'that the subjects and sentiments introduced into the volume before us are of a domestic and familiar character.'[6] To modern readers, the effect of such 'subjects and sentiments' is far less obvious. For we must learn to see in them the same combination of the real and the ideal that the Victorians saw. The ideal is apparent in the peace, love, harmony, and faith associated with home life, values very different from those of the larger social order, dominated as it was by classical economics and empiricist philosophy. These ideals the Victorians saw (or thought they saw, or wanted to see) made actual in what one reviewer called 'the truly English centre of thought and feeling ... the household fireside,'[7] and the 'household fireside' was common and familiar, not remote and exotic. Accordingly, the home was both an image of desire and aspiration, and a readily accessible experience. In literature, it duplicated almost exactly the function of the pastoral in Theocritus.

The Sicilian landscape of the Theocritean pastorals was real and accessible, and yet it was also an ideal retreat to which the too civilized inhabitants of Alexandria aspired when weighed down by the complexities of urban life. The strength of the pastoral in its pre-Arcadian days was its ability to suggest a fusion of the real and the ideal, to embody ethical and national aspirations in the common and the familiar. Such is the effect that the early reviewers suggest in Tennyson's use of domestic analogies, and it might be argued that, in using the home and the family in this way, Tennyson recovered the tone and feeling of the Theocritean pastoral, but recognized that he could do so in his age only by shifting the centre of attention from the field to the hearth. The result is a brilliant advance in the history of a genre: the replacement of pastoral conventions in the elegy by domestic references and images.

The basic structure of *In Memoriam* is that of the classical elegy, and Tennyson's chief models in English – Milton's *Lycidas* and Shelley's *Adonais* – are pastoral in their conventions, and belong to a long tradition through which the pastoral elegy may be traced back to Theocritus himself. The very length of the tradition meant that the pastoral carried with it associations, particularly of artificiality and insincerity, that Tennyson wished to avoid. Yet the effect of the earliest pastoral elegies was precisely the effect he sought, and the first reviews of the poem bear witness to his success. *The Atlas* speaks of the 'elegies' as 'the touching heart-utterances of a genuine and a noble sorrow' and continues: 'There is a homeliness and a simplicity about them which bear ample testimony to their truth. There is nothing ornate or elaborate in them; they are thoughtful, chastened, and subdued. The images are all of the domestic type – the associations are all redolent of home and the household affections. In this respect, the poems are the very antithesis of Milton's *Lycidas* – a kindred theme, treated with beautiful classicality, more imaginative, but much less true.'[8] Similarly, George Henry Lewes, reviewing the poem in *The Leader*, labelled Moschus' *Lament of Bion*, *Lycidas*, and *Adonais* 'the products of sorrowing Fancy,' and *In Memoriam* the product of 'genuine sorrow.'[9] The review in *The Times*, which may be by Manley Hopkins (father of Gerard Manley Hopkins), defines the conventions of the poem as suitable to the age. 'We regard it as a most happy judgment of Mr. Tennyson,' the reviewer wrote,

that he resolved to forget *Lycidas*, and to place the charm of his own longer elegy in its biographical passages and domestic interiors. We hear nothing of Damon, and are thankful for the silence. The age, whether for better or worse, has left the pastoral behind it. Corydon is forever out of the question with people who have anything to do; the close of the 18th century witnessed his burial. That rather insipid shepherd-swain, whom Pope patronized, will never lead his flock along the banks of the Thames since the South-Western crossed it at Twickenham. Not even Theocritus could have outlived a viaduct.[10]

The early reviewers' observations on the poem put it in a new perspective for us, who have tended to deal mainly with the exploration of faith and doubt, the treatment of evolution, and the use of particular images such as light and darkness. A study of the domestic aspects of the poem enables us to define its structure and character more precisely.

We might begin with Tennyson's own comments on the structure. His statement that the poem 'was meant to be a kind of *Divina Commedia*, ending with happiness'[11] suggests the structure of the classical elegy with its basic movement from grief to consolation, but it should also be noted that the happiness to which Tennyson refers lies in a marriage, described and celebrated in the epithalamium with which the poem concludes. Tennyson's divisions of the poem, moreover, are linked to some major domestic events in it: 'After the Death of A.H.H., the divisions of the poem are made by First Xmas Eve (Section XXVIII), Second Xmas (LXXVIII), Third Xmas Eve (CIV and CV etc.).'[12] It is unfortunate (as F.E.L. Priestley points out) that this chronology has so often been dismissed as 'artificial' because 'it does not correspond to the actual long time of [the poem's] composition.'[13] Tennyson's statement that 'this is a poem, *not* an actual biography'[14] must be constantly kept in mind, as the poet himself insisted, and hence we must recognize the chronology, in Priestley's words, as 'an essential part of the formal structure.'[15] Just how important it is becomes apparent when we consider the domestic nature of the Christmas poems: they not only mark the stages in the shift from grief to consolation, but also embody the spirit and dominant character of the poem. John Forster's review in *The Examiner* was the first to point this out:

And the successive pictures of the recurring festival, haunted by the remembrance of something for ever lost, but gradually softening while it deepens the memory of the dead, embody the spirit of the book and of the writer's intention, in a form which, without abating aught of grandeur or of elevation, imparts to them the most pathetic and homely interest. The genial old English season, with its blended solemnity and joy, comes back again and again, throughout, like the leading phrase in a masterpiece of music.[16]

The recurring pictures of a major domestic festival function in somewhat the same way as Milton's recurring invocations to the pastoral in *Lycidas*: they establish the dominant tone (which the poet may then modify, depart from, or transcend), and they embody themes and images which the poet may develop in each stage of the move from grief to consolation. For these reasons I should like to look at the Christmas poems in some detail.

Alan Sinfield has analysed one aspect of the structure by comparing the first stanzas of each of the three Christmas poems (xxx, lxxviii, and cv) where Tennyson is obviously emphasizing the importance of parallels with differences. 'The prime function of these sections,' Sinfield writes, 'is to provide a series of chronological fixing points against which the poet's changing attitude can be measured, the word order is used to throw into relief the most significant aspects of his response on each occasion.'[17] Thus, the opening phrases of each stanza ('With trembling fingers,' 'Again at Christmas,' and 'Tonight ungathered') suggest a movement from grief to dull repetition to something out of the ordinary. The prominent adverbs in the last lines of the stanzas ('sadly,' 'calmly,' and 'strangely') suggest a similar movement. But there is much more than these details of word order that defines the structure and character of the elegy. We note, in the first place, that the first Christmas poem (section xxx) is preceded by two others that also deal with Christmas, and that the first of these (section xxviii) is about 'The merry merry bells of Yule.' The second Christmas poem (section lxxviii) stands all by itself, and the sections around it are not specifically related to the season. The third Christmas poem (section cv) is, like the first, part of a set of three poems, of which the first (section civ), by repeating the first two lines of section xxviii, invites a comparison with the earlier poem. And when we hear bells again, they are the 'wild bells' of the New Year (section cvi). By extending this set of three poems to include the New Year celebrations, Tennyson is suggesting the progress of the poem from loss to gain. The pattern (three, one, and three) is formal and balanced, and combines in a complex way the changing and the unchanging.

The choice of Christmas itself is a significant one. It was the chief annual festival of family life in Victorian England, and it was permeated with a spirit that was certainly Dickens' chief ideal, and that appeared in many other writers as well – an ideal in which human relations were governed by sympathy and love, and were characterized by harmony and joy. These characteristics expressed themselves in the generosity, hospitality, and jovial goodwill that were appropriate to the holiday season, the 'showered largess of delight / In dance and song and game and jest' that Tennyson mentions in section xxix. But though these family celebrations are important in defining the ideal Tennyson is using in the poem, the archetype, the first Christmas, is equally important. Tennyson refers to 'the birth of Christ' in the first line of section xxviii, and the reference brings to bear on the family celebrations the whole of the Biblical account of this event. The pattern of this event – a pattern Tennyson never refers to explicitly, but which underlies his acceptance of Hallam's death – is, in terms of myth, the story of the birth of a child who will usher in a new golden age. The myth enables us to see the heroic dimensions of domestic life. However commonplace the home may be, it is also the place which nurtures the better, more fully developed man. In the child, then, present and future, domestic and heroic, are fused. This fusion, and its implicit reference to the myth of the birth of the hero, is one of the most frequently recurring aspects in Tennyson's treatment of domestic themes and images. Such treatment is the development of an older pattern. We recall how often the pastoral life was linked with, or was a preparation for, the heroic life, particularly in the classical figure of Paris, and in the Biblical figure of David. That pattern provides the context for these Christmas poems, and the basis for the elegy's conventional movement toward consolation. The consolation takes several forms: in the epithalamium, a child is conceived; Hallam is recognized as a type of the perfect man; and the poet himself, through an heroic inner struggle, has grown in spiritual strength, and is symbolically reborn.

The bells in sections xxviii, civ, and cvi are the evangelists of this pattern. In xxviii, the bells ring out the traditional Christmas message

('Peace and goodwill, to all mankind'), and their message contrasts with
the poet's mood, which is one of pain and sorrow. Nonetheless, says
Tennyson, they rule his 'troubled spirit' because 'they controlled me when
a boy.' The effect of the bells is curiously ambiguous: on the one hand, his
response suggests a reliance on habit and custom (a suggestion that is
developed in the account of the Christmas festivities in sections xxix and
xxx); on the other, he associates the bells with his own childhood and
development, and, just as the bells played a part in his growing up, so their
renewed influence here may play a part in yet a further stage of growth.
The kind of growth which in fact takes place is apparent in section civ.
The landscape of the poem is new and unfamiliar, since the poet has
moved away from his childhood home. Here there is 'A single church' and
'A single peal of bells' rather than 'Four voices of four hamlets round.'
Conditions are the same in the two poems ('The moon is hid, the night is
still'), but in xxviii the bells answer one another as if lost in the mist; in civ
the bells 'peal' rather than 'answer,' and they are 'folded in the mist.' The
phrase suggests both security and mystery (for the mist is related to the
veil image that Tennyson uses elsewhere) as opposed to the anxiety of
xxviii. There is even a pattern of irony in the reversal. The familiar bells in
xxviii ironically arouse in him a sense of fear; the unfamiliar bells in civ
have just the opposite effect. The linking of the familiar with grief and
anxiety, and of the unfamiliar with consolation, makes the general pattern of the elegy psychologically realistic. The same fleshing out of the
genre's skeleton is evident in other details. There is a sense in section
xxviii of the flux of things ('Each voice four changes on the wind, / That
now dilate, and now decrease') while in civ there is a sense of order and
calmness ('this hour of rest'). There is a sense in section xxviii of looking
backward, since the bells awaken memory and the emotions associated
with these particular sensations; in civ, however, 'not a memory strays': 'all
is new unhallowed ground.' The consolation which is apparent in the
second reaction to the bells Tennyson makes more precise in section cvi,
'Ring out, wild bells.' This time the bells are those of New Year's Eve
rather than Christmas Eve. They no longer evoke in Tennyson the associations of his childhood, but rather prophesy the moral and spiritual
development of man, development in which both Hallam and Tennyson
have had a part. The heroic and the divine are in a dynamic state of
becoming: 'Ring in the Christ that is to be.'

It is in the context of the bells and all that they signify that the actual
Christmas celebrations take place. In section xxix, the poet, as one would
expect, is bitterly conscious of Hallam's absence. The sense of emptiness,

of a place unfilled, is of course the chief way in which death manifests itself in the family circle, and absence is the 'compelling cause to grieve' which 'daily vexes household peace.' (The simple phrase, 'household peace,' is one of several such phrases in the poem that sum up the domestic ideal, and hence, in spite of the simple diction, it carries a considerable weight of meaning.) Moreover, the promised child is not yet born, as the 'cold baptismal font,' incongruously decked with holly boughs, suggests. The time corresponds to that stage in the old fertility rituals where the dead god is mourned, and the reborn god is not yet manifest. The strong emotions aroused by the absence and the sense of promise unfulfilled dominate the Christmas celebrations, and, as a result, the observances depend to a large extent upon habit, on 'Use and Wont, / That guard the portals of the house.' 'Use and Wont' are limited things, like the Will, but, also like the Will, they serve a useful function in the early stages of the poet's grief. Just as the Will strives for a knowledge of Hallam in the afterlife (a striving that becomes unnecessary when a vision occurs 'beyond the will' as in section lxx), so 'Use and Wont' maintain the form of the festivities, until a new spirit and understanding express themselves in new ways, and make the old forms unnecessary. Tennyson describes 'Use and Wont' as 'old sisters' and 'gray nurses.' Both sisters and nurses are domestic figures, and the latter in particular are associated with nurturing and growth. But this aspect of the image is only implicit. Tennyson emphasizes their 'loving nothing new,' their associations with the past. The ambiguity of the final sentence ('They too will die') suggests explicitly a parallel with Hallam's death, and implicitly a time when 'Use and Wont' will be superseded by something better.

I have already noted, by referring to Alan Sinfield's analysis, the way in which Tennyson provides a sense of movement and progression by varying words and phrases within parallel syntactical units. Devices such as this reinforce our sense of the extent to which the poem as a whole is based upon the traditional structure of the elegy, with its movement from grief to consolation. But when we examine the three Christmas poems carefully, we notice a curious thing: in spite of the sense of movement and progression, there is much in each poem that does not change. Each refers to death and to the sorrow of which it is the occasion; and each refers to various things which console and comfort the mourner. Each poem, in short, reflects in miniature the structure of the entire elegy. But each poem treats the elements of this structure (the expression of grief and the acceptance of death) in a different way. The tone is different in each poem; Tennyson emphasizes different aspects of the elegy in each;

and he combines in different ways the elements that he chooses to repeat. One might carelessly conclude that, in view of the repetition of these elements, the resolution is more apparent than real. But one should read more carefully. The stubborn affirmation which the family makes in the first Christmas poem must be filled out by experience, and harmonized with many other experiences of a different and seemingly irreconcilable kind. The best analogy for this movement is the Prologue and its place in the structure of the whole poem. If the elegy is a movement from doubt to faith, then the Prologue should be the epilogue, a statement of the position to which Tennyson fights his way. But Tennyson affirms his faith throughout the entire poem, and the statement in the Prologue is the position where he begins. The dryness of the statement indicates that it is (to change the metaphor) a skeleton which must be fleshed out by experience. The faith of the Prologue must be harmonized with doubt, sorrow, and a variety of other complex ideas and emotions, until a larger unity is achieved, until (in the words of the Prologue itself) 'mind and soul, according well, / May make one music as before, / But vaster' (27–9). A movement toward the same kind of resolution is apparent in the three Christmas poems.

The first Christmas (section xxx) is full of jarring incongruities. Christmas should be a time of joy, but the family's Christmas Eve fell 'sadly.' The holly, a symbol of continuing vitality through the winter months, is hung 'With trembling fingers.' Outside there is wind and rain, and the inclement weather is, as one would expect, associated with the family's emotions. 'A rainy cloud possessed the earth'; 'the winds were in the beech: / We heard them sweep the winter land.' The elements do not nourish the earth, but rather seem determined to maintain the sterility of winter. The 'old pastimes' suggested by 'Use and Wont' are permeated with a sense both of the death which has just taken place, and of the death which must claim each of the celebrants. Nonetheless, the family stubbornly affirms the ideal of family life and the idea of immortality. The former is evident when the members of the family sit 'in a circle hand-in-hand.' The circle is a familiar symbol of perfection and harmony, and the joining of hands suggests the love and intimacy of family life. Yet the gesture is not without incongruity. The family members are conscious of the threat of death, the 'one mute Shadow watching all' (the 'mute Shadow' may also be the dead Hallam), and their joining of hands is as much an expression of anxiety as it is of love. Nonetheless, this literal representation of the family circle provides a context in which the affirmation that follows can be made. They sing a song, talk about death, and sing a second song, and the sequence is clearly a movement toward

consolation. The first song fits the pattern of incongruity already established: it is 'A merry song we sang with him / Last year,' but its associations
make it in effect a lament for Hallam. The 'merry song' is accompanied by
tears; the tears and the song cannot be reconciled, and yet the song must
be sung and the tears shed. The incongruity itself leads to a 'gentler
feeling' and an affirmation which is a turning point: 'surely rest is meet.'
But this affirmation too is juxtaposed with tears, a very human reaction,
and with a silence that suggests doubt. The second song, which affirms
immortality and the progression of the soul through a series of spiritual
states, is given in some detail. The progression of the soul is an interesting
one, since it conforms to the pattern in which the heroic and the divine
develop out of the humble and the domestic (the dead man 'Pierces the
keen seraphic flame / From orb to orb, from veil to veil'). The emotion
which accompanies this song is not specified. The poet simply says, 'Our
voices took a higher range,' and the phrase 'higher range' is curiously
unemotional; it may refer to a higher musical key, or to a melody that
makes more varied use of higher notes, or to the more daring thought the
song deals with. At any rate, the song is an affirmation of faith that is not
yet reconciled with the complex emotions that must accompany it. The
incompleteness of the affirmation is again in evidence in the final stanza,
which introduces a favourite Tennysonian image, the dawn. It is generally recognized that light and dark are opposed at the beginning of *In
Memoriam*, but mysteriously fused as the poet accepts death as part of a
wider life, and doubt as part of a more comprehensive faith. Here the
imperative suggests a separation rather than a fusion: 'Draw forth the
cheerful day from night.' In spite of this incompleteness, the dominant
tone of the final stanza is a happy one, and the imperatives merge into a
collect, a petition for light and hope. Nonetheless, each part of the move
from grief to consolation in this section is separate and distinct. Each
stage, one hastens to add, does in some measure grow out of the preceding one, and the rhythm of the elegy's structure is there, but the
complex interweaving of thoughts and emotions is absent. Stage is added
to stage, but not yet fused and accepted as a total pattern.

The second Christmas poem (section lxxviii) also moves from grief to
consolation and, although it repeats many of the elements of the first
Christmas, it uses them in a different way. The sense of incongruity that
permeated the first Christmas has disappeared; a sense of the unity of all
things is potential but not yet actual. The second Christmas is, as one
would expect, transitional. The earliest stages of grief are passed; the
resolution has not yet come.

The activities of the first Christmas are repeated here, for 'Use and

Wont' are still playing their part: the holly is woven round the hearth; games are played; songs are sung. Outside there is 'silent snow' and calm air, and again these elements of the weather are associated with the family's emotions. The rain that has become snow recalls the 'chilling tears, / That grief hath shaken into frost!' of section iv, but the emotions here seem calm and dormant rather than pent up and frozen. There is now no suggestion that the winter landscape is a waste land. Instead, the poet is conscious of its beauty: 'The yule-clog sparkled keen with frost.' Other details suggest potential vitality. In section xxx, the wind which swept the land was linked with anxiety aroused by the sense of Death watching all. In section lxxviii this wind of death and destruction has disappeared, and, although the poet says there is no wind, there is at least the sense that a different kind of wind is present but not yet active. This sense is evident in the phrases 'wing of wind' and 'brooding slept.' The words suggest Milton's description of the Holy Spirit as a dove brooding over the vast abyss before the creation; 'slept' recalls the description of death as sleep which marked the turning point in section xxx; and the wind which is absent will eventually appear as the Pentecostal wind in section xvc. The images, then, suggest potential creativity, in spite of the negative 'No wing of wind,' and in spite of the fact that that which 'brooding slept' is 'The quiet sense of something lost.' This 'quiet sense' is very different from the 'awful sense / Of one mute Shadow watching all' in section xxx, and is a good indication of the change of tone.

Though the activities of the first Christmas are repeated, the emphasis now falls on different aspects. Song, which played such a major part in section xxx, is now simply one of a list of activities. The games in section xxx were a preliminary activity and represented a 'vain pretence / Of gladness'; in section lxxviii they are the main activity. They are still a pretence – the *tableaux vivants* are 'mimic' pictures – but the pretence has a curious vitality, as the phrase 'The mimic picture's breathing grace' indicates. It suggests not only the lifelikeness and skill of the performance, but inspiration, the breathing into the 'mimic picture' of life from a divine source. As such, it recalls the 'fair face' of the vision of section lxx, and foreshadows the vision of section xcv, where Hallam's letters (which might be considered a 'mimic picture') breathe grace to the poet.

The affirmations which the family made so explicitly in their second song in section xxx are not in evidence here, where the affirmation is more subtle and complex. The fourth of the five stanzas is a series of questions rather than assertions, and the questions recall, in form if not in substance, the uncertainties and speculations of the whole preceding part of the elegy. The assertions in the final stanza are not specifically about immortality, but affirm rather that there is a spiritual dimension to our being. 'Mystic frame' suggests a spiritual being; our physical frames, like words, 'half reveal / And half conceal the Soul within ' (section v). The word 'deep' in the phrase 'deep relations' is one of those deliberately vague words that suggest the unknown dimensions of spiritual reality. There is an acceptance in this stanza of the changes brought by time, an attitude that foreshadows the poet's acceptance of the ultimate change, death. The move from 'The quiet sense of something lost' to the affirmation of the reality of 'all this mystic frame' parallels the movement from the 'awful sense / Of one mute Shadow watching all' to the affirmation of the song in section xxx, but the poet is here aware of greater subtleties and complexities, and consequently the affirmation is both less dramatic and more assured.

The third Christmas poem (section cv) makes use of this same movement, but in a tone that is different again from that of the first two Christmases. This poem is permeated with a sense of strangeness, and this feeling comes about for a variety of reasons. The family is, first of all, now in an unfamiliar landscape ('We live within the stranger's land'). Moreover, they deliberately avoid their customary ways of celebrating Christmas (there is no holly, 'neither song, nor game, nor feast'), for 'Use and Wont' have now outlived their usefulness: 'For who would keep an ancient form / Through which the spirit breathes no more?' These lines indicate the main reason for a sense of strangeness: an awareness of the spiritual world manifesting itself in a manner so comprehensive that it transcends the familiar and the domestic.

Five and one-half stanzas of this seven-stanza poem are given over to a description of the ways in which the family will *not* celebrate Christmas. All of the domestic festivities which were so important in the first two Christmases are here rejected, and the imperative with which the poet begins ('let us leave') sets the tone for the whole section. The death to which Tennyson refers explicitly is not Hallam's, but rather that of the poet's father, and the reference is in the pastoral terms that, in *In Memoriam* generally, Tennyson treats as 'an ancient form / Through which the spirit breathes no more':

> Our father's dust is left alone
> And silent under other snows:
> There in due time the woodbine blows,
> The violet comes, but we are gone.

The poet specifies dust rather than spirit, and thereby sets the tone of the stanza as classical and pagan. In that context, the coming of spring is the traditional consolation, and the blooming of the violet the traditional symbol of renewed life. The concluding phrase, 'but we are gone,' indicates how limited this classical consolation is: nature renews herself, but the individual, once gone, is gone forever. The phrase serves other purposes here as well. It refers literally to the family's move to its new home, away from the place where their father is buried. It contributes to the general movement in this section away from the familiar and the customary and toward the strange and the mysterious.

Just as the second stanza of this section refers explicitly to the death of the poet's father, so the fourth stanza refers obliquely to Hallam's death. The image Tennyson uses is one used widely throughout *In Memoriam*: darkness. 'Cares that petty shadows cast' is a generalization that diminishes the importance of the chief care which *In Memoriam* commemorates. The second line of the stanza, however, accepts these cares as the agents of human development. It is they 'By which our lives are chiefly proved'; that is, tried and made good (the gloss is Bradley's).[18] These cares are to be held in abeyance on Christmas Eve, 'the night I loved,' because it commemorates the past. The commemoration seems to be largely a matter of memory, for the activities that had almost become rituals are explicitly rejected in the next stanza.

An examination of these direct and oblique references to death reveals a pattern in the poem which parallels the movement from grief to consolation in the other Christmas poems. The last phrase of the second stanza ('but we are gone') has a tone of finality that suggests a complete break with the past. In the fourth stanza, however, cares have a purpose, and Christmas Eves (particularly those following Hallam's death, with all their complex emotions) are to be held 'solemn to the past.' The conclusion of the poem completes the pattern. Past, present, and future are indeed linked in a cyclic pattern which, because it moves toward an appointed end, is in fact a spiral: 'Run out your measured arcs, and lead / The closing cycle rich in good.' The lines suggest a cosmic dance, and the image has the same significance here that it had for the Elizabethans. It pictures a universe that is both orderly and dynamic. The dance that is part of the Christmas festivities might have been a reflection of this dynamic order, but the poet deliberately rejects it ('No dance, no motion'). He emphasizes instead an aspect of the image that would have been foreign to the Elizabethans, but not to the nineteenth century: the concept of development through time. Earlier in this same section Tennyson uses the phrase 'growth of time,' and it sums up his affirmation of a purposive movement upward of all living things. The same idea is suggested in his agricultural metaphor ('Long sleeps the summer in the seed') and by the chief symbol with which this section ends: the dawn. There is no sense here that the light is abstracted from the surrounding darkness. Rather, it gathers up everything in a unity so comprehensive that it can be suggested only by symbol: 'What lightens in the lucid east / Of rising worlds by yonder wood.' The periphrasis is deliberate. 'What lightens' is too incomprehensible to be specified in any more precise way, yet he perceives it with absolute clearness, as the phrase 'lucid east' suggests. 'Rising worlds' is juxtaposed with 'Yonder wood,' and the contrast suggests both vastness and the limits of our earthly perspective.

The general effect of the third Christmas poem is a curious one. Death is something in the distant past, and the emotions associated with it are no longer immediate. The poet emphasizes the consolation he has reached, but it is a consolation so vast in scope that it seems difficult to relate ordinary human activities to it. This sense of a gap between the cosmic progression which he affirms and the domestic activities that have provided the context for his experience is magnified by his rejection of the Christmas rituals, each specified and named. The third Christmas, then, is by no means the conclusion of the elegy. What is still required is the bringing together of the cosmic and the domestic, so that vast purposes may be seen working themselves out in the familiar and the ordinary. Tennyson fulfils this requirement in the epithalamium with which he concludes the poem, because, in John Killham's words, 'in marriage we come closest to participating in the cosmic purpose.'[19]

It should now be apparent that the Christmas poems are not simply the marks of an 'artificial' chronology imposed on the elegy, but one of the essential features of its structure, repeating with variations the basic rhythm of the elegy, the movement from grief to consolation, and giving at crucial points (though in different ways) the domestic tone and the domestic ideal that permeates the work. Before examining the completion of the pattern in the epithalamium, however, we must discuss the function of the domestic in each of the divisions of the poem.

We might begin with what the *Eclectic Review* called 'the ideal analogies to itself, [which] the creative sorrow realizes, in familiar life,'[20] particularly as they appear in the first division (sections i to xxvii). Sections vi and viii are especially interesting examples of this particular use of the domestic, because they provide a context for one of the best-known sections, the 'Dark house' lyric (section vii). Of the three sections, vii is the most complex, the most personal, and the most immediate. It is a description of the poet's visit to his friend's house, but, as Sinfield says, 'we feel that the emotional pressure behind the writing is so high that [the description] must refer to something beyond itself'; 'the lack of explicit connections between clauses' encourages us 'to reconstruct from his immediate sensations the poet's state of mind,'[21] and hence the lyric is essentially a symbolist poem. In sections vi and viii, however, there is not the same sense that the poet is trying to convey his immediate experience. The grief is distanced. Though the emotion is the same in all three sections, and is as deeply felt in all three, the technique of the framing sections is very different from that of the central one. The organization is more formal, the structure more logical, the emotion described rather than conveyed. The domestic thus functions in these sections in much the same way as the pastoral conventions would have: it makes universal the poet's private grief. Sections such as these make actual Tennyson's statement: '"I" is not always the author speaking of himself, but the voice of the human race speaking thro' him.'[22]

Section vi begins with commonplaces: 'One writes, that "Other friends remain," / That "Loss is common to the race."' The effect is impersonal and abstract, when compared with the symbol that introduces personal experience in section vii: 'Dark house, by which once more I stand.' The poet does not deny the truth of the aphorisms, but he asserts that they are no comfort to him personally. In the lines 'That loss is common would not make / My own less bitter, rather more,' the last phrase is crucial to both the thought and the structure of this section. The sorrow of others does not diminish but rather intensifies his private grief. Hence the importance of the domestic analogies. The sorrows in these other family situations are not only like his sorrow, but (given his belief in the importance of the home and the family) a part of it, so that his grief is not just personal but comprehensive. Moreover, these analogies appeal to common experiences in his readers, and thus evoke in them something of the quality and intensity of his grief. The artistic problem that Tennyson faced in making this difficult transition from the particular to the general was a loss of the sense of immediate experience, and a tendency towards the abstractions that are commonly the result of an attempt to generalize. Tennyson solves the problem brilliantly, not by rejecting the abstractions with which he begins, but by asserting their truth in exploring the actual emotions over which the language of generalization seems to slide so easily. That is why the phrases 'rather more' and 'Too common!' are crucial, for they turn our attention to the many particular situations that prove the truth of the aphorisms. Tennyson introduces these situations with his own version of the second aphorism: 'Never morning wore / To evening, but some heart did break.' This phrasing, by using the cycle of the day, and by referring to loss as a breaking heart, makes the first more concrete and immediate. The three analogies that follow have the same effect. Each suggests the immediacy of a particular loss, partly because the dramatic apostrophes help create the illusion that the father, mother, and maiden addressed are individuals, and partly because the pattern of irony in each situation conveys the complexity, and evokes the complex responses, of actual experiences.

In spite of these particularizing devices, the effect of section vi is quite different from that of section vii. The organization is more formal and more logical. In effect, Tennyson states a commonplace, and then illustrates it with three little pictures. Each of the first two illustrations fills a single stanza; the third, which is more important in the pattern of the whole elegy, takes up four stanzas. In the final stanza, the poet asks a question about the maiden and about himself, and gives answers to both questions. The syntactical parallels emphasize the similarities among particular losses, and make actual the truth of the exclamation, 'Too common!' There is a linear progression here quite different from the emotional structure of section vii, where our attention is focused on a single complex experience, the house and its associations.

Section vi introduces patterns that are of some importance in the poem as a whole. First, the analogies between the poet and the maiden, and between the poet's loss and her 'perpetual maidenhood,' prepare the way for the pattern whereby the poet pictures himself as a female figure. Secondly, at the beginning of the elegy, we have families broken up or marriages prevented by death; at the end, we have families re-established and a marriage celebrated. Thirdly, in each of the three analogies in section vi, Tennyson focuses, not on the figure who is lost, but on the figure who is left behind at home, like himself. And, in each case, he emphasizes the irony of each figure's lack of knowledge about the death that has taken place, just as he himself thought about Hallam's return when Hallam was in fact already dead. The irony is, rather unexpectedly, an early version of the affirmation with which this first division of the poem ends: ' 'Tis better to have loved and lost / Than never to have loved at all' (section xxvii). In the three cases, the lack of knowledge does not cancel out the love expressed in the three actions: pledging, praying, and adorning oneself to please a lover. The affirmation is only implicit, however, and the chief function of the analogies is to illustrate loss and to suggest the grief that accompanies it.

The structure of section viii is equally formal and logical. The poem falls into two parts of three stanzas each, and each part is devoted to a domestic analogy. The syntax makes the logic apparent. Tennyson begins the first analogy with 'A happy lover,' and then turns to himself: 'So ... I ...' The 'Yet ... So' construction of the second analogy is equally logical, but whereas in the first part of the section he devoted two stanzas to the 'happy lover' and one to himself, in the second he devotes one to the beloved and two to himself. The structure is ordered, balanced, and formal, and it is interesting that it should be so when the thought of the section is a comment on his experience in section vii, where the structure is emotional rather than logical. The theme has to do with perception and with the changed way in which one sees familiar things when a loved one is no longer present. In section vii, Tennyson conveys the experience itself, and it is immediate and personal; in section viii he describes the experience through domestic analogies which, like the analogies in section vi, make the experience both common and particular.

The twentieth century is likely to prefer section vii, and to reject sections vi and viii as examples of Victorian sentimentality. But these sections have an important function, as I have tried to demonstrate, and the domestic analogies would appeal to Victorian readers in a way in which they no longer appeal to us. The same point might be illustrated by comparing sections xix and xx. In section xix, Tennyson likens the alternation of 'my deepest grief,' on the one hand, and 'lesser griefs' and 'lighter moods,' on the other (the last two phrases are from section xx) to the ebb and flow of the rivers Severn and Wye. Section xx makes the same point, but in domestic terms. There Tennyson explores the difference by contrasting the reaction of servants and children to the death of a man who was both master and father. The second poem is no less specific, nor is it even less personal, but in its appeal to common experience and to a common ideal it fills a function that we tend to distrust in poetry. If we are to read the elegy properly, we must attempt to see it in its historical context.

Our sense of historical context is most sorely tried when we come to deal with that pattern which is introduced in this division of the poem, in which Tennyson uses marriage to describe his relationship with Hallam, and, moreover, frequently pictures himself as the female figure. The implications which Freud has taught us to see in such imaginings are simply not relevant here.[23] Tennyson uses marriage because he wants to suggest the kind of relationship which involves the deepest human emotions; he also wants to suggest the ideal nature of the relationship – its creative blending of two diverse natures – and knew that he could count upon the Victorian idealization of marriage to evoke such a response. Moreover, the blurring of the sexual identity of the 'I' in the poem helps make the elegy universal, and the speaker the voice of the human race. The 'I' is masculine in section i, 'the man that loved and lost' (the phrasing is echoed by the affirmation in section xxvii), and in the fully developed analogy between himself and the widower in section xiii. The 'I' is feminine in sections vi and viii, where there is the analogy between the poet and the maiden, and in sections ix and xvii, where the poet refers to himself as a widow. The phrase 'Till all my widowed race be run' appears in both sections ix and xvii, and deserves some consideration. In its context in section ix it appears thus:

> My Arthur, whom I shall not see
> Till all my widowed race be run;
> Dear as the mother to the son,
> More than my brothers are to me.

One notices, first of all, that marriage is one of several family relationships here, and that the mother-son relation has already been used in section vi. Yet marriage seems the most important relationship, because it is introduced first, and because the line itself is repeated elsewhere in *In Memoriam*. The phrasing ('race be run') has Biblical overtones, and Hebrews 12:1 seems particularly relevant: 'Let us lay aside every weight, and the sin which doth so easily beset us, and let us run with patience the race that is set before us.' The race is metaphorically the course of life he must pursue, and although he will clearly be active, the passive verb suggests progress toward an appointed end. 'Widowed race' is thus a very complex image, suggesting both loss (a marriage broken by death) and consolation (rather like that of the Biblical 'fulness of time'). The affirmation of faith is apparent too in the wider structure of the sentence: he will 'not see' Hallam 'Till ...', and the construction indicates a time when Hallam will be restored to him. The phrasing extends the marriage vow ('Till death us do part') through time and into eternity, and suggests both the grief of his present loss and the joy he will ultimately experience.

If we consider Tennyson's use of the marriage metaphor in relation to the older pastoral conventions in the elegy, we can see more clearly how the metaphor works. It is conventional for the pastoral bard to reminisce about his life with the dead shepherd, and their relation is usually that of close friends. Indeed, in sections xxii and xxiii of this poem, Tennyson explicitly uses the older convention, by describing 'our fair companionship,' and by associating it with that most central of all pastoral myths, the Golden Age. The landscape is deliberately Arcadian ('all the lavish hills would hum / The murmur of a happy Pan') and the life ideal:

> And many an old philosophy
>   On Argive heights divinely sang,
>   And round us all the thicket rang
> To many a flute of Arcady.

In section xxiv, Tennyson rejects the myth of the Golden Age by looking at the past more objectively. Similarly, in section xxi, he exposes the inadequacy of the pastoral. There, he portrays himself as a pastoral bard piping a song of mourning for his dead friend. Three passers-by harshly criticize the song, one for its undesirable effect, one for its apparently private and selfish concerns, and one for its failure to take into account wider public concerns. The bard defends his song, but the defence is not very convincing ('I do but sing because I must'). In thus using pastoral elements, Tennyson both links his elegy with the older tradition, and suggests his distance from it. The particulars of the older tradition are to be rejected, but its spirit is to be revitalized by the shift from the pastoral to the domestic. Hence the conventional friendship of rural bard and dead shepherd is replaced by the unconventional marriage by which a poet devoted to the domestic ideal describes his relations with someone who might have been a member of his family.

The effect of such a shift is apparent in Tennyson's domestic treatment of another conventional element of the pastoral elegy, the procession with the bier. To describe Hallam's burial as a procession of shepherds and nymphs would make it seem remote and unreal. Instead, he describes the movement of the ship bringing Hallam's body back to England, and his own reactions as he contemplates that voyage in his imagination. He gains a firm sense of immediacy, and avoids a sense of artificiality, by focusing on the domestic function of the ship, as he does, for instance, in section x:

> Thou bring'st the sailor to his wife,
>   And travelled men from foreign lands;
>   And letters unto trembling hands;
> And, thy dark freight, a vanished life.

'So bring him ...' These words introduce the third stanza of the section, and it is a stanza full of complexities and contrasting emotions. The tone of the imperative may, on the one hand, be a rising tone of expectation; just as the ship reunites families or sustains them with news of family members, so it will bring the 'dark freight' back into the poet's family circle. On the other hand, the imperative is preceded by the qualifying phrase, 'a vanished life,' and that 'vanished life' contrasts with the continuing lives in the other three lines of the stanza. In this context, the tone of the imperative may be a flat tone of resignation. It is not necessary to decide which tone prevails. Both resignation and expectation are present as the poet struggles with the gap between what he wants and what he knows must be. What he wants he calls 'dreams,' and though he labels them 'idle,' the label is not to be taken at face value, nor are the dreams so easily rejected. Tennysonian dreaming is usually the activity of the imagination, and the imagination, among other things, shapes the domestic ideal which presides at the burial. In this context Tennyson refers to the dream as 'Our home-bred fancies,' and they are responsible for the poet's description of the burial place he desires for Hallam. There are two possibilities:

> To rest beneath the clover sod,
>> That takes the sunshine and the rains,
>> Or where the kneeling hamlet drains
> The chalice of the grapes of God ...

Both possibilities symbolize the domestic virtues of peace and order, and both suggest a continuing vitality that foreshadows the consolation at the end of the elegy. Sunshine and rain are the life-giving forces of nature, and the clover sod suggests a continuance of some form of life after death as much as does the more conventional violet that is to spring from the grave in section xviii. 'The kneeling hamlet' is a community united in a common purpose, and that purpose is the celebration of the central sacrament of the Christian church. That sacrament, too, symbolizes life out of death. The opposite of both the church and the churchyard is the undersea world, which is without order and vitality, and characterized by random motion and helpless drifting. This waste land (or, rather, waste sea) is best described by a phrase which appears in section xxxv: 'the homeless sea.' When the actual burial takes place in section xviii, the description is permeated with a sense of peace, order, and rest. Both Bradley and Sinfield discuss the tone of resolution in this section,[24] and it is not too difficult to see how it is achieved: the burial makes actual the desires of 'Our home-bred fancies' and completes the progress toward home which is the chief movement of this first division. This movement is, we note, balanced by the movement with which the elegy concludes, a return to a wider world. As we should expect, Tennyson presents that movement in domestic terms too.

In the second division of the poem (sections xxxi to lxxvii), which is dominated by speculation on such subjects as evolution and the progress of the soul after death, the domestic references and analogies have a new function. Tennyson's central concern is the passage of time: is it meaning-less flux, or is it the condition that makes possible the moral and intellec-tual progress of the race? If it is the latter, what evidence do we have of such a divine purpose? To these questions Tennyson brings domestic answers: time is shaped by the generations that link the ages; and it is redeemed by a state of mind which in the pastoral tradition would be associated with contentment, but which in the Victorian age is the basis of the affirmation of faith.

The image of the family circle is a spatial image, but the family has a temporal dimension as well. Parents and children represent two genera-tions, and their sense of embracing, in the family circle, a time longer than the individual life of any of them is something Tennyson uses to good effect in the elegy. Towards our parents and all their forbears we feel a sense of piety and gratitude; and for our children and our children's children we have cares and hopes. In the *Memoir* Hallam Tennyson quotes his father as saying of babies, 'There is something gigantic about them. The wide-eyed wonder of a babe has a grandeur in it which as children they lose. They seem to me to be prophets of a mightier race.'[25] The 'mightier race' was not just an idle dream. In the child Tennyson saw a link between the present and the future, and it is by such a linking of genera-tions that time is redeemed. To the ordinary eye, time is meaningless flux ('the sliding hour,' section xliii, or, more violently, 'a maniac scattering dust,' section l), or endless recurrence ('the rolling hours' in section li; those who are passively caught up in this motion Tennyson describes in section liii as 'those that eddy round and round'). To the eye illuminated by the domestic ideal, time is shaped by the begetting of children.

This pattern is clearest in section xl, where the wife and mother, in nurturing and teaching her children, becomes 'A link among the days, to knit / The generations each with each.' It is the word 'link' which suggests the pattern, a shaping which takes place in time and saves it from mean-ingless process. By the end of the poem, this link will be the basis of the consolation, but here Tennyson sees only a contrast between the wife and mother, and himself. In the surrounding sections he has been speculating at length on the possibility of some kind of link between Hallam's living soul and his own, still confined to earth. In this section, that speculation takes the form of a wish which he expresses in domestic terms:

> Could we forget the widowed hour
> And look on Spirits breathed away,
> As on a maiden in the day
> When first she wears her orange-flower!

The marriage which takes place here is an image of order and fulfilment, and by bearing children, the bride links the generations and shapes the future. She is a link not only with the future but also with the past, as her visits to her own parents and her 'old fireside' indicate. It is here, however, that the analogy breaks down, and Tennyson's words, 'Ay me, the difference I discern!' mark the turning point of the section. For while the maiden may return to her parents, Hallam may not return to the poet.

Nonetheless, Tennyson comes to see Hallam as a link analogous to the child. In the epilogue he calls Hallam 'a noble type / Appearing ere the times were ripe' of the 'crowning race' that is to come. This division of the poem prepares for that affirmation, for here Hallam's superiority to the poet is a constant theme. In section xlii, Hallam is 'A lord of large experience' who may 'train / To riper growth the mind and will.' In section lx, Tennyson explores this same idea by means of a domestic simile: his own spirit is 'Like some poor girl whose heart is set / On one whose rank exceeds her own.' The same simile underlies section lxii, where Hallam rejects 'some unworthy heart' and 'lives to wed an equal mind.' In section lxiv, the imagery shifts to the pastoral; Hallam is like 'some divinely gifted man, / Whose life in low estate began / And on a simple village green.' He becomes a powerful statesman while his friend remains a ploughman. In all of these sections the poet explores the distance between himself and his friend, and gradually comes to recognize in Hallam the type of the future man. He is, says Tennyson in section lxi, 'the perfect flower of human time,' and 'human time' is 'the sliding hour' perceived, not as slipping away from man, but as providing the opportunity for the fullest human development.

The forging of links is, in many ways, the central activity of this second division of the poem, and to make connections requires a particular state of mind. Tennyson defines this state by contrasting it with its opposite, and this contrast is an interesting development of the pastoral tradition.

The state of mind which is associated with the pastoral is familiar enough. Hallett Smith defines it as 'the state of content and mental self-sufficiency which had been known in classical antiquity as *otium*,' and contrasts it with the aspiring mind which was motivated by ambition and greed.[26] The one is characterized by peace, order, and harmony, the other by restless striving. When Tennyson replaces the pastoral with the domestic, the contrast remains, though the terms shift. The contentment and harmony associated with pastoral life become the faith associated with domestic life; and the restless striving of the aspiring mind becomes the restless struggle of doubt.

We in the twentieth century are more familiar with doubt, largely because it is closer in character to our sense of alienation, our feelings of anxiety, and our view of the world as absurd. This state of mind is suggested by the 'subtle thought' and 'curious fears' to which Tennyson refers in section xxxii; it is more apparent in the dramatic image with which Tennyson concludes section liv:

> but what am I?
> An infant crying in the night:
> An infant crying for the light:
> And with no language but a cry.

The image suggests a state where one is full of urgent desires but is unable to affirm that they have any validity in the general scheme of things. (The affirmation, using this same image, will come later in the poem.) This failure comes about because the validity of the desires cannot be verified empirically. Hence this state of mind is primarily concerned with what Tennyson calls knowledge, and is at the same time agonizingly conscious of its limitations. Knowledge provides a view of Nature as a blind amoral process, the character of which is summed up in Tennyson's famous phrase in section lvi. With no 'intelligible First Cause deducible from the phenomena of the Universe' (the words are from the proposition debated by the Apostles),[27] one is constantly threatened by an alien and meaningless Nature, and so fear and anxiety (the 'calm despair and wild unrest' of section xvi) are the chief emotions of this state.

Its opposite is faith (though Tennyson will affirm that doubt is part of the larger life of faith), and faith is associated with the domestic ideal. Tennyson defines this state of mind in his treatment of the story of Lazarus in sections xxxi and xxxii. The Biblical story is archetypally domestic in character, and contrasts Martha and her household cares with

Mary's choice of the better way. In retelling the story, Tennyson concerns himself primarily with Mary, but in such a way as to suggest that her state of mind is the highest form of domestic life. The first line of section xxxii, 'Her eyes are homes of silent prayer,' is deceptively simple. It defines faith as perception, as a way of seeing the world. The word 'home' here is used as a metaphor for the eyes, and suggests both the propriety of prayer's dwelling place and the centrality of the home in any world view. The 'silent prayer' is a comprehensive act which the rest of this section defines. It involves adoration, as the second stanza indicates, for there 'her ardent gaze' is motivated by 'one deep love.' It involves thanksgiving and joy, as the last three lines of the first stanza indicate; and her motivation for the bathing of the Saviour's feet is her 'gladness ... complete.' It involves petition and supplication, not in the form of private requests, but in the form of intercession, a petition for blessings on others. In the last stanza, Tennyson confirms the importance of the word 'prayer' in this section with a new Beatitude: 'Thrice blest whose lives are faithful prayers.' Throughout this section one senses the wholeness of Mary's response; it comprehends life and death, sorrow and joy; it intuits a wider unity in the disparate experiences of human life; it sees in all things the working of a divine purpose, and hence takes a sacramental view of life. The same view is evident (though with some differences) in the sister in section xxxiii: 'Oh, sacred be the flesh and blood / To which she links a truth divine!' Calmness, joy, comprehensiveness, insight, love: these are the attributes of the state of mind proper to the home.

The fact that this state of mind manifests itself in a particular kind of perception is apparent in Tennyson's references to eyes, references for which there are parallels in his earlier poetry. One recalls, for instance, *Supposed Confessions of a Second-Rate Sensitive Mind*, and the 'trustful infant' who 'knows / Nothing beyond his mother's eyes' (49–4). The speaker recalls how he

> beheld
> Thy mild deep eyes upraised, that knew
> The beauty and repose of faith,
> And the clear spirit shining through.   (73–6)

One recalls, too, the portrait, *Isabel*, which opens with a description of her eyes. Here the eyes reveal 'pure vestal thoughts' (4), and her virtues make her 'the queen of marriage, a most perfect wife' (28).

Tennyson approaches this ideal state of mind in his own affirmations, particularly in his use of the verbs 'trust' and 'feel.' Again, the words are deceptively simple. They express an affirmation for which there is no proof, but which rests upon an intuitive response to life on earth, a response which asserts human values and divine purposes. We cannot prove these values or purposes, and yet it is they that give shape and meaning to our lives. Tennyson's use of these words, and his appeal to the state of mind they represent, is clearest in the sections dealing with evolution: 'Oh yet we trust that somehow good / Will be the final goal of ill'; 'I can but trust that good shall fall / At last – far off – at last, to all' (section liv); 'I ... call / To what I feel is Lord of all, / And faintly trust the larger hope' (section lv).

In time, this stubborn affirmation of faith develops into intimations of immortality, and again 'link' is a key word. In section xli the poet complains that 'I have lost the links that bound / Thy changes,' and he longs 'To leap the grades of life and light, / And flash at once, my friend, to thee.' As this division proceeds, the poet's wish is fulfilled, though the link is not precisely what he expected, nor is it something that can be forged at will. The link takes the form of a vision, largely mystical in character, which provides insight into the spiritual life, the reality lying behind the appearance of this world. It is apparent in section lxvii, where the 'mystic glory' that illuminates Hallam's tablet in Clevedon church is a mysterious fusion of darkness and light that brings comfort, rest, and sleep. It is apparent again in section lxx, where the vision is more explicit: it is a vision of Hallam's 'fair face,' it is accompanied by 'a wizard music,' and it happens 'beyond the will.' The setting in section lxvii is explicitly domestic ('When on my bed the moonlight falls') and the same setting is implicit in section lxx. The visions are closely related to memory and desire, and certainly these two forces are at work at the beginning of section lxx: 'I cannot see the features right, / When on the gloom I strive to paint / The face I know.' Memory and desire are the prime motivating forces of this elegy. Memory preserves a past in which the poet recognizes much that is ideal; it is the dominant force in the early part of the elegy. Desire looks to a future in which that ideal is more fully realized; it is the dominant force in moving toward the consolation. Memory and desire link past and future, and forge the link between this world and the spiritual one. As he makes the connections, Tennyson moves closer to the affirmations of the final sections of the poem.

In the third division of the poem (sections lxxix to ciii), Tennyson returns to one of his major concerns in the first division – his companionship with his dead friend – but treats it in domestic rather than pastoral terms. The repetition, but with the shift in treatment, has a number of important effects. First of all, the reader's sense of verisimilitude is greatly strengthened. Though the domestic is just as artful as the pastoral, the pastoral lyrics in the first division of the poem seem artificial. With his keen sense of his audience and his age, Tennyson would have been aware of that effect, and aware, too, of how he could use it in the pattern of his poem. Hence he balances the account of himself and Hallam as shepherds with a fuller description of himself and Hallam as members of families soon to be joined in the marriage of Hallam and the poet's sister. But verisimilitude was not Tennyson's only concern. The pastoral lyrics suggest a one-to-one relationship that was private and exclusive; the domestic lyrics are concerned with a family circle, and, through it, with the social and political life of the nation. This shift is apparent primarily in the change in the way the poet and Hallam communicate. In the pastoral lyrics, the two are one in thought and imagination, and seem to have little need of words. In this division of the poem, discourse is the major activity, and ordinary speech is the recurring means of communication. The shift prepares us for the poet's conventional return to the world of familiar activities at the end of the elegy. But it is a return in which Tennyson embraces the world with new and deeper understanding, and this he develops by exploring in some detail the nature of family life.

The first of these detailed domestic pictures is in section lxxxiv, where Tennyson imagines Hallam's domestic bliss had he lived to marry the poet's sister and have children. The picture is one of an ideal domestic existence, but it is, unfortunately, a picture of a home which can never be. As such, it is a 'backward fancy' that brings 'The old bitterness again,' and breaks 'The low beginnings of content.' In short, desires of this kind have, like the will, already played their part in the elegy by presenting an ideal, and now the ideal must be realized in new ways. Throughout this section, however, the poet's fancy drives him to daydream.

The opening lines suggest the inadequacy of the fantasy: 'When I contemplate all alone / The life that had been thine below...' The picture is as private as the poet's song in section xxi; it lacks the domestic context of the vision of section xcv, where the poet is also 'all alone' (20), but in quite a different way. The rhythm of the line in section xcv ('Went out, and I was all alone') is regular and gives the effect of confidence; the rhythm of the opening line in this section is irregular, and the phrase 'all alone,' with its long vowels and heavy accents, slows the line and, in doing so, draws attention to itself. It suggests a degree of self-pity and perhaps an excessive self-regard.

The poet describes Hallam's domestic life in terms of light, and specifically in terms of the progress of the moon and sun. The youth which the poet knew is 'thy crescent,' the new moon which would have grown full. In the second stanza Tennyson presents Hallam as a sun god like Apollo, 'sitting crowned' and providing for his family 'A central warmth.' Domestic relations are described in terms of the sun's creative and sustaining powers. The sun god's life is in effect a Golden Age which is brought to an end by 'that remorseless iron hour' of Hallam's death. This fantasy is complete by line 16, a completion which is emphasized by the three parallel phrases all dependent on the verb 'Made':

> But that remorseless iron hour
> Made cypress of her orange flower,
> Despair of Hope, and earth of thee.

The last phrase in particular has a tone of finality about it, because it presents so bluntly the physical aspect of death. But Tennyson continues with the fantasy: 'I seem to meet ...', 'I see myself ...' The attractive and charming picture of Hallam's children is undermined by reminders of the actual situation ('I see their unborn faces shine / Beside the never-lighted fire'), but the drive is toward the fantasy, which begins anew – and without reminders of the actual – at line 21.

In this second part of the fantasy, the image of Hallam as the sun god is still implicit, particularly in lines 25 to 36, but is fused with the more realistic picture of Hallam the thinker, the intellectual:

> I see myself an honoured guest,
>   Thy partner in the flowery walk
>   Of letters, genial table-talk,
> Or deep dispute, and graceful jest ...

The accomplishment of Hallam's life on earth would be 'great legacies of thought.' Though these gifts of Hallam are presented in a domestic context, they are clearly the same gifts that would have made him great in public life, and so the link between the family man and the statesman is made. It is worth noting that, when Tennyson first describes Hallam's intellectual abilities, no such link is suggested. In section xxiii, where he described his past life with Hallam as a Golden Age, their understanding of each other had little need of words. It was a time

> When each by turns was guide to each,
>   And Fancy light from Fancy caught,
>   And Thought leapt out to wed with Thought
> Ere Thought could wed itself with Speech ...

There Hallam's gifts had no bearing on public life. Their communication was something private and almost mystical. But in section lxxxiv the discourse is more ordinary, and is clearly related to wider social concerns.

It would perhaps be easy to assume that, in thus developing his account of his relations, actual or fancied, with Hallam, Tennyson is leaving behind the kind of communication that goes beyond words. But that is not so. Section lxxxv corrects this assumption, just as it corrects section lxxxiv by focusing on the image of Hallam which is conceived, not by a 'backward fancy,' but by faith. In this section, the poet describes Hallam received in heaven, gaining at once 'All knowledge that the sons of flesh / Shall gather in the cycled times,' and becoming half-divine: 'O sacred essence, other form, / O solemn ghost, O crownèd soul!' Hallam cannot give such knowledge to the poet, but he sets a standard that both inspires his friend and assures him that the perfect man is an attainable goal for the race. The result is that Hallam becomes an icon, influencing those who, like the poet, must continue to struggle on earth. Tennyson's phrase for this role of Hallam is 'An image comforting the mind' (51), and it is well to remember that 'comforting' means 'giving strength with.' This strength goes beyond words, but, in ordinary social relations, it manifests itself in words.

Thus, when Tennyson in section lxxxvii again describes Hallam as he knew him, he concentrates on his skill in debate and on the influence of his spoken words. The occasion, a visit to Hallam's former rooms in Cambridge, might have given rise to another 'backward fancy,' but that does not happen here. Instead, Tennyson describes Hallam in such a way that he is 'An image comforting the mind,' and he does so by picking up the image of Hallam as Apollo that he had used with ambiguous results in section lxxxiv. Here he treats Apollo less as the sun god and more as the god of the arts of civilization, particularly speech, poetry, and music, all of them arts requiring inspiration. The bow and arrow are attributes of Apollo, and Hallam is depicted here as a 'master-bowman' whose words and ideas are like arrows that pierce the very centre of the target. His 'rapt oration flowing free' is associated with 'power and grace / And music in the bounds of law,' so that logic and rhetoric are fused in one highly effective art. The light image signifies the god within: the listeners saw 'The God within him light his face, / And seem to lift the form, and glow / In azure orbits heavenly-wise,' and the macrocosmic view with which this image ends suggests both the insight and the comprehensiveness of Hallam's thought. The reference to a particular feature of Hallam's physiognomy, 'The bar of Michael Angelo,' suggests mighty thought, deep insight, and a mastery of the arts. Of such materials is the icon constructed; in such a way does the familiar friend become a hero.

When the poet returns to domestic life in section lxxxix, his realistic picture of a rural retreat is permeated with this sense of the heroic dimensions of ordinary experience. The section is an idyl which, as we shall see, has a great deal in common with Tennyson's other idyls. For it pictures a retreat into the country, and contrasts the quiet and contentment of rural and domestic life with the roar and unrest of the wasteland-like city. The landscape here is similar to that of section xcv, a lawn surrounded by trees, the whole a pattern of shade and light ('Witch-elms that counterchange the floor / Of this flat lawn with dusk and bright'). Much of the first part of this section is devoted to the contrast between this landscape and the city: it is 'this retreat,' as opposed to 'The dust and din and steam of town'; the activities proper to it are 'simple sports' as opposed to 'brawling courts / And dusty purlieus of the law.' The next three stanzas each begin with exclamations ('O joy,' 'O sound,' 'O bliss'), and each states or suggests a contrast: the 'ambrosial dark' and the 'cooler air' of the retreat as opposed to the heat of the broader landscape; the sounds of field and garden as opposed to 'the brood of cares'; the family circle, literally represented as the family listens to Hallam reading the 'Tuscan poets,' an image of perfection that implies its opposite, other less orderly relations. The 'all-golden afternoon' too suggests an ideal period of time. The last six stanzas of the section are devoted to the 'banquet in the distant woods,' a rural excursion in which the poet and his friend engage in discourse and debate:

> Whereat we glanced from theme to theme,
>   Discussed the books to love or hate,
>   Or touched the changes of the state,
> Or threaded some Socratic dream ...

The chief topic – or at least the one of which Tennyson gives a detailed account – is a debate about the relative merits of town and country. The poet praises 'the busy town,' but apparently only to draw Hallam out in defending the country. The country, Hallam argues, allows individuality and eccentricity, whereas the town demands conformity: 'ground in yonder social mill / We rub each other's angles down.' This is an important distinction, given Tennyson's sense of the uniqueness of personality and its value in the general scheme of things. The individual flourishes, and best retains his identity, in a rural setting, and (given the degree to which pastoral and domestic are merged in the poem) at home as well. The debate between the poet and his friend needs no spoken resolution, for the experience described in this idyl itself resolves the debate in favour of the country.

In spite of the idyllic tone, the ending of the section is not unmixed. There is much to suggest the passing of time, and the decay and death that accompany it. The first indication of a threat to this idyllic world appears almost incidentally during the debate: 'We talked: the stream beneath us ran, / The wine-flask lying couched in moss, / Or cooled within the glooming wave.' The stream is a natural part of the pastoral landscape, but it is also a familiar image for the passing of time; 'the glooming wave' is an accurate description of the water which shades the wine-flask and cools it, but 'glooming' suggests an ominous link with the images of darkness elsewhere in *In Memoriam*. These lines are followed by the picture of 'the crimson-circled star' falling into 'her father's grave' (that is, Venus following the sun down in the western sky), and the passing of time is more explicitly linked with death, as are love (the 'star' is Venus) and the family (suggested here by the daughter-father relationship). The section ends with a return from 'the distant woods' to the home, and that return foreshadows a return to the wider world of the town. The return seems to be described in simple terms, but the words are full of subtleties and suggestions. There is much to suggest blessings realized in what the Bible calls 'the fulness of time': the flowers, which the poet asked Spring to bring in section lxxxiii, are 'ankle-deep'; milk and honey, with their Biblical associations with a Promised Land, are both mentioned, the milk being actual, and the honey an image for the sweetness of the time in his rural retreat. But the ideal is never quite complete. The milk is not seen, though the milking is heard 'behind the woodbine veil,' a phrase which echoes the 'behind the veil' phrase which concludes section lvi, and suggests that the blessing is not yet fully experienced. The 'buzzings of the honied hours' suggest both fulfilment and the relentless passing of time, and conclude the section on a note that is a careful blending of the realistic and the idyllic. This mixture of tones in this final stanza suggests that this rural retreat, though seemingly ideal, is not an end in itself, and must be completed by a return to a wider life which unifies the extremes of human experience. One senses a pattern taking shape in this retreat which will do just that. That pattern is apparent in the relationship of Tennyson and Hallam, particularly as it manifests itself in their discourse, for their talk is wide-ranging and comprehensive, and yet it is part of a harmony of personalities with differing thoughts and feelings. The value of this relationship has already been suggested by a phrase in section lxxxv, 'A friendship as had mastered Time.'

Tennyson's full account of the nature of the relationship with Hallam makes the forging of a new link with him more important than ever. In section xc, he denies that the return of the dead would, as in other families, 'shake / The pillars of domestic peace.' In section xci, he twice asks Hallam to return: once, in the spring, in 'the form by which I know / Thy spirit in time among thy peers,' and once, in summer, 'in thine after form.' As Sinfield points out, there is in the description of spring 'a certain sparseness, a lack of abundance,' while the summer is 'overflowing with abundance.'[28] In fact, the phrase 'summer's hourly-mellowing change' suggests the summer of section lxxxix, with its fusion of the blessings of ripeness and its sense of the relentless passing of time. It remains now for the poet to affirm, in the passing of time since Hallam's death, the continued blessings of their relationship, and, indeed, the continuing of the relationship itself, though in a different form. He does so in the familiar section xcv.

Section xcv is preceded by a section in which Tennyson describes the state of mind necessary for the individual who 'would hold / An hour's communion with the dead,' and the description picks up and extends the state of mind he attributed to Mary in section xxxii. It is the state of mind which is proper to the domestic life, and its chief characteristics are inner peace and harmony. The poet must be able to say, 'My spirit is at peace with all.' This calmness Tennyson defines precisely. It involves, first of all, being 'pure at heart and sound in head.' The first phrase echoes one of the Beatitudes, and in doing so suggests the insight which is the result of such purity; the second phrase is curiously matter-of-fact in tone, and, in its affirmation of soundness, answers the doubts about visions which the poet raised in section xcii. Thought and feeling are brought together in the two phrases. There is a third attribute of this state of mind: 'divine affections bold.' The 'divine affections' are related to the 'one deep love' of section xxxii, because they are unselfish, and involve adoration and insight; 'bold' suggests resolution and activity, and indeed both the active and the passive are involved in 'communion with the dead.' In the second stanza the poet will 'call / The spirits,' but in the third he must be still, as one must be to hear the voice of God, to be conscious of the spirits: 'They haunt the silence of the breast.' The consciousness of the spirits involves a memory which is clear, 'like a cloudless air,' and a conscience which has no need to goad or warn. The spirits themselves are 'Imaginations calm and fair,' and the word 'Imaginations' suggests that both memory and desire are operating here. But they are now harmonized as part of the state of mind associated with the domestic ideal. The poet is ready for the vision of section xcv.

The extent to which we are familiar with section xcv should not blind us to the way in which the vision and the circumstances surrounding it gather together the themes and images we have been tracing in this division of *In Memoriam*. The setting is the same as that in section lxxxix, a lawn surrounded by trees. The lawn links the pastoral and the domestic, since it is between the house mentioned in line 19 and the field mentioned in line 16. There is the same pattern of light and shade, but the two seem more fused here, particularly as the night is softened by the 'silvery haze of summer.' And the summer itself, as we have already seen, is associated with 'the fulness of time.' The occasion is a family gathering. The harmony and peace suggested in the family grouping imply a state of mind that meets the conditions specified in section xciv. The activity ('we sang old songs') looks back to the first Christmas, where the songs developed into an affirmation of immortality, and to section lxxxix, where the song contributes to the mood of well-being. Consequently, when the family members withdraw and the poet is left 'all alone,' there is no sense of self-pity and self-regard as there was when the phrase was used in the first line of section lxxxiv. Instead, it indicates a stillness like that described as necessary in the third stanza of section xciv. Hence it is a condition not of a 'backward fancy' but of a vision. The vision is based on 'The noble letters of the dead,' which have the same function here as discourse and conversation had when Hallam was alive. They give evidence of a relationship that is both dynamic and harmonious, and they prepare for a new relationship that goes beyond 'matter-moulded forms of speech.' It would be easy to dismiss the reading of Hallam's letters as a sentimental act, and the letters themselves as the sentimental outpouring of one friend to another. But that is not so. The letters give evidence of Hallam's gifts in argument and debate, his intellectual abilities and his sensitivity:

And strangely on the silence broke
  The silent-speaking words, and strange
  Was love's dumb cry defying change
To test his worth; and strangely spoke

The faith, the vigour, bold to dwell
  On doubts that drive the coward back,
  And keen through wordy snares to track
Suggestion to her inmost cell.

The use of the word 'strangely' here anticipates its use in the third Christmas poem. Out of something as familiar as Hallam's letters, the poet has a sense of something mysterious taking shape. When the vision occurs, it is sudden and complete. The one brief stanza in which the poet moves from 'The dead man' to 'The living soul' is the turning point of the entire poem.[29] The vision confirms his faith in Hallam's continued existence, and so provides the consolation toward which the poem has been moving. It also picks up and transforms the discourse between the poet and his dead friend. The 'great legacies of thought' that Hallam might have left behind (section lxxxiv) pale before the 'empyreal heights of thought' to which this vision raises the poet. And the recurring themes implicit in all their discourse – 'The steps of Time – the shocks of Chance – / The blows of Death' – are now recognized as phenomena through which the spiritual world manifests itself, and hence as necessary parts of the unity of all things. In a similar way the landscape, with all its elements of the pastoral and the domestic, is transformed too. The lawn, the trees, the field, and the cattle are all seen now as symbols that both hide and reveal spiritual unity. The domestic and the pastoral, always recognized as ideals, now become vital forces as well. The change is most clearly apparent in the breeze which begins to blow at the end of this section. 'A more than ordinary breeze,' it 'arouses distinctly Pentecostal associations';[30] it is an 'ancient symbol of the spirit,'[31] and it seems to be here specifically the Holy Spirit, inspiring, invigorating, sustaining, creating. It merges extremes and fuses opposites, so that darkness and light, 'like life and death' (the simile is a crucial one), are seen as one, manifestations of a mysterious spiritual world.

The advance that section xcv represents can be seen best by comparing it with sections xci and lxxxix. In xci, Tennyson contrasted Hallam's familiar form and his 'after form.' Section lxxxix is devoted to Hallam's familiar form, which there he remembers in full daylight; the section ends with the coming of dusk and the sense of the passing of time. In section xcv, Hallam's 'after form' appears in a flash that transcends the 'silvery haze,' and the section ends with the coming of dawn and a sense of eternity. The vision, however, does not lead Tennyson to reject this world. Malcolm Ross has pointed out that 'the experience of the timeless moment is ... the way not out of time but into time,'[32] and indeed Tennyson does see new purpose and significance in the things of this world, and in continuing human life. This new acceptance he explores in the extended domestic analogy in section xcvii. Here his spirit and Hallam's spirit are described as 'Two partners of a married life,' and the poet's spirit is the wife, an analogy that Tennyson has already used in earlier parts of the poem. He glances first at the past: 'Their hearts of old have beat in tune, / Their meetings made December June, / Their every parting was to die.' The lines give, in terms of the marriage metaphor, the poet's past life with Hallam, a life he described largely in pastoral terms in the first division of the poem. When he describes the present, he picks up the picture of Hallam as a superior being and of himself as 'some poor girl' that he had already used in section lx, but the poor girl is now a wife, and he and Hallam are still married though Hallam is absent and 'rapt in matters dark and deep.' Section xcvii focuses on the wife's attitude in this situation, and it is an important one because it includes the determination to continue in time and in this world. The wife continues to love, though 'She knows not what his greatness is'; her love goes beyond understanding, and is hence related to Mary's attitude in section xxxii and to the state of mind defined in section xciv. 'She knows but matters of the house.' The line is crucial, because it helps define the new function of the domestic in the poem. The domestic becomes a metaphor for a continuing life on earth, but a life permeated with the sense of how the spiritual manifests itself in earthly things – a manifestation so intimate that marriage is the best metaphor for it. The union described here is metaphorically the marriage of the poet and Hallam, but it is also the marriage of the spirit and flesh. This world, then, though limited and limiting, is of immense value and significance, and the attitude of the wife is the proper one:

> Her faith is fixt and cannot move,
> She darkly feels him great and wise,
> She dwells on him with faithful eyes,
> 'I cannot understand: I love.'

The vision, then, impels Tennyson back into the world of time and death, and this direction is complemented by the movement with which the elegy ends: a move from the familiar and the domestic into a wider public world, a return from the retreat to ordinary life. It is the traditional movement with which an elegy ends, but Tennyson as always uses the tradition in his own way.

The return Tennyson describes as the family's move from the old home, and this move away from home balances the move toward home (the coming of the funeral ship) at the beginning of the elegy. And just as a group of poems was devoted to the funeral ship, so a group of poems (sections c to ciii) is devoted to the move. The direction is set by section cii, which begins with the sentence, 'We leave the well-belovèd place,' and ends with: 'I turn to go: my feet are set / To leave the pleasant fields and farms.' The group of poems looks both backwards and forwards. Section c, for instance, is largely pastoral in character, and looks back to section xxiii. Each feature of the landscape – the 'old grange,' the 'lonely fold,' the 'sheepwalk,' the 'pastoral rivulet,' the flock itself – 'reflects a kindlier day,' and there is a sense of looking back to a Golden Age. But the landscape in section xxiii is deliberately idealized and Arcadian, while the landscape here is an actual English landscape: the wold is 'windy,' the daw 'wrangling,' the knoll 'hoary.' The sense of time passing, however, is as keen here as it was earlier, and that sense gives the landscape a poignancy not apparent in the Arcadian landscape of section xxiii. Section ci also looks backward, and describes another aspect of the move: it is not just a matter of leaving home, but also a separation of the poet's thoughts and feelings from the familiar landscape with which he associated them. Each of the first four stanzas begins with a word drawing attention to the separation: 'Unwatched,' 'Unloved,' 'Unloved,' 'Uncared for.' The pattern is introduced strongly in the first stanza, where the first line begins with 'Unwatched' and the third with 'Unloved.' The landscape is predominantly an autumn landscape, and Tennyson selects and orders the details of it in such a way as to emphasize the passing of time. The passing of time is not a linear movement here but a cyclical one, and the circle is the central image in this section. The first stanza establishes the pattern:

> Unwatched, the garden bough shall sway,
>   The tender blossom flutter down,
>   Unloved, that beech will gather brown,
> This maple burn itself away ...

The seasons turn from spring to autumn, and bring with them decay and death. The villain in the process is time, which is a force not outside the trees mentioned here, but a part of their very being. Ironically the trees , in fulfilling their natural purposes, also destroy themselves. The verbs here are all active, and the activity both nourishes and consumes, like the fire in Shakespeare's sonnets. (One sees the opposite of this sort of thing in section xv, where the storm destroys and the landscape is passive.) The sun-flower in the second stanza is circular in shape (she shall 'Ray round with flames her disk of seed') and associated with the cycle of the sun whose movement she follows. The brook in the third and fourth stanzas has already been associated with the passing of time in section lxxxix, and its movement is both ominously linear (it will 'Babble down,' 'gird,' 'flood,' and 'break') and helplessly cyclical (it is associated with a constellation, the 'lesser wain' which 'Is twisting round the polar star'). In the final two stanzas the complementary activities of growing and fading are part of a cycle, the turning of which is emphasized by the repetition of the phrase 'year by year.' 'The labourer tills / His wonted glebe, or lops the glades,' and the springtime and autumn suggested here bring the section itself back in a circular pattern to where it began, just as the very last phrase, 'the circle of the hills,' points to a feature of the actual landscape that represents in a static way the movement of the poem. Once this pattern is recognized, it enables us to see the first words of the first four stanzas ('Unwatched,' 'Unloved,' 'Unloved,' 'Uncared for') in a new way. At first glance, the words seem to indicate that the poet is withdrawing from the cycle. In fact, his separation from the landscape is part of the cycle, as the last two stanzas with their pattern of growing and fading indicate. In spite of the regret, there is a tone of acceptance, a sense that the pattern which makes separation as necessary as union is nonetheless good and right.

This acceptance is confirmed in section ciii, the account of his dream vision on the last night in the old house. The dream reveals the significance of the end of the retreat: the return is a stage in the growth of the individual and of the race, and, though it takes place in time, its goal is eternity. In the dream, time does not simply swing round again in a cyclical pattern, but spirals into eternity. The dream thus completes the description of nature in section ci, and in doing so it picks up some images from the earlier poem. Of these, the most important is the river. At first it is an image of the inevitable passing of time, and the phrase 'sliding by the wall' even suggests involuntary movement. But when the figures set out in the 'little shallop,' the river seems to be flowing with a purpose. The 'flood'

begins to roll 'in grander space,' and the water begins to suggest something infinite and eternal, which Tennyson calls here and elsewhere 'the
deep,' the mysterious source and end of all life, physical and spiritual.
There is much in this section that foreshadows *The Passing of Arthur* in
Idylls of the King, and the similarities indicate the extent to which Tennyson
is describing in yet another way the apotheosis of his dead friend: 'The
man we loved was there on deck, / But thrice as large as man he bent / To
greet us.' Moreover, the development of a man of heroic proportions is
not confined to the dead friend. It is to be the lot of all men, and of the
poet himself:

> And I myself, who sat apart
>   And watched them, waxed in every limb;
>   I felt the thews of Anakim,
>   The pulses of a Titan's heart ...

This then is the proper end of the retreat: the home and the country are a
preparation for a fuller life, places which nurture 'that great race, which is
to be.' And so the link between the domestic and the heroic is forged. With
this vast perspective and mighty development in view, it is no wonder that
the third Christmas Eve falls 'strangely.'

The final division of the poem (sections cvii to cxxxi) is the final
movement of the elegy, and, as we should expect, it is full of links with all
that has gone before. In section cvii, for instance, the poet observes
Hallam's birthday with some of the customs and activities which he had
rejected for the third Christmas; section cxix, like section vii, is another
visit to Hallam's house in London, but the description is full of images of
renewal; the violet, already used to suggest new life from the grave in the
first division of the poem, becomes, in section cxv, a symbol of renewal
within the poet himself. It is in this context that Tennyson examines once
again the significance of Hallam's earthly life. This examination is that
part of the elegy that would, conventionally, be the apotheosis of the dead
friend. But Tennyson has in effect already dealt with Hallam's apotheosis
in the third division of the poem, where the visions are visions of Hallam's
'after form,' and the dream a picture of an heroic Hallam, 'thrice as large
as man.' Here he concentrates on Hallam as he was, but such a picture is
no longer a 'backward fancy.' Rather, it is an understanding of the way in
which the ideal is made actual, in which the spiritual manifests itself in the
world of phenomena. Hallam is not here the hero of myth or Arthurian
romance; he is, rather, the more familiar ideal that is signified by the label

'gentleman.' This treatment of Hallam (like the dream of Arthur returning as a 'modern gentleman' in *The Epic*) fuses the ordinary and the
domestic with which the poem began with the heroic and the ideal which
Tennyson intuits by the third Christmas. And so the conclusion of the
poem brings us back to the ordinary and the familiar, but with a new sense
of its significance.

The sections dealing with Hallam's character (cix to cxiii) are central to
this division. Tennyson defines that character to a large extent by describing opposite or contrasting qualities. The pattern is set in section cx,
where Tennyson mentions 'The proud,' 'The stern,' 'The flippant,' 'the
brazen fool,' and 'The feeble soul,' and contrasts these labels with 'The
grand old name of gentleman' (cxi). The structure of section cxi is based
on this same contrast, with the first two stanzas devoted to 'The churl in
spirit' and the last four to Hallam as gentleman. Section cxii is more
complex, but it has the same contrast as its basis, as the 'But thou' at the
beginning of the second stanza indicates. The last stanza associates Hallam with 'Large elements in order' and with 'tracts of calm' that are made
'from tempest.' Section cxiii contrasts social upheavals (described here in
terms of noise and movement, but represented best by 'the red fool-fury
of the Seine' in section cxxvii) with Hallam's civic role:

> A life in civic action warm,
>   A soul on highest mission sent,
>   A potent voice of Parliament,
> A pillar steadfast in the storm ...

The qualities of mind and character that Tennyson attributes to Hallam in these sections are qualities which combine the ideals of the domestic life (calmness, order, the attributes of the gentleman) with the more
active qualities of the man who undertakes a wider public life. This
combination Tennyson describes in section cix, where he lists Hallam's
gifts: 'critic clearness,' 'Seraphic intellect,' 'Impassioned logic' (note the
fusion of thought and feeling here), 'High nature,' 'passion pure,' 'love of
freedom,' and 'manhood fused with female grace.' It is the first quality
Tennyson lists which is, for our purposes, the most interesting, because all
the rest are implicit in it: 'Heart-affluence in discursive talk / From
household fountains never dry.' These lines may be, as Sinfield says,
'Tennyson at his worst,'[33] but the diction becomes a good deal more understandable in the light of the patterns we have been tracing. 'Discursive
talk' is, as we have seen, the chief form of the link between Tennyson and

Hallam; it was actual experience in the past, and it is the basis (through the letters) of Tennyson's visions in the present. 'Discursive talk' is the expression of thought, just as 'Heart-affluence' is the generous overflowing of feelings, and thought and feeling are fused in the more comprehensive quality that Tennyson will soon call Wisdom. 'Household fountains' are the source of Wisdom. The home is associated with the harmony of head and heart, and hence the influence it has prepares the individual for a wider public life. The link between the home and society is the stream image, which appears here as the stream's source, fountains. The stream was earlier associated with the passing of time, but the linking of Hallam's talk with fountains suggests time shaped by Hallam's influence. It is, I think, significant that section cxiv, with its definition of Wisdom, ends the group of poems describing Hallam's character. Wisdom is a comprehensive quality that fuses knowledge with love and faith, and it is the same mysteriously effective fusion of qualities that Tennyson is trying to describe in Hallam.

The sense of the home as both source of and context for the qualities that enable an individual to cope with the broader human problems is apparent once again in section cxxiv. Tennyson affirms his faith in familiar terms:

> A warmth within the breast would melt
>   The freezing reason's colder part,
>   And like a man in wrath the heart
> Stood up and answered 'I have felt.'

It should perhaps be pointed out that Tennyson is not rejecting reason here, but only reason's 'colder part.' He is fusing reason with love and faith, and the fusion is the basis of his affirmation. In making such an affirmation, Tennyson picks up a major domestic analogy. He rejects his first simile ('like a man in wrath') and elaborates on the domestic one ('like a child in doubt and fear'). The simile enables him to make the point that doubt and fear are part of the life of faith. Unlike the child in section liv, the child here has a context: 'Then was I as a child that cries, / But, crying, knows his father near.' The context is the family, and the associated ideals of love and security; the context also suggests the whole Judaeo-Christian tradition, with its emphasis on the paternal, particularly as it manifests itself in Providence. The simile, moreover, completes the stories of domestic disasters in the parts of the poem (sections vi and xx, for instance) where children are separated from parents. The separation is part of a broader unity here. The repetition of the hand image ('And out of darkness came the hands / That reach through nature, moulding men') affirms God's purposes working through all things.

Tennyson's statements about the ending of *In Memoriam* are well known: 'The poem concludes with the marriage of my youngest sister Cecilia. It was meant to be a kind of *Divina Commedia*, ending with happiness';[34] 'It begins with a funeral and ends with a marriage – begins with death and ends in promise of a new life – a sort of Divine Comedy, cheerful at the close.'[35] The statements emphasize not only the structure of the elegy (the move from grief to consolation) but the extent to which it is shaped by major domestic events. The epithalamium, moreover, brings to a highly satisfactory conclusion the patterns we have been tracing in the poem.

In the first place, the marriage which actually takes place here is a type of the marriage which Tennyson uses metaphorically throughout the poem to describe the relationship between himself and Hallam. Moreover, the marriages which were broken up or prevented by death in the first part of the poem (in section vi, for instance) are here balanced by a marriage which is celebrated and consummated. The marriage itself is like a return to the state of original creation, and as such it is related to the Golden Age Tennyson associated with his past companionship with Hallam. The bride, for instance, 'enters, glowing like the moon / Of Eden on its bridal bower,' and when the eyes of husband and wife-to-be meet, the bride's 'brighten like the star that shook / Betwixt the palms of paradise.' The ceremony is a celebration of life, yet it is inextricably connected with death:

> Her feet, my darling, on the dead;
> Their pensive tablets round her head,
> And the most living words of life
>
> Breathed in her ear.

A little later 'They leave the porch, they pass the grave / That has today its sunny side.' And we begin to realize that, just as the two are made one, so opposites of other sorts are brought together. The marriage is in fact the type of the fusion of opposites that we have been tracing throughout the poem. This fusion is apparent in many ways here. The wedding bells, for instance, recall the Christmas and New Year's bells that sound throughout the poem, and, in signifying joy, they affect 'The blind wall' and 'The dead leaf.' The same combination of moods is apparent in the movement of the epithalamium itself. The 'drinking health to bride and groom' is full of joy; the departure of the pair is 'A shade' that 'falls on us like the dark / From little cloudlets on the grass.' Then the guests 'range the woods' and 'roam the park,' and the walks are in effect a pastoral retreat (similar to that described in section lxxxix) which brings them to accept the sadness of parting and prepares them for renewed feasting. Then, in a now familiar pattern in the poem, the poet retires, and, when he is alone, gives himself up to contemplation. The contemplation takes place in moonlight, which is also the occasion for the vision of section lxvii, and which is like the 'silvery haze' of section xcv; there is a vision here as well, though it is not so mysterious and indefinable as the earlier ones. The moonlight becomes a 'splendour,' linked with 'star and system rolling past,' and the vision marks the transition from the local to the cosmic, from the setting of the marriage and the honeymoon to 'the deep' or (as here) 'the vast.' But the transition does not mean that the poet has left the local and the particular behind. Rather the spiritual is fused with the material in the conception of a child: 'A soul shall draw from out the vast / And strike his being into bounds.' As before, the vision propels the poet not out of time but into it, just as the spiritual is constantly manifesting itself in the matter of this world. With the conception of the child and the manner in which it is described, we begin to realize that the epithalamium celebrates more than just the marriage of a particular couple. It is in fact a celebration of the marriage of Heaven and Earth, and one of Blake's proverbs from *The Marriage of Heaven and Hell* is particularly apt: 'Eternity is in love with the productions of time.' The child is to be, in fact, 'a closer link / Betwixt us and the crowning race,' of which the 'noble type' was Hallam. The poem thus concludes with a vision of a dynamic universe, where diverse forces move in order and harmony toward 'one far-off divine event.' It is this dynamic movement which gives the home and the family such tremendous significance. Just as Hallam is the type of the 'crowning race,' so the home is the type of that dynamic harmony by which 'the whole creation moves.' We have come a very long way from the household whose peace was destroyed by Hallam's death. And, fantastic as this concluding vision may seem, the poem's steady focus on the home and the family keeps it always within the bounds of the actual or possible. The domestic thus serves Tennyson's purposes well, and, in using this central ideal of Victorian life, he found a tremendously effective way of speaking to his age.

2

Idyl and Epyllion

The conjunction of domestic and heroic is by no means confined to *In Memoriam*. Domestic concerns are pervasive in Tennyson's poetry, and the poet's imagination was preoccupied with the home and the family. This preoccupation was not unique – it is apparent, for instance, in the work of Felicia Hemans, Martin Tupper, and Coventry Patmore – but Tennyson's treatment of these themes sets his poetry well above that of his contemporaries. For Tennyson was unusually sensitive to the values and effects of form and style, and when his readers, like many modern undergraduates, seemed to think ideas were the central concern of poetry, he was quick to object. Edmund Gosse records the poet as saying, 'The dunces fancy it is the thought that makes poetry live; it isn't, it's the expression, the form, but we mustn't tell them so – they wouldn't know what we meant.'[1] Hallam Tennyson's *Memoir* records a good many comments on the importance of style and structure, the most interesting appearing in the Appendix to the first volume. There Aubrey de Vere writes, 'An anecdote will illustrate his solicitude on the subject of poetic form, the importance of which was perhaps not as much appreciated by any other writer since the days of Greek poetry.' De Vere tells his anecdote, and then records Tennyson as saying, 'Every short poem ... should have a definite shape, like the curve, sometimes a single, sometimes a double one, assumed by a severed tress or the rind of an apple when flung on the floor.'[2] And in the second volume of the *Memoir*, we find F.T. Palgrave's record of the poet's views of *Balder* and *Aurora Leigh* as works which 'might rather be defined as "organizable lymph" than as compacted and vertebrate poems.'[3] 'Compacted and vertebrate poems' – we cannot be sure that the words are Tennyson's, but they certainly indicate his chief concerns in the shaping of a poem: condensation, and a firm structure. That structure, I shall argue, is based upon a recurring action in domestic relations – a rhythm of separation and reunion – while the desire to condense led the poet to the idyl* and the epyllion.

In dealing with these matters, we are close to the centre of Tennyson's art. Northrop Frye has argued that every poet has a certain structure of imagery, certain myths or recurring shapes in his poetry, 'as typical of him as his handwriting.'[4] I want to examine some of the typical figures and myths that are the basis of Tennyson's domestic concerns, and then analyse in some detail the various forms and styles in which Tennyson realizes those concerns.

THE MYTH: *DORA* AND *DEMETER AND PERSEPHONE*

It has long been recognized that the pastoral, however ideal the existence of which it is an image, is not always an end in itself. The pastoral is an ideal because its happy simplicity contrasts with the disheartening complexities of urban life, but it is an ideal which is meant to inform and re-create that more complex life. Thus the escape to the country is usually balanced by a return to the city, and pastoral life itself is usually a preparation for something else. Traditionally that something else is a life of heroic action, and this link between the pastoral and the heroic accounts for the importance of figures who move from the one way of life to the other, like Paris in the classical tradition (though he is a flawed link), and David in the Biblical tradition. In the Renaissance view of the pastoral, the Judgment of Paris was a principal myth.[5] Here was a king's son turned shepherd, whose choice not only determined the course of his own life, but also precipitated the Trojan War. David is the Biblical equivalent of Paris, the shepherd and poet who becomes king, and founds a house into which the Messiah is born. Because the domestic is a version of pastoral, it is not surprising that we should find a similar link between the domestic and the heroic in Tennyson's poetry. And, just as in the older tradition, the link is embodied in two central figures. But in Tennyson these figures are female rather than male, and their heroic actions take the form of wanderings and childbearing rather than military exploits and affairs of state. These two figures are Ruth and Demeter, and their

---

* I follow Tennyson's practice in spelling this word, and use 'idyll' only for *Idylls of the King*.

significance can best be seen in a detailed examination of one of the *English Idyls*, *Dora*, and a late poem, *Demeter and Persephone*.

In style, *Dora* is the least typical of the *English Idyls*, but its central character is a type who appears again and again in Tennyson's work, and the pattern of its narrative recurs in other more complex poems. The importance of the poem for Tennyson himself may be indicated by its appearance in the title of the trial edition of eight poems in 1842. The volume was called *Morte d'Arthur; Dora, and other Idyls*. It is interesting that Tennyson should single out the poem in this way, especially since critics have almost ignored it ever since Matthew Arnold's damning distinction between the 'natural simplicity' of Wordsworth's *Michael* and the 'artificial simplicity' of this poem. Tennyson's own statement about the poem draws attention to his difficulties with the style: ' "Dora," being the tale of a nobly simple country girl, had to be told in the simplest possible poetical language, and therefore was one of the poems which gave most trouble.'[6] The statement, it should be noted, raises a question of decorum: what style is appropriate to 'the tale of a nobly simple country girl'? If we ignore for the time being questions about Tennyson's success (or lack of it) in solving that problem, and concentrate instead on what it is that makes Dora 'nobly simple,' we may get at some important aspects of Tennyson's concept of his central character. It is the pattern of the narrative that reveals these most clearly.

The narrative falls into a pattern of separation and reconciliation: as in *In Memoriam*, a family is broken up and reunited, largely through the efforts of the central character whose own disappointed hopes are fulfilled vicariously. In effect, the pattern is made up of two interwoven strands: the story of Dora herself, and the story of William's family. The latter is the story of a family quarrel and reconciliation; the former is the story of selfless love. The first section (lines 1 to 8) introduces both strands: the family (farmer Allan, William his son, and Dora his niece), and Dora's love for William. The father's intention – to have Dora and William marry – precipitates the story, since his wish has unexpected results: the break-up of his family and the disappointment of Dora. The second section (lines 8 to 38) develops the first narrative strand in telling of William's refusal to marry Dora, and of his impulsive marriage to Mary. This marriage is described in only four lines, but the quarrel between father and son is given in some detail, through dialogue. The emphasis on the details of the separation, rather than on a union which might balance the parting or even compensate for it, is appropriate to this stage of the story. The same emphasis is apparent when the narrative returns to Dora (lines 39–45). The farmer forbids Dora to see William and Mary, and thus cuts her off from the newly married couple in the same way that he has cut himself off from them. But the ultimate separation is yet to come, and that is William's death. Lines 46 to 53 are the darkest part of the story, and also the part most briefly told. The summary gives all the aspects of the separation: suffering, hardship, hard feelings, broken hearts, and finally death.

'Then Dora went to Mary' (54). This is the action which starts to bring the family together again. Dora refuses to let her own disappointment and grief rule her actions, and constantly serves a higher domestic ideal. In the sections from lines 54 to 107 we are told of Dora's proposal to take William's child and 'set him in my uncle's eye / Among the wheat' (65–6), and of its partially successful outcome: the farmer is united with his grandson but estranged from Dora. 'Then Dora went to Mary's house' (108). The echo of line 54 is deliberate, and the reverberations are in part ironic. Dora, loyal to the domestic ideal, goes to Mary because Mary is the only family she has left. There is irony, too, of a very human kind, in the reversal of Mary's attitude. Earlier she 'thought / Hard things of Dora' (55–6), but now she acts on Dora's behalf. The reconciliation of Mary and Dora foreshadows the reunion of the entire family. In the final sections of the poem, partial reconciliation with the father (through the boy) gives way to full reconciliation, and remorse and forgiveness forge a new unity. A large part of the narrative is devoted to the speeches and dialogue by which the reconciliation is effected, and again the emphasis is appropriate to this stage of the story. The conclusion (lines 164 to 167) both draws attention to the reunited family, and suggests the heroism of Dora and the pathos of her situation.

Such is the pattern of the story, a pattern of separation and reunion. Tennyson draws attention to it by giving the story in chronological order, rather than beginning in midpoint, using flashback, and then proceeding to the conclusion, as Mary Russell Mitford does in *Dora Creswell*, the story which is the poet's source. Another of Tennyson's changes emphasizes this same pattern. Mitford explains Dora's relations with her uncle thus: 'The young girl, Dora Creswell, was the orphan niece of one of the wealthiest yeomen in our part of the world, the only child of his only brother; and having lost both her parents whilst still an infant, had been reared by her widowed uncle as fondly and carefully as his own son Walter.'[7] But Tennyson makes the uncle's motive for raising Dora quite different:

'She is my brother's daughter; he and I
Had once hard words, and parted, and he died
In foreign lands; but for his own sake I bred
His daughter Dora ...'   (15–18)

'This quarrel,' Tennyson wrote in his notes in the Eversley Edition, 'is not in Miss Mitford.'

Dora is 'nobly simple' because she is the agent of the reconciliation and renewal. The strength of what the Victorians would have called the 'domestic affections' prevails, and brings harmony and order out of suffering and frustration. This ideal is embodied in an image which is at the centre of the poem: the picture, given twice, of Dora and the child sitting on a little mound in the wheat field. In describing this picture, Mitford draws parallels with Proserpina, Shakespeare's Lavinia, and Ruth. Tennyson, however, lets the situation and the style suggest these types. The flowers which Dora makes into a wreath for the child suggest the flowers in the field of Enna, and the poppies which grow on the mound Dora chooses to sit upon are traditionally associated with Demeter. The figure of a woman in a harvest field, surrounded by reapers who are kind to her, calls to mind the figure of Ruth. The austere style suggests the economy of Biblical narratives, and Ricks in his edition gives useful parallels for the Biblical turns of phrase. It is not surprising, then, that readers should think of the Book of Ruth. In a letter of 7 December 1842 Carlyle told Tennyson that 'Your "Dora" reminds me of the *Book of Ruth*,'[8] and Gilfillan pointed out the resemblance in his *Second Gallery of Literary Portraits* (1850).[9] The parallel is a most important one. If the twenty-third Psalm is the chief Biblical source of the pastoral tradition, the story of Ruth is the chief Biblical type of the domestic idyl.[10] By giving the picture of Dora and the child such a central place in his narrative, Tennyson in effect creates an icon, an image which is complex enough to sum up the main features of the Biblical idyl.

These features are familiar enough. Ruth (whose name means 'the beloved') embodies the virtues of loyalty, charity, and self-sacrifice. Her refusal to leave her mother-in-law takes on added significance when she chooses Yahweh over the Moabite gods. Through her marriage to Boaz she becomes an ancestress of David and ultimately of the Messiah, and this fruitful marriage is often taken as evidence of the working of Providence in raising an heir to save Elimelech's name from extinction, and in providing a ruling house for Israel. So, too, Dora shows the virtues of family loyalty, charity, and self-sacrifice; so, too, she restores the grandson to his rightful place as heir, forges a link between the generations, and ensures the continuation of the family. Tennyson's changes in the final reconciliation scene confirm this theme. In Mitford, the scene takes place in the fields; but in Tennyson, the scene takes place in the family home, by the fireside, and the two women see the picture framed by the door:

> They peeped, and saw
> The boy set up betwixt his grandsire's knees,
> Who thrust him in the hollows of his arm,
> And clapt him on the hands and on the cheeks,
> Like one that loved him: and the lad stretched out
> And babbled for the golden seal, that hung
> From Allan's watch, and sparkled by the fire. (127–33)

The child's attraction to the golden seal, the symbol of the farmer's possessions, indicates his acceptance as heir, and the sparkling of the fire on the seal makes it not just a symbol of material possessions but also a sacred object, full of the vital energy that the home fire represents.

For Tennyson, the value of the domestic affections was twofold: they were, in his view, the chief basis of harmonious human relations, and hence on them the order of civilization depended; and out of them came the children who were the visible links between his own generation and the 'crowning race' envisioned at the end of *In Memoriam*. The importance of the domestic affections in shaping and ordering civilization is a constant (though largely unrecognized) theme in Tennyson's poetry. 'Upon the sacredness of home life he would maintain that the stability and greatness of a nation largely depend,' wrote Hallam Tennyson in his *Memoir* of his father, 'and one of the secrets of his power over mankind was his true joy in the family duties and affections.'[11] These duties and affections regularly centred on a child, and hence the child is often the specific agent of social order and harmony through the feelings and emotions that he arouses. The child has a major role in *Dora* and in *The Princess*, and a similar function in other poems.

In treating the child in this way, Tennyson was drawing upon a literary tradition of some antiquity: the pastoral tradition in which the birth of a child is heralded as the dawning of a new Golden Age. The Biblical source of the tradition is the recurring prophecy of a Messiah in the Old Testament (especially Isaiah), while the classical source is Virgil's fourth Eclogue. Both sources celebrate the expected birth of a child who will better the lot of mankind and raise man to new heights morally and spiritually. The Christian interpretation of Virgil, as early as the reign of the Emperor Constantine, fused the Biblical and classical traditions, and one of the best examples of the fusion in English is Pope's *Messiah: A Sacred Eclogue in imitation of Virgil's 'Pollio.'* Virgil's Eclogue has an important place in the history of the pastoral elegy, for it, along with the fifth Eclogue, establishes the pattern by which lamentation gives way to joy and consolation. This pattern Tennyson follows in *In Memoriam*, and he is working entirely within the fusion of the classical and Christian traditions when he makes so much of a marriage and the birth of a baby at the end of his poem.

The picture of Dora and the child in the field, then, is especially rich in meaning. It is, in effect, a sacred picture, and he who looks at it aright feels the civilizing influences of love and the heartening influence of hopes for the future. The picture is fraught with vitality, and it is therefore no accident that the setting is a wheat field in harvest time. Even though Dora herself is condemned to perpetual maidenhood, her appearance with the child in a harvest setting associates her with something vital. We sense that this vitality goes beyond the domestic affections to a more elemental fertility, to a nature which is kind and bountiful, and ordered so as to provide for the needs of man. Here we are close to a concept of nature which is just the opposite of that one which is 'red in tooth and claw / With ravine,' a nature whose order is closely associated with the arts of civilization. Classical myth provides us with a figure who links civilization with the bounty of the earth, and she is Demeter. She seems to have held as central a place in Tennyson's imagination as Ruth, for she embodies those aspects of human experience which were the basis of Tennyson's faith and of his constant assertions of the value of life.

The epyllion *Demeter and Persephone* was not finished until 1887 and not published until 1889, but it dealt with a figure for whom Tennyson apparently felt a special attraction throughout his life. It is worth recalling that his earliest extant poem, and hence the first printed in Ricks' edition, is a translation of the opening part of Claudian's *De Raptu Proserpinae*. And Hallam Tennyson's comment on the poem in the *Memoir* is worth repeating: 'The poem from which the book was named was written at my request, because I knew that he considered Demeter one of the most beautiful types of motherhood.'[12] The myth, like the story of Ruth, is rural and domestic in character, and yet its pattern and rhythms, we soon discover, embrace the whole life of nature and the whole of human experience. Like the story of Ruth, the myth follows a pattern of separation and restoration which is in fact a symbolic death and rebirth. The chief action during the period of separation is the quest for a lost child. The motive of the quest is maternal love, and the reunion of mother and daughter corresponds with a renewal of fertility in nature. The relation of Demeter and Persephone does not just cause the fertility; it *is* the fertility. A human relationship which is the basis of civilization is thus identified with the bounty of nature – Tennyson's version of the classical identification of Demeter with both the fertility of the land and the arts of civilization. The single heroic action with which an epyllion traditionally deals is, in this case, an unusually rich one. The loss and recovery of a child becomes the type of human experience, embracing the cycle of the day (darkness and light), the cycle of the seasons (a period of sterility and a period of fertility), and the cycle of human experience (life, death, and a new life beyond both). Though the dominant pattern in the myth is a cyclical one, Tennyson replaces the classical pattern of endless recurrence with a spiral, a movement upward toward a new Golden Age.

The structure of the epyllion is one that Tennyson had rejected for *Dora*: he begins *in medias res*, with Persephone's return; the central part of the poem is a flashback in which Demeter tells of her grief and wanderings, while the conclusion is a prophecy of an age of 'younger kindlier Gods.' This kind of structure makes somewhat less of the pattern of separation and reunion, and somewhat more of progress toward a brighter future.

Demeter begins the epyllion by describing Persephone's return in terms of rebirth and resurrection. Darkness changes to light, and the change is accompanied by music; winter gives way to spring, and a dormant nature wakes to generation. The change is summed up in the line, 'Queen of the dead no more – my child!' (18), where the renewal of the human relation subsumes all other changes. Nonetheless, the renewal is not a precise repetition. Persephone has been Queen of the dead, and she has 'imperial disimpassioned eyes' (23) because she has lived in the underworld and has learned secrets hidden from the living. Demeter's reaction to this change in Persephone is one of awe. It is the reaction of a parent who sees a child advancing beyond her own knowledge, achieving a wisdom more comprehensive than her own. Yet Demeter has advanced too. The period of separation from her daughter has been a kind of death for her, and the experience of reunion is a major step forward:

> But when before have Gods or men beheld
> The Life that had descended re-arise,
> And lighted from above him by the Sun? (29–31)

The opening sections of the poem, then, not only celebrate Persephone's return, but suggest human progress.

The wandering of Demeter is the main action of the epyllion, and her account of it is a description of a waste land that is both a landscape and a state of mind. The land is not literally waste until after the dream, but the theme of alienation and a sense of the absurd are present from the beginning. The dialogue is a desolate antiphony consisting of Demeter's question 'Where?' and the recurring answer 'We know not.' This answer is given by winds, waves, and Fates, and their lack of knowledge about the meaning and purpose of their actions is a reflection of the condition the twentieth century calls alienation. In a situation like this the chief emotion is anxiety. The serpent, the scorpion, and the tiger all indicate an inhospitable and threatening universe.

In the midst of her epic wanderings, Demeter dreams that she sees the 'likeness' of Persephone, and the dream is crucial. In epic, a dream is a prophetic device, like the dreams of Dido and Eve. So here. The appearance of Persephone in the dream obviously foreshadows her actual reappearance. But the dream is rather more complex in its foreshadowing than that. Persephone's shadow is represented as saying:

> 'The Bright one in the highest
> Is brother of the Dark one in the lowest,
> And Bright and Dark have sworn that I, the child
> Of thee, the great Earth-Mother, thee, the Power
> That lifts her buried life from gloom to bloom,
> Should be for ever and for evermore
> The Bride of Darkness.'   (93–9)

The words are ambiguous, and Demeter takes them in their worst light, believing that Persephone is lost to her forever. But in fact the words suggest not just a restoration but a new life entirely. Zeus and Aïdoneus, says the shadow, are brothers, and the family relationship suggests not just the closeness of 'Bright' and 'Dark,' life and death, but also their common parentage, the totality of human experience. In fact, these opposites, the basis of the separation which causes Demeter's grief, are to be recognized as complements, as part of a wider unity. The fusion of these opposites is figured as a marriage: Persephone is to be 'for ever and for evermore / The Bride of Darkness' (98–9), a relation closer than that of brother and brother. The parent is 'the great Earth-Mother,' Demeter herself. Her happiness and grief, and the things associated with them – light and dark, fertility and sterility – are all summed up in this marriage.

Demeter, however, does not yet recognize the significance of the marriage. She is conscious primarily of the 'hard Eternities' (105) of the adverbs 'for ever and for evermore' (98), and this consciousness leads her to sympathize with the flexibly human rather than with the inflexibly divine. What follows, therefore, is Demeter's account of her alienation from the gods and her increasing sympathy with man. The crucial lines are these: 'The man, that only lives and loves an hour, / Seemed nobler than their hard Eternities' (104–5). These lines are followed by her account of how she caused the earth to become sterile:

> My quick tears killed the flower, my ravings hushed
> The bird, and lost in utter grief I failed
> To send my life through olive-yard and vine
> And golden grain, my gift to helpless man. (106–9)

At first glance the sentiment and the action seem contradictory. If she sympathizes with man, why should she affect his welfare so severely? But what seems to be a matter of cause and effect is in fact something else. Demeter's grief does not cause the sterility; it *is* the sterility, and the identity of the two makes Demeter the type of human suffering. In arguing that man is nobler than the gods, and in experiencing a very human grief, Demeter is in effect advancing a new concept of the heroic, a concept in which the hero (or heroine) encompasses in his experience all the changes that time brings, including death itself. It is a sense of the unity of this experience that is the truly heroic.

The intervention of Zeus confirms this concept. By decreeing that Persephone spend nine months of the year with Demeter and three with Aïdoneus, he gives divine sanction to cyclic recurrence. What looks like a compromise in fact is an arrangement figuring the true heroic that Demeter has come, slowly and painfully, to accept.

In the final section, Demeter foretells a time when the rhythm of change will give way to a blessed eternity, presided over by 'younger kindlier Gods' (129). About this passage Hallam Tennyson quotes his father as saying, 'When I write an antique like this I must put it into a frame – something modern about it. It is no use giving a mere *réchauffé* of old legends.' And Tennyson would give as an example of the frame lines 126 to 136.[13] The passage is usually interpreted as a foreshadowing of the Christian concept of immortality,[14] and the word 'frame' unfortunately suggests something put round the story which is not in the story itself. What Demeter foretells, however, is the fusion of light and dark, life and death, in a greater unity. The image is typically Tennysonian: 'Till thy dark lord accept and love the Sun, / And all the Shadow die into the Light' (135–6). Through the growth of love, the totality of human experience is to be fused in blessed immortality. The affirmation is of the same kind, and given in the same images, as that at the end of *In Memoriam*.[15] Robert Stange finds this affirmation unsatisfactory because it seems to lack assurance: 'Tennyson's desire for certainty, when he felt none, mars the last lines of *Demeter*.[16] But in fact this idea of a greater unity is prepared for by the dream and by the concept of the heroic that Demeter comes to, so that the 'frame' is not just an addition but the necessary conclusion to the movement of the poem. Such an affirmation is inherent in Tennyson's concept of Demeter, just as it is explicit in the story of Ruth.

These two poems, *Dora* and *Demeter and Persephone*, provide us with two types of the figure who stands at the centre of Tennyson's domestic imagination. This is the figure of a woman, with a child, set in a field of flowers and grain. The figure is associated both with the fertility of nature and with the order of civilization, largely through her love for the child, and through the feelings which that relationship arouses in others. In the myth about this woman, the child is lost and regained, and the separation and reunion are a symbolic death and rebirth. The woman embraces, then, the whole of human experience, and in her love fuses the opposites, sorrow and joy, life and death. The child is closely associated with this unity, and is the 'prophet of a mightier race' because he will make the unity real for all men. The figures of woman and child, and the myths associated with them, are the literary forms of Tennyson's many affirmations in other poems of the value of life (particularly family life), of the efficacy of love, of the certitude of immortality, and of the moral and spiritual advancement of man. In these figures and stories Tennyson realized some central aspects of his thought.

THE MYTH: *THE DAY-DREAM*

So far, I have dealt only with the female figures of Tennyson's domestic imagination, but the male has a role in the myth too, and it is a role which embraces the heroic in action just as the female figures embrace the heroic in the range of their experiences. The action is primarily the romance quest, and in Tennyson it customarily takes the form of penetration into a secret or forbidden place where the hero discovers and releases the mysterious sources of fertility and vitality. These forces are usually embodied in a female figure who, like Persephone, is identified with the fertility of nature, dormant in the winter months, and active in the spring and summer. The myth of a male who awakens this force has, of course, sexual significance, and some of the variations of the myth – the *hortus conclusus* passage of the Song of Songs, for instance, or the *Romance of the Rose* – are highly charged with sexual relations. But the origin of the myth is the sun awakening the dormant life in the seed. In *Demeter and Persephone*, the agent of Persephone's return is Zeus, but he is not called Zeus in the poem. Instead, he is 'The Bright one in the highest' (93), and he is described primarily in terms of light. In the pure myth, then, the male figure is the sun god; in Tennyson's romance versions, he is a prince or a knight, and his solar origins are suggested by his glittering armour or his blond hair. This myth is the basis of *The Lady of Shalott*, *Maud*, and *The Princess*, but it is most accessible in Tennyson's retelling of the story of Sleeping Beauty, *The Day-Dream*.

The centre of the poem is the section called *The Sleeping Beauty*, which was published in 1830 (the complete poem was published in 1842). The three stanzas of this section give us a picture of vitality suspended. The maiden herself sleeps a dreamless sleep, and she is 'A perfect form in perfect rest,' but her hair continues to grow – Tennyson describes it as 'streaming' forth – and the light around it is 'rich and warm.' The colours are black, white, and purple, the colours of winter and death. Sleeping Beauty's hair is 'jet-black,' and it streams forth from 'a braid of pearl'; her coverlet is purple. Though the colours are harsh, the effect of the description is by no means so. Shapes are rounded, lines are flowing, and the whole scene is bathed in the kind of light that, in modern photography, would be created by soft focus. Lines 15 and 16 are at the centre of the picture: 'Her constant beauty doth inform / Stillness with love, and day with light.' One has a sense of vital energy forming things from within. The myth deals with the way this energy is released and made productive.

Tennyson's additions elaborate this picture of suspended vitality and give the myth in its complete form. *The Sleeping Palace* gives us more details of the setting in which Sleeping Beauty herself is at the centre. The first two lines of the section deal with the familiar cycle of nature: 'The varying year with blade and sheaf / Clothes and reclothes the happy plains.' This pattern of recurrence contrasts with the Sleeping Palace, where time stands still. All action is suspended, so that 'like a picture seemeth all.' The whole scene is, in fact, like a work of art, and a comparison with Keats' Grecian urn seems inevitable. The scene has the same advantages and disadvantages. Everything is always fresh, and never grows old or decays; the brilliant colours, predominantly green and gold (the colours of youth) and red, never fade; it is always summer. As on Keats' urn, there is a man and a maid; he is always pursuing her, and his desire never falters; she is always 'blooming fair' (28). Nothing, however, changes, and so there is no opportunity for fulfilment, growth, or development. It is a static rather than a dynamic world: 'Here all things in their place remain, / As all were ordered, ages since' (53–4). In spite of the similarities with Keats' urn, there are dissimilarities as well. The pictures on the Grecian urn, though lifelike, are a 'cold pastoral,' but in the palace life is only suspended, and one has a sense of tremendous energy waiting to be released. Everything is waiting, in effect, to be born again. Hence the simile used to describe the palace and its inhabitants: 'spirits folded in the womb' (8); hence the picture, at the beginning of the third stanza, of birds sitting on their eggs: 'In these, in those the life is stayed' (18) – 'stayed' but not extinguished. And there is other evidence of immense potential energy: 'Here rests the sap within the leaf, / Here stays the blood along the veins' (3–4); 'The fountain to his place returns / Deep in the garden lake withdrawn' (11–12); the beams of light are scattered by the prisms of wine glass and beaker.

The release of all this energy is possible only in time, and hence the Prince is associated with change and the variety that it brings: 'Come, Care and Pleasure, Hope and Pain, / And bring the fated fairy Prince' (*The Sleeping Palace* 55–6). Change is associated with the cycle of the sun, and the Prince has some of the attributes of the sun god: 'He travels far from other skies – / His mantle glitters on the rocks' (*The Arrival* 5–6). But he is also the 'fairy Prince' of folk tales, the hero of romance who undertakes a difficult task and succeeds. The nature of this task is defined by the aphorisms with which the section called *The Arrival* begins:

> All precious things, discovered late,
>   To those that seek them issue forth;
> For love in sequel works with fate,
>   And draws the veil from hidden worth.   (1–4)

The action has to do with discovering hidden treasure, or, to put it another way, with penetrating to the heart of a mystery. The aphorisms indicate the conditions: activity on the part of the seeker, and a motive, love. Love works hand in hand with fate, and the relentless passing of time is shaped and redeemed by the activity of man. The specific image which inspires the Prince is very similar to that which inspired William Morris: the image of brave and loving men perishing in 'their daring deeds' (14), and of one brave and loving man persevering and succeeding.[17] The antagonist the Prince faces is 'the thorny close' (11), a deadly barrier that has claimed many victims. There is no logical reason why the Prince should succeed where the others have failed, but we must remember that logic has little place in the pattern of wish-fulfilment which governs romance. *The Arrival* is essentially the story of a successful quest; cause and effect, and the interaction of character and event, do not figure very largely here. We know nothing about the Prince except that he is helped along by a charm, 'words of promise' (23), 'whispered voices' (24), and 'Magic Music in his heart' (26). And we know little about the crucial struggle – the breaking through the deadly barrier – because it is narrated with such economy. The shape of the action overrides all other aspects of it: the approach, the crucial struggle, and the discovery, which leads to the release of the only true wealth, life itself. It is significant here that life comes out of darkness. When the Prince kisses Sleeping Beauty, he makes much of this pattern: 'Love, if thy tresses be so dark, / How dark those hidden eyes must be!' (31–2).

Tennyson divides his account of the results of the kiss into two sections (*The Revival, The Departure*) that present a contrast in style and effect. *The Revival* focuses on the return to the ordinary round of daily activities in the castle. The verse not only describes the sudden activity but reflects it, in piling up a list of things, animals, and people in speeded-up motion (the connective is 'and' in the first four lines; then even that is dropped in the breathless description of renewed activity), and in the cacophony of sounds (the words are full of plosives and sibilants, particularly in the initial consonants). The effect is comic. The account ends with the king's jovial let's-get-on-with-it attitude and with the chancellor's wily evasiveness. They and the others go on as if nothing had happened; no new worlds have opened up for them, and so the reader begins to sense a submerged metaphor here, in which ordinary waking life and sleep are identified. The result is quite different for the lovers. *The Departure* describes the exaltation of hero and heroine in terms of a new and better life for them. But the phrase 'that new world which is the old' (4) reminds us that the exaltation is largely an inner illumination which enables them to see old things in a new way. In effect, they now perceive the old world symbolically – a true awakening – and it reveals to them a spiritual world of almost unimaginable dimensions and bliss. The language becomes more general – as in 'Across the hills, and far away' (5) – to suggest vast spaces, mysterious distances, and perspectives of infinite promise. The

Prince's links with a sun god are again suggested, since the lovers appear to travel through the sky, and through a cyclical pattern of darkness and light, night and morning. But the moment the narrator characteristically focuses on is that point in the cycle when one becomes the other: 'The twilight melted into morn' (16); 'The twilight died into the dark' (24). Finally the cycle gives way to what is apparently endless day: 'Beyond the night, across the day, / Through all the world she followed him' (31–2). The dialogue between the lovers is mainly exclamations, and exclamations are appropriate to the ecstatic experience being described. The penetration of the secret place, then, releases energy, and reveals something even more mysterious: a dynamic universe that is somehow hidden by the round of daily life.

In *Demeter and Persephone*, the 'something modern' is integrated in the myth itself. In *The Day-Dream*, however, the myth and its nineteenth-century parallel are formally separated by the device of a frame. But though formally separated, the relation between the frame and the fairy tale is complex, and goes considerably beyond Fitzgerald's suggestion, recorded in the Eversley Edition, that the frame is simply 'an excuse for telling an old-world tale.' An examination of the relation between the frame and the tale helps us to understand the problems Tennyson faced in retelling myth, in providing in the retelling 'something modern.' 'It is no use giving a mere *réchauffé* of old legends.' The retelling is firmly based on Tennyson's sense of the continuing vitality of myth, and on its continuing ability to illuminate the essential patterns of modern life. But it is just as firmly based on his sense of the necessity to reshape the myth, to give it a structure and idiom that unmistakably represented the nineteenth century. Hence the curious combination, in so much of Tennyson's poetry, of what Victorian critics called the 'real' and the 'ideal.'

In the *Prologue* to this poem, the speaker is a young man, and he is with a young lady, Flora, to whom he is apparently engaged. The setting is out of doors, presumably a lawn, with a natural backdrop: 'behind, / A summer crisp with shining woods' (7–8). The activities are the domestic activities of the leisure class: for the young lady, embroidery, and a languid afternoon with her lover; for the young man, sleeping and dreaming, and telling stories. The sequence of activities (or non-activities) leading up to the fairy tale is worth noting. The speaker has been watching his lady while she sleeps. He describes her as being like a flower (as her name indicates) and specifically a rose, for she has a 'damask cheek' (3), the 'dewy sister-eyelids' (4) lie on her cheeks like petals, and she reclines 'by the lattice' (5). The speaker lets his mind and feelings drift ('I went through many wayward moods' 6) until 'I too dreamed' (9). The dream matures into a vision:

> And I too dreamed, until at last
>   Across my fancy, brooding warm,
> The reflex of a legend past,
>   And loosely settled into form.   (9–12)

It is worth noting that the dream is not the legend itself but its 'reflex'; that is, the type reflected in a particular occasion and circumstances. It is obvious enough that the actual occasion is the basis of the dream. Flora, the rose at the centre of the garden, is Sleeping Beauty (in the German version of the story, as told by the Brothers Grimm, Sleeping Beauty is Dornröschen), and the lattice becomes the deadly barrier. The languor of the summer day is reflected in the hundred-years' sleep. And the speaker is the Prince whose kiss brings Sleeping Beauty back to life. The fairy tale, then, presents actual circumstances in their imaginative form. It takes the 'real' and shapes it into the 'ideal.' It reveals the essential pattern in a familiar situation. But if the tale is the essence of that situation, it also affects that situation in unexpectedly complex ways. The *Moral, L'Envoi*, and the *Epilogue* all explore the application of the tale to the lives of the lovers. The *Moral* looks back, by implication, to Perrault's telling of the story in 'La belle au bois dormant,' which he concludes with some general truths that are meant to be a guide to conduct. The title of this section of Tennyson's poem is ironic, for the speaker points out that there is no moral, and refuses to 'hook [the story] to some useful end' (16). Instead, he advises Flora simply to take the story as story, and draws an analogy with her beauty: 'Go, look in any glass and say, / What moral is in being fair' (3–4). In giving this advice, the speaker apparently fears that if Flora reduces the story to a moral, she will then think she can discard the story itself, and all its imaginative energy will be lost. The next two sections explore some of the ways in which that energy illuminates their situation. In *L'Envoi*, Flora clearly expects something more from the story, and the young man comes up with a suggestion that is half in jest, half in earnest: 'were it not a pleasant thing / To fall asleep with all one's friends,' he asks, 'And every hundred years to rise / And learn the world, and sleep again' (3–4, 7–8). The suggestion is clearly a spur-of-the-moment one, and not totally applicable to the story, because everyone in the Palace (except Sleeping Beauty herself) is totally unaware of the passing of time, and carries on as if the hiatus were only half an hour. But the suggestion is a serious one, too. Such an arrangement would enable an individual to grasp 'The flower and quintessence of change' (24); that is, something which is both the product of time and yet is timeless; in short, a myth which is revealed in recurring patterns in particular situations. The pattern the speaker sums up is the essence of the Sleeping Beauty story, which he wishes to see in his being attracted to Flora:

> My fancy, ranging through and through,
> To search a meaning for the song,
>   Perforce will still revert to you;
> Nor finds a closer truth than this
>   All-graceful head, so richly curled,
> And evermore a costly kiss
>   The prelude to some brighter world.   (34–40)

The last two lines give the essential pattern, which the speaker then finds in other situations: the kiss of Adam and Eve in the Garden of Eden, and their own kisses that foreshadow their approaching marriage. But in the last lines of this section the irony of the situation becomes apparent. The actual situation falls considerably short of the ideal one, for Flora is no Sleeping Beauty when it comes to perceiving things imaginatively, and she simply does not know what her lover is talking about. Her waking life is like that of the king and the court in the tale, and she is metaphorically asleep. She is, in her lover's words, 'all too dearly self-involved, / Yet sleeps a dreamless sleep to me' (49–50). Nor is she to be awakened by the essential action of the story, a kiss. Hers is 'A sleep by kisses undissolved, / That lets thee neither hear nor see' (51–2). The fact that the actual situation falls short of the ideal one does not detract from the ideal, but the ideal does serve as a standard by which the actual is judged. That judgment is clear-sighted but not harsh, and the general effect is poignantly ironic rather than bitingly satiric. It is, after all, characteristic of the human situation that the ideal is always imperfectly realized. The speaker's attitude toward the actual situation is close to what Meredith was later to call the comic spirit, a spirit which is both clear-sighted and ready to accept imperfections. In the *Epilogue*, the speaker changes his initial advice ('Go, look in any glass') so that it indicates Flora's vanity ('what wonder, if he thinks me fair?' 4). He says that he himself was 'all unwise / To shape the song for your delight' (5–6) because it didn't touch her in any significant way, but was simply an ornament like 'long-tailed birds of

Paradise' and 'old-world trains.' But he gives her the story anyway, 'earnest wed with sport, / And either sacred unto you' (11–12). In effect, the
story is an offering to an ideal that Flora both reflects and departs from.

The *Day-Dream* allows us to see clearly two patterns that are central to
Tennyson's imagination. One is an action: the hero's approach to a
maiden in a forbidden garden; the other is a structural principle: the
modern response to an old story. The action, as we shall see, is typical of
the *English Idyls,* and it appears in more complex ways in longer poems,
like *The Princess* and *Maud.* In *Maud,* for instance, there are two principal
settings, the little wood and Maud's garden; the former is full of dangers
(like the briar wood or the thick forest in the Sleeping Beauty story) and
the latter promises rewards. The shifting significance of the two settings
makes up the 'main movement of the poem.'[18] This same action occurs in
The Lady of Shalott, where Lancelot's approach is the turning point in the
story; and it is an action which Mariana longs for, though she remains
enclosed in her moated grange. The modern response to an old story is
equally important in Tennyson's work. The formal device of the frame is,
as we shall see, used in *The Princess* and *The Epic,* where we have realistic
reactions to old romances. The frame separates the response from the
story, but Tennyson fuses the two in a complex way in *Idylls of the King.*

THE FORM: *THE MILLER'S DAUGHTER, THE GARDENER'S DAUGHTER,* *THE BROOK*

If the stories of Ruth, Demeter and Persephone, and Sleeping Beauty are
the types in which we see some of Tennyson's chief concerns as a poet,
then we can begin to understand his requirements in poetic form. Clearly
he needed a form in which he could explore the relations between domestic and heroic, real and ideal. Clearly, too, he needed a form which would
embrace a wide range of human experiences, for the stories I have just
been examining involve separations and reunions, sorrows and joys. If
one were to examine these stories by using the modes distinguished by
Northrop Frye, tragedy, comedy, irony, and romance could all be found
in them. Such a range of patterns and effects requires an encyclopedic
form, like the epic. But Tennyson was not attracted to such a long form.
For the most part, he preferred the small and finely finished to the large
and ungainly. Looking back on 1838, he told his son, 'I felt certain of one
point then ... if I meant to make any mark at all, it must be by shortness, for
the men before me had been so diffuse, and most of the big things except
"King Arthur" had been done.'[19] And in the context of a conversation

with Browning in the 1870s Tennyson is quoted as saying: 'An artist should get his workmanship as good as he can, and make his work as perfect as possible. A small vessel, built on fine lines, is likely to float further down the stream of time than a big raft.'[20] Tennyson's classical education made him familiar with a form which fitted his preferences and requirements unusually well. It was a shorter rather than a longer form, and yet it retained something of the comprehensive quality of the epic, and of the epic's wide-ranging treatment of human experience. This form was the idyl. The epyllion is closely related to the idyl, as we shall see, but it is with the latter that we must begin.

Critics have long recognized that the idyl is (to use Gilbert Lawall's description) a 'composite or eclectic form.'[21] Some of the *Scholia* which accompany the poems of Theocritus date back to the first century before Christ, and even these statements describe the idyl as a mixed form. Herbert Snow, a Victorian editor of Theocritus, translates a statement from the *Codex Ambrosianus*:

All poetry has three styles: the descriptive, the dramatic, and the mixed. Now the bucolic is a mixture composed, as it were, of every form: consequently it is more agreeable from the variety of its manner, consisting at one time of the descriptive, at another of the dramatic; and anon of the mixed, or combination of descriptive and dramatic; and sometimes of something else ... It should be known, moreover, that the name Idyll means 'the little poem', from the word εἶδος, a representation or picture ...[22]

The idyl was thus an unusually rich and flexible form, and its special marks were concentration rather than expansiveness, and comprehensiveness rather than narrowness. It allowed the poet to deal, in a brief form, with a range of experience as broad as that observed by the Lady of Shalott. She, we recall, sees among the 'mirror's magic sights' funerals and marriages, reapers and shepherd-lads, market girls and knights. The idyl, like the web, brings all these together, the various combinations making possible a wide range of effects.*

---

* The characteristics of the idyl are dealt with in much greater detail by Robert Patti-son, whose book, *Tennyson and Tradition* (Cambridge, Mass.: Harvard University Press 1979) appeared while this book was in the process of being published. His second chapter ('The Sources of Tennyson's Idyll') is an excellent account of the genre which was the poet's favourite. Pattison points out that the chief characteristics of the form are self-consciousness and eclecticism. Self-consciousness is apparent in the display of erudition (largely through allusion, which 'compels the work to be studied as artifact

The way in which Tennyson used the genre can be demonstrated by an analysis of three idyls, *The Miller's Daughter*, *The Gardener's Daughter*, and *The Brook*. The three idyls belong together, because they all present versions of the Sleeping Beauty story; that is, in each there is a lady who is to be found in a garden, or in a rural setting that is like a garden, and each describes the approach by the lady's lover, who is hindered sometimes by a parental figure (as in comedy) and sometimes by his own inexperience in perceiving the ideal. All three are a mixture of the dramatic, the narrative, and the descriptive, and some have intercalary songs as well. Through this mixture, Tennyson explores the various ways in which idealized love is realized in actual circumstances.

The Miller's Daughter is a typical mixture. The poem's dramatic elements are those which are often identified with the dramatic monologue. There is a speaker (the husband), a listener (Alice, the miller's daughter), an occasion ('after-dinner talk / Across the walnuts and the wine' 31–2), and some action (the gesture that accompanies 'In yonder chair' 9; 'Yet fill my glass: give me one kiss' 17; the going forth to the mill at the end). Mixed with the dramatic is the narrative. It is a story of courtship and marriage which focuses on the courtship: the wanderings of 'the long and listless boy' (33), the fishing expedition on which he catches his first sight of Alice, the wooing, and the introduction of Alice to his mother. Mingled with these two elements are descriptions of the landscape, especially the landscape around the mill. And two love songs are introduced in the course of the idyl. It is not enough, of course, simply to list the various elements in this mixture. Tennyson combines them in a particular way for precise effects.

The theme of the poem is happiness in love, particularly married love, and this idealization of marriage is a theme that was especially appealing to the early Victorian reader. There were precedents, of course – the 'Hail wedded Love' passage in *Paradise Lost* is one – and, like Milton, Tennyson links marriage with an idealized rural landscape, and thus makes the domestic a version of pastoral. The landscape here is not just a setting for the courtship and marriage, but a reflection of it, 'not merely in harmony,'

---

instead of as inspiration' p 20) and in distancing (which is achieved through the use of a frame, or of allegory). As for eclecticism, the idyl 'is culturally omnivorous, and it plays with its sources ...' (p 20). It is 'epic in intent' (p 22), and it 'seeks universality in a comprehensive survey of the continuum of human feeling' (p 23), but at the same time the idyl is relatively brief and concentrated. Above all, it reflects 'the Alexandrian preoccupation with genre and poetic form' (p 18) – a preoccupation of Tennyson, too.

to use Hallam Tennyson's words, 'but in direct sympathy with the subject of the poem.'[23] The idyl celebrates love, not as a revolutionary force or as 'rage' (the word is used at line 192 of the poem), but as order, the kind of order nineteenth-century writers meant when they talked about the strength of the domestic affections. The nature of that order is evident in the courtship itself. Its chief manifestation is human development, which takes the forms of increasing understanding, maturing emotions, and quickening perception: it moves toward fulfilment in marriage and in all the joys and sorrows that that state brings. The literary opposite of the wooing described here is the ritualized movement of the courtly love tradition, particularly as we see it in works influenced by Petrarch. There satisfaction lies, not in marriage, but in prolonging the courtship itself. The lady is conventionally as cold and remote as she is beautiful, and scorns the attentions of her lover. The lover despairs of any return of his feelings, but finds a static satisfaction in faithful worship of his beloved. In contrast, Tennysonian love is fruitfully dynamic. It grows and matures with time. Like Browning, Tennyson often makes human love a witness of divine love, revealing a spiritual world lying in and around and behind the phenomenal world. Hence love makes up for the deficiencies of time (for a great deal of time has passed in the poem, and husband and wife are now old), or (to use an older phrase) it redeems time. It is possible to see this idyl as Tennyson's treatment of the Petrarchan theme of the triumph of love over time. For time is a major element in this poem, and is slowly bearing the lovers toward death. Love gives shape and purpose to this inexorable movement. This shape appears in Tennyson's treatment of two major images in the poem: eyes, and the circle. The sense impressions of the eye give way to vision; and the circle develops out of random movement and coincidence, as the speaker's passivity gives way to purposeful activity.

The idyl combines a wide range of experiences and responses: there is the sadness and decline of old age ('There's somewhat flows to us in life, / But more is taken quite away' 21–2) and the sense of an earthly existence that does not fully meet human desires ('There's somewhat in this world amiss' 19). There is the joy of the marriage and the celebration of its continuing vitality ('Such eyes! I swear to you, my love, / That these have never lost their light' 87–8). And there is joy in the speaker's retelling the story of his courtship as a romance quest. This mixture Tennyson extended in his revisions of the poem for the edition of 1842. He added the account of Alice meeting the speaker's mother (137–60), an account where light touches of humour are combined with tender feeling, and he added two stanzas (223–38) describing the birth and death of the child. Joys and sorrows are thus mingled in the idyl, and given an order in art as they are in the speaker's experience, where (to quote another addition of 1842) 'Past and Present, wound in one, / Do make a garland for the heart' (197–8).

The Gardener's Daughter is listed among the English Idyls in Tennyson's 1884 edition of his works, the first edition in which he used that label for a group of his early poems. Here, too, there is a mixture of elements, but the effect is quite different. The dramatic element includes a speaker, the 'I' of the poem; a listener who is not named but referred to specifically in lines 264–9; and an occasion, the showing of the portrait of Rose. Aside from our sense of the narrator recounting his experiences, these dramatic elements are not apparent until the very end of the poem, although the occasion (the anniversary of his first meeting with Rose) is mentioned in the first line. The unveiling of the picture commemorates that meeting, and both it and the telling of the story (like the narration in The Miller's Daughter) are a ritual commemorating a happy courtship and marriage. The narrative element, like that of the earlier poem, focuses on the courtship, especially the first sight of the beloved. The narrative presents a particular pattern of separation and reunion, which might be called a pattern of approach and retreat. There are meetings with Rose and partings from her, actions described in terms of retirement to a garden and return to a city. The narrator chooses not to tell in detail about any meeting except their first, and he refuses to narrate or describe the events of their marriage. The narrative and the dramatic elements of the idyl are complementary. The story centres on the approach to Rose, while the drama centres on a commemorative approach, the unveiling. The descriptions in the poem support both these ritual movements. Hallam Tennyson quotes his father as saying 'The centre of the poem, that passage describing the girl, must be full and rich. The poem is so, to a fault, especially the descriptions of nature, for the lover is an artist, but, this being so, the central picture must hold its place.'24 The central picture is the description of Rose in the garden, which is also, apparently, a description of the painting of Rose (hence the subtitle of the poem, The Pictures). Both the description and the painting itself are icons, images 'comforting the mind,' to use the phrase from In Memoriam. The painting represents someone whom the speaker in effect regards as sacred, and hence her image is honoured with worship and adoration, as the unveiling indicates. The fullness and richness of this idyl, then, in effect ritualize the Sleeping Beauty story by focusing on the pattern of approach, unveiling, and retreat.

The Brook is a later poem than the two I have just dealt with, and was not published until 1855. When it first appeared, it was subtitled 'An Idyl.' As we should expect, its form is mixed: there is both the dramatic (the first 196 lines of the poem are the speech of Lawrence Aylmer, and there is a good deal of dialogue either reported or given in the course of the story) and the narrative (the story of a love affair), as well as intercalary songs (in which the brook is represented as speaking). In addition, the poem begins with an elegy for the speaker's brother Edmund, moves on to the comic story of the speaker's role in the courtship of Katie and James, and ends with another story that is essentially romance rather than comedy. The mixture embodies patterns and figures we are now familiar with: separation (which takes the form of death) and reunion, an approach to a lady in a garden, and a child who is associated with the fertility of nature.

The first thirty-six lines of the poem are an elegy for Edmund, the poet. This part of the idyl begins and ends with a separation: at the beginning, it is a leave-taking as each brother departs on a journey; at the end it is Edmund's death in Italy. Both separations are associated with the brook: the brook is the scene of the parting at the beginning, and at the end it is the subject of Edmund's song which the speaker quotes in his brother's memory. The theme of this song is a traditional part of the elegiac lament: 'For men may come and men may go, / But I go on for ever' (33–4). At first glance the refrain seems to be a version of the old thought that nature renews herself, but man once gone is gone always. But the lines are preceded by a phrase that is also repeated in all the other songs: 'I flow / To join the brimming river' (31–2). The 'brimming river' is a version of the 'great deep,' the mysterious source and end of all life. In this context, the brook is a metaphor for human life, which, through children and the generations they represent, goes on forever. The brook is thus a complex symbol, suggesting both the passing of life and the preservation of it.

The main story (given in lines 36–196) has to do with the speaker's part in the courtship of Katie and James. This story is comic, and follows the traditional pattern of comedy: a young man and a young woman are in love, but their courtship is hindered by the young woman's garrulous father; with the help of the speaker, they get round the father, and the courtship concludes happily in marriage. Katie is the beautiful girl in the middle of a garden, and her lover (with the connivance of Katie and the speaker) overcomes the chief obstacle in his approach to her, and proposes. The description of Katie (lines 67–73) is worth noting, since she is associated with the fertility and bounty of nature, and hence with Ruth and Persephone. One might even go so far as to suggest that the speaker's account of his part in the story is a comic version of the Demeter and

Persephone myth. It is, after all, a story of separation and reunion, in which Katie leaves the speaker and then returns to him. The period of separation is the comic equivalent of a symbolic death as the speaker listens to Philip talk: 'O Katie, what I suffered for your sake!' (119). The conversation takes so long that the speaker fears 'to die a listener' (163). Though the sun is literally setting, the reunion is described in terms of a rising sun: the speaker and Philip 'found the sun of sweet content / Re-risen in Katie's eyes, and all things well' (168–9).

In the final section of the poem (lines 197–228) Tennyson steps back from Lawrence Aylmer (who has been the speaker in the poem to this point) and, through an anonymous narrator, gives an account of Aylmer's meeting with Katie's daughter, who looks just like her and bears her name. And through her, Aylmer is invited to a reunion with Katie herself. The broader pattern of the poem now becomes apparent, and it is, as we should expect, a pattern of separation and reunion. Katie and James emigrated twenty years before the actual time of the idyl, and have now returned to England. The meeting with the daughter takes place in a rural setting, and it is harvest time. The child is here old enough to be on her own, but she does what we would expect of a child in an idyl: she preserves her mother's beauty, and maintains the fertility associated with it. As such, she is associated with both the Demeter and Persephone myth and the Sleeping Beauty story. Her hair, like that of her mother, is an image of a bountiful harvest, and she is associated with flowers that are both actual (in the hedge) and suggested (in Aylmer's apostrophe, 'Too happy, fresh and fair' 217). When Aylmer first sees her, he is 'seated on a stile / In the long hedge' (197–8), and her appearance is heralded by a trembling of air in the hedge itself (lines 201–4) – a much displaced version of the breaking up of Sleeping Beauty's hedge. These suggestions, however, are submerged in the particulars of the narrative, which is essentially a romance version of the comic story in the central part of the idyl. As we should expect in romance, cause and effect are dispensed with. The meeting is sheer coincidence, and it represents a fulfilment of a long-standing desire of Aylmer. Hence the analogy with a dream: Aylmer 'Laughed also, but as one before he wakes, / Who feels a glimmering strangeness in his dream' (215–6). Aylmer's remembrance of things past is thus completed by a re-creation and (as one has come to expect in Tennyson's idyls) that re-creation takes the form of a family reunion.

The Brook is thus a fairly complex treatment of the pattern of separation and reunion, linking as it does an elegiac treatment of the pattern with a comic one, and enclosing both within the wish-fulfilment pattern of romance. The link among all these various elements is of course the brook itself. I have already indicated how the refrain suggests both the passing of life and the preservation of it. But we also note, as we move through the songs, that the movement of the brook becomes less direct and more subtle and complex, like the poem itself. Compare, for instance, the initial words of the four songs: 'I come' (23), 'I chatter' (39), 'I wind about' (55), and 'I steal by' (170). In the first song, the brook's movement is swift and easy, and there is a directness about its flowing from source to river that is emphasized by the varied verbs (for instance, 'sparkle out,' 'bicker down,' 'hurry down'). In the second song, the verbs for the most part describe the sound of the brook, and the repetition of the verb 'chatter' leads directly into the account of Philip's garrulousness. In the third song, the movement is more varied and apparently random. It begins with 'I wind about, and in and out,' and the phrase 'here and there' is repeated twice. Like the second song, it anticipates the main part of the idyl in foreshadowing the evasive action of the story. That story, it should be noted, is full of references to water. James appears 'like a wader in the surf' (117), Philip walks 'babbling as he went' (123), and the story of selling the colt is told in terms of fishing. In the final song, the movement of the brook becomes much more subtle and airy. It seems to pervade everything, to tie everything together; like Carlyle's organic filaments, it is a metaphor for the mysterious connections among human lives; and, like those filaments, it has many curious links with the mysterious sources of life itself. If we were to look for a single image which might be considered essential to the combination and fusion of patterns the Tennysonian idyl deals with, we have come very close to finding it in the brook.

THE FORM: ŒNONE

When the idyl deals with, or suggests, material that might be appropriate to the epic – heroic figures, great actions, and events upon which the fate of a society or nation depends – it is more properly called an epyllion, though the techniques of the two forms are very similar. (MacCallum's comment that the idyl is 'an epic in miniature' is a good indication of the closeness of the relationship.)[25] Like the idyl, the epyllion has its origin in the Greek literature of Alexandria, and the genre was the subject of the famous quarrel between Callimachus and Apollonius of Rhodes. Apollonius took Homer as his model, and insisted that the long narrative poem was still a vital form, as he tried to demonstrate in his own *Argonautica*. But Callimachus argued that the age of the epic was past. 'A big book is a big nuisance' is the saying that sums up his view. He argued instead for brevity and polish, and in this matter he was apparently supported by Theocritus, if we are to judge by some of the comments in the idyls. Tennyson's preference for a shorter form places him in the same camp, and Theocritus was one of his favourite poets. He liked in particular the thirteenth idyl, the epyllion about Hylas. We know that he translated it aloud in 1855, and that he translated it again for Palgrave about 1857, saying, 'I should be content to die ... if I had written anything equal to this.'[26] Tennyson was likely attracted by both the polish and the richness that were achieved through condensation and allusion. The technique of suggesting the whole action of an epic, with all of its varied implications, in a single incident or event provided an opportunity for experiments of many sorts, but in particular the kind of experiment where he could reveal the heroic dimensions of a single or common action. His means, as Marshall McLuhan has pointed out in his important introduction to the Rinehart edition of Tennyson's *Selected Poetry*, were 'discontinuity, flashback, digressions, and subplots. Dramatic parallelism, multileveled implication, and symbolic analogy, rather than linear perspective or narrative, characterize the little epic at all times.'[27] Marjorie Crump's definition of the epyllion is worth quoting at length, because it sums up much that I have been saying:

An epyllion is a short narrative poem. The length may and does vary considerably, but an epyllion seems never to have exceeded the length of a single book, and probably the average length was four to five hundred lines. The subject is sometimes merely an incident in the life of an epic hero or heroine, sometimes a complete story, the tendency of the author being to use little-known stories or possibly even to invent new ones. The later Alexandrians and Romans preferred love stories and usually concentrated the interest on the heroine. The style varies; it may be entirely narrative, or may be decorated with descriptive passages of a realistic character. The dramatic form is frequently employed, and it is usual to find at least one long speech ... The general style of the epyllion is that of all Alexandrian poetry, formal, allusive, learned. The language and atmosphere are more homely than those of grand epic, and a graceful use of realism gives great charm to the work of some poets.[28]

This definition indicates that the epyllion is a mixed and flexible form like the idyl, and that it too suggests the great and heroic in the common and familiar. I have already called *Demeter and Persephone* an epyllion, and it is not too difficult to see why: in the dramatic form Tennyson uses, the speaker is the heroine of the story; the theme is love (primarily maternal love); the narrative is the story of a single incident (the recovery of Persephone), which is told in part by means of flashback; and, in Tennyson's treatment of that incident, it becomes the type of the whole of human experience. Tennyson's earlier epyllia are equally interesting. I propose to examine one of them, *Œnone*.

As an epyllion, *Œnone* corresponds closely to Marjorie Crump's definition. It deals with a single incident (the Judgment of Paris); it concentrates on the heroine; and it is a love story. It foreshadows the action of the *Iliad* and the destruction of Troy, and does so through the devices that McLuhan has listed. Moreover, the form is composite or mixed. The narrative includes the story of the Judgment of Paris, with which the story of Œnone is inextricably linked. The poem is dramatic, for Œnone herself is the speaker throughout most of it, and her story includes dialogue and speeches that are dramatic. There are detailed descriptions of the landscape. In addition, there is a movement from a pastoral love lament to an account of an event which is in essence heroic, and this movement is accompanied by a shift towards an epic style. Paul Turner is critical of 'some lack of uniformity in style,'[29] but the mixed style is in fact appropriate to the mixed form, and gives Tennyson the opportunity to achieve a range of effects that suggests the encyclopedic quality of the epic proper. The action of the poem demanded such treatment. The Judgment of Paris had long been an especially attractive story, because such vast consequences and such important issues were bound up in it, and so it is a natural subject for an epyllion. Renaissance writers viewed the Judgment of Paris as a link between the pastoral and the heroic, and Tennyson treats it in this way in his epyllion. As such, the poem is an interesting parallel to the link between the domestic and the heroic that I have been tracing.

The introduction (lines 1–21) gives the context for Œnone's long speech, and here the chief patterns of the poem are established. The foreground is a quiet pastoral scene; the background includes dangerous precipices, an ominous mist, and the city of Troy itself, 'Ilion's columned citadel' (13). The mournfulness and disconsolate wandering of Œnone are thus seen against a background of great heights and depths, and of prospects that are heroic and sublime rather than sheltered and pastoral. The epyllion will explore the links between foreground and background, links established by Œnone in the important analogy which she uses, at the outset, to describe her own lament:

'Hear me, for I will speak, and build up all
My sorrow with my song, as yonder walls
Rose slowly to a music slowly breathed,
A cloud that gathered shape ...'   (38–41)

Œnone thus compares the making of her lament with the building of
Troy, and sets up the parallel between her own situation and that of the
city. It was the music of Apollo that constructed Troy,[30] but Œnone gives
the analogy in such a way as to link it with the mist imagery. Her song is
like Apollo's music, 'slowly breathed,' and the vapour suggested here is
made explicit in the phrase, 'A cloud that gathered shape.' Œnone is
herself 'the daughter of a River-God' (37), and that associates her both
with Venus, who was born from the waves of the sea, and with the mists of
the mountain setting. Of these her hair in particular seems to be a part,
since it 'Floated ... or seemed to float in rest' (18). One has a sense of
something taking shape out of mist, existing precariously, and then dissolving again. The analogy defines both the shape of the poem and the
nature of the epyllion. Œnone's song gives shape to her emotion, but that
shape will soon give way to unreasoning passion which marks the disintegration of her personality. The refrain 'harken ere I die' thus defines the
structure of the poem: a shaping at the beginning and a falling apart at the
end. The mist image links this structure with Troy itself, which was once
shaped by music and is soon to be destroyed by a war caused by unreasoning passion. The mist image, with its shapes that appear and dissolve, is
thus the chief link between the personal and the general, and forces us to
see parallels between the situation of an individual and the fate of a city.
That kind of parallel is part of the essential nature of an epyllion.

   Equally essential is Tennyson's use of allusion. The encyclopedic quality of the epyllion depends to a large extent on this device, which is so
pervasive that Paul Turner has argued that the poem 'is a distillation, not
of life, but of literature.'[31] For instance, the description of Œnone's hair,
which I have already quoted, suggests both Virgil's description of Dido
and Ovid's description of Cassandra, so that Œnone becomes a type of the
abandoned woman. The speeches of the three goddesses give Tennyson
the opportunity to sum up two major schools of classical philosophy (for
Here's diction is 'adapted from Lucretius' description of the Epicurean
gods,' while Pallas uses the concepts and language of Stoicism),[32] and to
present a third choice which is, in Turner's words, 'entirely unphilosoph-
ical' but 'still profoundly literary.'[33] References, allusions, and echoes thus

combine in a concentrated way to define the nature and importance of the central action.

This, then, is the manner in which Tennyson has Œnone tell the story of the Judgment of Paris. This story has been traditionally interpreted as the choice of one of three courses in life, as an individual's shaping of his future. But that future is not an isolated one, and on this choice the fate of a nation depends. The pattern that Tennyson seems most interested in is the pattern whereby both individual well-being and a whole civilization are destroyed. He works out this pattern by treating the Sleeping Beauty story as tragedy. Œnone is another version of the maiden in a pastoral retreat, and her lover has not only come but gone, so that she is left isolated. The 'fragment twined with vine' (19) on which she is leaning is what is left of the woods surrounding her bower, a barrier now in ruins. The same tragic treatment is evident in the main story itself. During the principal action, Œnone is, at Paris' command, hidden 'within the cave' (85), and she herself says that she was waiting 'underneath the dawning hills' (46). It is from these same hills that the fountains of Mount Ida spring, and Œnone is closely associated with these waters, because she is 'the daughter of a River-God' (37) and because she invokes 'many-fountained Ida.' Waters springing from the ground usually symbolize vitality and fertility, dormant during the winter, and released by the sun god upon his return in the springtime. Paris has some of the characteristics of the sun (note in particular Œnone's description of him in lines 56 to 59), but he orders Œnone to remain in the cave. His coming, then, is not release but entrapment; not a reunion, but a separation. Tennyson draws attention to this division by having Œnone use, twice in two lines, the rhetorical device called a polyptoton: though she may 'behold' the action, she herself is 'unbeheld'; though she may 'hear,' she is 'unheard' (87–8). Such separation and such entrapment are the marks of tragedy.

The last parts of the epyllion look forward to the results of this isolation and imprisonment, and, in doing so, suggest the broader epic action. There are signs of discord and destruction, and one senses both an individual and a world breaking up. This sense is conveyed largely in the images. The kisses that Œnone lusts for are like a 'quick-falling dew' (200), and they are to be 'thick as Autumn rains / Flash in the pools of whirling Simois' (201–2). The mist image is now associated with the end of the cycle of the seasons, and with rains that cause destructive floods. The cutting of the pine trees has destroyed the pastoral landscape, and has left 'ruined folds' (217), 'fragments tumbled from the glens' (218), and 'dry thickets'

(219). The mist becomes an 'ever-floating cloud' (234) that is an image of death. And the final lines of the poem are dominated by the fire image. Œnone has 'fiery thoughts' (242), 'A fire dances' before Cassandra (260), and to Œnone herself 'All earth and air seem only burning fire' (264). Such burning traditionally represents lust, and it is extended here to foreshadow the destruction of Troy. That destruction has its source in Paris' passion for Helen, of which the parallel is Œnone's passion for Paris. Such passion is the opposite of domestic love, and it is significant that Œnone finds the idea of bearing Paris' child a nightmare (lines 246–51). Here there is to be no child to shape the future. The epyllion began with Œnone's wandering in a rural landscape, but it ends with her going down into Troy. The movement confirms a link which the whole epyllion has been exploring in a variety of ways.

SATIRE: *EDWIN MORRIS, WALKING TO THE MAIL,*
SEA DREAMS, AND AYLMER'S FIELD

Victorian readers often thought that the idyl ought to deal with the idyllic; that is, with a pastoral landscape which offered the possibility of a contented human existence. But such expectations ignored a good part of the pastoral tradition in poetry, for some of Theocritus' idyls are bitterly critical of actual social conditions; Petrarch, Boccaccio, and Mantuan use the pastoral as a means of expressing their political, religious, and moral ideas; their works lead in turn to the pastoral eclogues of Spenser, Sidney, and Drayton; the satiric function of the pastoral informs parts of Milton's *Lycidas*, and the pastoral, though often ridiculed as a form in the eighteenth century, was still sometimes used to attack follies and vices. Satire thus has a fairly established place in the pastoral tradition, and, though Tennyson shifts the ideal from pastoral to domestic, it is not surprising that a concern with follies and vices should turn up in his idyls as well. The fault he attacks is neatly summed up in a phrase in *Aylmer's Field* – 'marriage-hindering Mammon' (374) – and the point of view from which he attacks it is specified in the phrase itself. Marriage is the expression of human love; the relationship establishes a social unit characterized by peace, contentment, and harmony, and hence the family is both the model for society and the stabilizing and inspiring force in it; the children of a marriage are prophets of a mightier race and living links with it. In hindering marriage, then, Mammon undermines both present and future society, and replaces family ties with the 'Cash-payment' as, in Carlyle's words, 'the sole nexus of man with man.' The speaker in *The Golden Year* describes his period as an age

> That, setting the *how much* before the *how*,
> Cries, like the daughters of the horseleech, 'Give,
> Cram us with all. ...'   (11–13)

This sense of an age which is grasping and selfish is a familiar enough feature of Tennyson's work. The speaker in *Maud*, for instance, rails against his age, and the figure of Mammon whom he invokes in the first section of the poem – a figure with whom Maud's brother is associated – is the chief barrier between the speaker and the beloved maiden. Similarly, in *Northern Farmer, New Style*, the son confronts Mammon in his father, who is determined to prevent a marriage with the poor parson's daughter, and to promote marriage to a girl with property, like the mother: 'Warn't she as good to cuddle an' kiss as a lass as 'ant nowt?' (24).

The theme is secondary in *The Brook*, but it is pervasive, and appears in all three parts of the idyl. In the elegy, the speaker contrasts his brother the poet with 'the strong sons of the world' whose lives are apparently governed by the cash nexus:

> One whom the strong sons of the world despise;
> For lucky rhymes to him were scrip and share,
> And mellow metres more than cent for cent;
> Nor could he understand how money breeds,
> Thought it a dead thing; yet himself could make
> The thing that is not as the thing that is.   (3–8)

Underlying this description is a Ruskinian sense of life (especially the life of the imagination) as true wealth. Well-being is alone productive, while money is 'a dead thing.' In the central story, Philip's tiresome talkativeness arises out of his obsession with material things: 'He praised his land, his horses, his machines; / He praised his ploughs, his cows, his hogs, his dogs' (124–5), and so on. His longest story is the account of bargaining for the colt. But Philip's obsession does not extend to his daughter Katie, nor does he see her marriage as a means of improving his material welfare. Hence the treatment of his obsession as a comic eccentricity. In the final section of the idyl, Katie and James have apparently earned money abroad that enables them to buy, on their return, the farm they once tenanted. Here the money serves the broader human purposes of their lives, and is associated with the bounty of the land, which alone is true wealth. The idyl's initial contrast between human creativity and dead money is thus resolved when money assumes its proper and subordinate place in the arrangements of human life.

'Marriage-hindering Mammon' is a more central theme in *Edwin Morris*, where Tennyson's treatment of it is less comic, and more melodramatic and ironic. The presiding deity of the story is a type of Mammon, 'The rentroll Cupid of our rainy isles' (103), and financial considerations and the business arrangements of life constantly undermine romantic ideals. The theme is potentially tragic, but the treatment here is a mixture of melodrama, irony, and comedy. The narrator speeds up the action so that the changes and reversals happen quickly, a comic technique that emphasizes incongruities. The first action of the story – the crossing of the lake to see Letty – is an action undertaken in the service of an ideal, and the simplified emotions involved in a forbidden meeting of this sort smack of melodrama. There are some familiar patterns and images. The journey across the lake for a dangerous meeting with a loved one in a garden is yet another version of the Sleeping Beauty story. And there is a specific allusion to the Demeter and Persephone myth: 'she moved, / Like Proserpine in Enna, gathering flowers' (112). Ricks points out the allusion to Milton's Eve in Paradise, 'with suggestions of precariousness' (p 712). The meeting will soon give way to a parting as Letty is snatched away from the narrator. This separation is potentially tragic, but in fact the account of it has a comic effect. The vows of eternal love are exaggerated:

> 'Leave,' she cried,
> 'O leave me!' 'Never, dearest, never: here
> I brave the worst ...'   (116–18)

The exaggeration makes the reversal all the more sudden and complete. The whole edifice of romantic love comes crashing down with a rout of 'pugs / And poodles' (119–20), 'Trustees and Aunts and Uncles' (121). Their exaggerated gestures and speeches make the discovery comic, and the shrilling of 'the cotton-spinning chorus' (122) anticipates Gilbert and Sullivan. The consequences follow just as quickly. Letty is wed within a month 'to sixty thousand pounds' (126) while the narrator is broken by 'an ancient creditor' (130) – both victims of that ironic figure, 'rentroll Cupid.' The narrator treats Letty's marriage ironically and his own flight melodramatically: 'Her taper glimmered in the lake below: / I turned once more, close-buttoned to the storm' (135–6).

The experience does not, as one would expect, make the speaker a confirmed cynic. Instead, he has pardoned Letty and accepted what happened, because 'She seems a part of those fresh days to me' (142). Ironically, this story of disappointed hopes ends with the reassertion of an ideal, which he now sees symbolized by the landscape. The swallow 'dips his wing' (145) in the lake, and the image, as in *In Memoriam*, suggests hidden depths; and fire, which is only suggested in the colour of 'the gold-lily' (146), but appears more specifically in the cloud ('overhead / The light cloud smoulders on the summer crag' 145–6), is an image for the vitality of a transcendent spiritual world. Like the speaker in *Locksley Hall*, this young man finds consolation in his own ability to integrate griefs and disappointments into a more comprehensive understanding of man's lot.

The ability of the speaker in *Edwin Morris* to harmonize disparate experiences, and to see things from more than one point of view, is an illustration of a particularly important aspect of Tennyson's approach to satire in the idyls. Like many of his contemporaries, Tennyson thought satire a very limited genre, and if he were to rank the literary kinds as Arnold did, he would likely place it in an equally low position. For satire, though right in what it attacked, was wrong in the attitude it displayed. The satirist was sometimes thought of as being unfair, but Tennyson saw him as limited in a much more fundamental way. The satirist tends to categorize and classify, to treat men as types rather than individuals; he lacks pity and sympathy, and his appeal is to feelings that divide us rather than 'the according hearts of men' (another useful phrase from *Aylmer's Field*, 453). In Tennyson's view, then, it is not so much the objects of attack that must be corrected as the satirist himself. The speaker in *Locksley Hall* says, 'So I triumphed ere my passion sweeping through me left me dry, / Left me with the palsied heart, and left me with the jaundiced eye' (131–2), and that is what the satirist must do too. The standard is the temper of mind which is associated with the home.

In the pastoral tradition, as I pointed out in chapter 1, the state of mind associated with the life of the shepherd was called *otium*; its opposite was the aspiring mind, which manifested itself in pride, ambition, and relentless striving at the expense of others. In *In Memoriam*, such restlessness was associated with doubt; in the idyls, it is associated with the 'lust of gain, in the spirit of Cain' (the phrase is from *Maud*). The contrast is summed up in John Sterling's review of Tennyson's *Poems* (1842):

Little therefore as is all that has been done towards the poetic representation of our time ... it is hard to suppose that it is incapable of such treatment. The still unadulterated purity of home among large circles of the nation presents an endless abundance of the feelings and characters, the want of which nothing else in existence can supply even to a poet. And these soft and steady lights strike an observer all the more from the restless activity and freedom of social ambition, the shifting changes of station, and the wealth gathered on one hand and spent on the other with an intenseness and amplitude of will to which there is at least nothing now comparable among mankind.[34]

This restless striving Tennyson explores in some poems that are related to the idyls. In the ballad-like *Lord of Burleigh*, for instance, 'shifting changes of station' are responsible for the lady's death, while undue considerations of rank are corrected by the statement in *Lady Clara Vere de Vere*: 'Kind hearts are more than coronets, / And simple faith than Norman blood' (55–6). The striving is sometimes motivated by pride, as it is in *The May Queen*, but it is more typically motivated by the desire to acquire wealth, as in *The Flight*, a poem similar in style and stanzaic form to *The May Queen*, and also written in the 1830s (though not published until 1885). The title refers to the escape of a girl from a marriage arranged by her father to pay off his gambling debts. In spite of the melodramatic treatment of the story, the pattern is one which recurs again and again in Tennyson's poems. Mammonism leads to the manipulation of people as things; it narrows and confines and reduces as much as home life nurtures and develops and generates. The correction of the temper of mind that characterizes such striving is a major concern of *Walking to the Mail*, *Aylmer's Field*, and *Sea Dreams*.

Walking to the Mail takes the form of a dialogue between two friends, so that it is in effect a little dramatic scene similar to those Theocritean idyls (the fifteenth, for instance) that the Victorian critics sometimes called 'mimes,' though the correct term is amoebean verse. The dramatic is the most prominent element in this idyl, but Tennyson also makes use of narrative, and the ghost story and the story of the pig are mixed with references to incidents and events that, if given in more detail, might have been little stories in themselves. The narrative element plays rather a larger part here than in Theocritus' fourth idyl, with which Ricks suggests a comparison. It too is a conversation between two friends, Battus and Corydon, and consists largely of gossip about acquaintances and references to events. Their remarks might variously be described as cutting, knowing, sarcastic, and leering, and there is a current of bitchiness throughout the whole conversation that makes the idyl seem realistic. The rustic coarseness of this particular idyl of Theocritus is paralleled in Tennyson by the carelessness and unfeelingness of the undergraduate high jinks described, and the tone of the conversation is one that mingles bitchiness and banter. The effect is similar to Theocritus: one has the sense of listening to an actual conversation, a sense that is enhanced, here as in the classical poem, by the apparently random flow of gossip. But conversation generally proceeds by the principle of association. Movement from one topic to another is not fortuitous, and depends upon the continuous linking of topics in the minds of both speakers. The dialogue, then, serves its traditional dramatic function: it reveals something of each speaker's mind and character. Gilbert Lawall analyses Theocritus' fourth idyl from this point of view, and argues for a common theme. The apparently 'loose organization' is, he writes, 'a tightly organized unity' which explores the links and parallels between human and animal loves.[35] The common theme of Tennyson's idyl is quite different and rather more complex, and is revealed not so much in the subjects of the conversation as it is in the way they are treated. The idyl is in fact about the treatment of people, about various ways of viewing them, and about various ways of acting in relation to them. Inadequate feelings of common humanity, or a failure to sense a complex whole, result in cruel or unfeeling treatment, or in black and white concepts that reduce and simplify a complex situation. This point of view is, like the striving for wealth, a threat to the rural and domestic ideal. Tennyson's conversation with Hallam in the section of *In Memoriam* that is in itself an idyl (section lxxxix) explores the same theme. Hallam criticizes urban life because 'We rub each other's angles down,' while the country preserves eccentricities and places considerable value on a true sense of individuals as individuals. As in Theocritus' idyl, the theme is realized in the two characters – indeed, it has no life apart from them – but Tennyson gives more shape to the dialogue than his predecessor. His conversation moves toward a moment of insight that is accompanied by a change of heart. The conversation is in fact an education, at least for one of the speakers (John), and his speech at the end is both the moral of the piece and the birth of better feelings. This recovery is the ethical and psychological equivalent of the return of spring in myth, but it is accomplished here in ways that are appropriate to the realistic cast of the poem.

The occasion of the idyl is a country walk, but the walk has rather a different purpose from rural journeys elsewhere: not to discover a maiden in a garden nor to picnic in the woods, but to meet the mail coach.

This utilitarian purpose is accompanied by a deadline: they must meet the coach at 1 PM. They pause to talk about Sir Edward Head only because they have fifteen minutes to spare. Underlying the poem is a sense of urgency, of time passing quickly, and this sense seems to make it necessary to deal summarily with people and events. That there might be other perspectives and other kinds of time is something the two friends must learn.

The conversation about Sir Edward Head is full of things that match this sense of time passing: careless judgments, jumping to conclusions, the readiness to make the most of what is bad or sensational or funny, the understandings that are clichés because they are based on stereotypes and popular patterns, the tired expressions of proverbial wisdom. James is guilty of these things throughout; John is guilty at first, but comes to recognize their common fault. The conversation about Sir Edward is initiated by John's question, 'Whose house is that I see?' (7). The answer and the information accompanying it ('he's abroad: the place is to be sold' 11) provoke a comment from John which is full of unspoken assumptions: 'Oh, his. He was not broken' (12). 'Oh, his' suggests a recognition that sets a man in his place without further thought. Equally thoughtless is the assumption that a man who is getting rid of his estate must be bankrupt. But John already knows that this is not Sir Edward's situation, and his comment is in fact a request for more particular information. James explains that Sir Edward has 'a morbid devil in his blood' (13), and 'He lost the sense that handles daily life' (16). James presents this information as fact, with very little intermingling of sympathy or indeed any emotion. This lack of feeling is confirmed by his offhand comments in answer to John's question about where Sir Edward is now: 'Nay, who knows? he's here and there. / But let him go' (19–20).

The ghost story, which James tells about Sir Edward's tenant, Jocky Dawes, is a comic story about 'a jolly ghost' (28), comic because of the action and the reversal of expectations. It is a good story, and well worth the entertainment it provides, but its context in the conversation places it in a rather different light. James tells the ghost story because he is reminded of it by the fact that Sir Edward is haunted by his devil, but the association is one of subject only, and glosses over the fact that Sir Edward's devil is akin to madness, while Jocky Dawes' ghost is a figure out of folk tales. The latter provides amusing action, but the former is an image of a tortured personality. The conversation slides easily over these differences, just as it slides easily to the subject of Sir Edward's wife. She too is introduced by association, which here takes the form of contrast. Jocky

Dawes could not rid himself of his ghost, but 'He left his wife behind; for so I heard' (39). The words are John's, and it is in his mind that the association takes place. James gives a quick judgment of her character ('A woman like a butt, and harsh as crabs' 41), but he has met her only once. John tries to give a fuller account by describing the lady as she was 'ten years back' (42), and that leads James to tell about Sir Edward's wife as 'the daughter of a cottager' (51) who married above her rank. James' account of the results of this event is full of tired old sayings and worn-out images: 'the blossom fades' (49), 'they that loved / At first like dove and dove were cat and dog' (49–50), 'Like men, like manners: like breeds like, they say' (55). These generalizations tell us nothing about the tragedy of a marriage that has failed and of a woman who has soured. In spite of these generalizations, however, Sir Edward's going abroad must still be explained, and that keeps the conversation going by turning it to Sir Edward's politics.

In recalling what the lady was like 'ten years back,' John has already established himself as the individual who pushes for fuller explanations, who is more aware of the complexity of human motives and character. He plays the same role here by canvassing politics as an explanation for Sir Edward's conduct, by suggesting that the Reform Bill and 'fear of change at home ... drove him hence' (60). That leads James to describe Sir Edward when confronted with 'A Chartist pike' (63). This incident James actually witnessed ('I once was near him, when ...' 62), but he attributes to Sir Edward thoughts and feelings he cannot know of. They are simply a melodramatic elaboration of John's suggestion ('fear of change at home') and they lead to another generalization (68–70) that anticipates Disraeli's famous statement about the 'two nations' in *Sybil*. The accompanying generalization – that young radicals become old conservatives – leads James to the story about the sow. It is the story of a schoolboy trick, and its motive is to get back at a man who is 'a flayflint.' It shows the schoolboys' readiness to attach labels to people, and to treat them accordingly. The results are both unfeeling and cruel. But there is daring and high spirits in this story as well, and the treatment is in part mock-heroic, as the allusion ('the Niobe of swine' 91) suggests. The high spirits attract the narrator, but he is apparently unaware of the lack of feeling.

Not so John. John comes to realize what they have been doing in ranging over all these topics and stories; their judgments have been too facile, their generalizations too easy; they have been too ready to attribute motives, to reduce, to simplify. His words are both the idyl's moral and an account of the treatment their gossip has accorded to all the topics they have touched upon:

What know we of the secret of a man?
His nerves were wrong. What ails us, who are sound,
That we should mimic this raw fool the world,
Which charts us all in its coarse blacks or whites,
As ruthless as a baby with a worm,
As cruel as a schoolboy ere he grows
To Pity – more from ignorance than will.   (94–100)

What John asserts is the mystery of individuality and the value of sympathy with one's fellows – a perspective and a feeling quite different from that of 'this raw fool the world.'

The speech casts light on both the theme and treatment of the entire idyl. It also points to another pattern, the tendency to 'chart us all in ... coarse blacks or whites'; that is, the readiness to simplify relationships by reducing them to opposites or pairs. The speakers do this throughout the idyl. There are Sir Edward and his devil, Jocky Dawes and his jolly ghost, Sir Edward and his wife, the 'two parties' that 'divide the world' (69) ('those that want, and those that have' 70), conservative and radical in politics. In all these cases the easy similarity or contrast masks complex links: Sir Edward cannot leave his devil, just as Jocky Dawes cannot leave his ghost behind; Sir Edward's marriage has made his wife what she is; in a society where the acquisition and distribution of scarce means depend upon supply and demand, having something means that someone else does not have it; and, in the process of developing and maturing, destructive tendencies are transformed into Toryism. In each pair the two halves are linked in mysterious and complex ways. This pattern also applies to the two speakers, John and James. The give and take of casual conversation (the constant prodding of John's questions and comments, the stories of James) lead to a moral realization, a moment of enlightenment for John and (presumably, through John's words) for James. The diversity and complexity of life constantly elude the attempt to fit them into so neat a pattern as pairs.

The appearance of the mail coach confirms this lesson. It comes 'With five at top: as quaint a four-in-hand / As you shall see – three pyebalds and a roan' (103–4). The coach is deliberately asymmetrical and quaint. Its appearance gives an ironic twist to the sense of urgency with which the idyl began. In one sense the coming of the coach simply marks the inexorable passing of chronological time; but John's words emphasize the coach's uniqueness, so that what time brings is a sense of something out of time, something that is itself and nothing else. In a different kind of idyl, the coach might be a vision of some sort, but it is simply a coach here. The important thing is that John has escaped from the point of view which Tennyson associates with the satirist, and which we see here primarily in the words and attitudes of James.[36]

Growth of this sort is Tennyson's main concern in *Sea Dreams*. The bulk of the poem is made up of a dialogue between husband and wife, a dialogue which deals with the recounting and interpreting of dreams. It is similar (as Ricks points out in his notes, p 1096) to Theocritus' Idyl xxi, but Tennyson goes much beyond Theocritus in showing the husband experiencing a change of heart. In portraying such moral growth, Tennyson attacks Mammonism. And he does so primarily by attacking the temper of mind which it fosters, a temper of mind which he attributes to the satirist. The treatment of people as individuals Tennyson associates with rural and domestic life, as we know from section lxxxix of *In Memoriam*. To treat people as abstractions, or as the embodiment of one or two characteristics, is the technique of satire. *Walking to the Mail*, which is full of imputations based on partial knowledge and characterized by a lack of feeling, is an implicit rejection of satire. In *Sea Dreams*, satire is explicitly rejected. It, and the subject to which it is applied, Mammonism, are rejected by being placed in a context primarily domestic in character, a context which acts as a standard by which the incomplete viewpoint of the satirist is corrected.

All of these complex concerns Tennyson embodies in some familiar patterns. The idyl describes a retreat from the city to the country, or, more specifically, from 'the giant-factoried city-gloom' (5) to the sea. The retreat is a vacation. It is conventional in such an idyl for the business arrangements of life to be left behind, and for the vacation to be a period of 'fallow leisure,' as in *Audley Court*. But here the husband takes with him his concerns over the business arrangements of life. The poem presents the resolution of these concerns, and does so through a three-day pattern that is (as we shall see) typical of romance. On the first day the family travels to the sea-side; on the second they attend church, walk on the shore, and dream their crucial dreams; and on the third (presumably) they awake renewed. The poem focuses, however, on the crucial struggle that takes place on the second night.

Tennyson treats this struggle within the husband in a more complex way than is at first apparent. To begin with, the dialogue is pervaded with dramatic irony. The wife knows, though her husband does not (nor does the reader), that the man who persuaded her husband 'To buy strange shares in some Peruvian mine' (15) has just died of a heart attack. But she withholds the knowledge from her husband because she wants him to forgive the man freely. After the knowledge the forgiveness is less a moral triumph: 'We *must* forgive the dead' (261). Coupled with this dramatic irony is the sense that the wife represents a standard to which the husband must bring himself. She is ready to forgive; she is full of Christian charity; and her faith allows her to set this particular falling out in a wider context:

> she, who kept a tender Christian hope,
> Haunting a holy text, and still to that
> Returning, as the bird returns, at night,
> 'Let not the sun go down upon your wrath,'
> Said, 'Love, forgive him:' but he did not speak;
> And silenced by that silence lay the wife,
> Remembering her dear Lord who died for all,
> And musing on the little lives of men,
> And how they mar this little by their feuds.　　　　(41–9)

By thus establishing the wife as the standard of conduct, Tennyson both judges the husband and defines the state of mind to which he must come. Setting up such a standard is one of the techniques of the satirist. But Tennyson does not, as one might expect, satirize the husband by presenting a highly selective portrait of him. Instead, he uses techniques of romance to represent the husband's change of heart. These techniques are responsible for our sense that the husband is undertaking an inner quest; that the quest involves a confrontation with his deepest concerns; and that its type is a descent into an underworld or hell. The descent appears in this poem in the images of rack and ruin that pervade the whole idyl. It is heralded in the sermon about 'the ruin of a world' (30), in the going down of the sun, in the violent energy of the full tide, and in the crying of the child. Counterpointing this inner descent to an underworld is the outer retreat to the seashore from the city. The sea is the most prominent feature of both the retreat and the descent, and its associations with both destruction and renewal are an important part of the poem. Dramatic irony, satire, and romance are thus fused in Tennyson's treatment of the husband's struggle, a fusion apparent in the recounting of the two dreams themselves.

The husband's dream is a quest which follows a course just the reverse of the usual cycle of water: instead of going down a stream to the sea, he is brought in by the tide toward land, carried through a cave, and sent up a stream. Climbing a mountain under the guidance of a giant woman, he looks back toward the sea, and sees a fleet of glass founder on a reef of gold. His own interpretation of the dream is heavily moral:

'Now I see
My dream was Life; the woman honest Work;
And my poor venture but a fleet of glass
Wrecked on a reef of visionary gold.'   (132–5)

To this dream Tennyson's own comment in the Eversley edition seems best to apply: 'The glorification of honest labour, whether of head or hand, no hasting to be rich, no bowing down to any idol.' But though the husband deliberately abstracts the moral from the dream, the dream embodies other more important things. One has only to ask why, when the husband states the moral, the poem does not come to an end, and then one begins to sense that the husband's understanding is incomplete. His is, in essence, the stance of the satirist, and though he can condemn hypocrisy and folly, and give intellectual assent to moral truths, he lacks sympathy and love. His view from the mountain-top is a version of the Olympian viewpoint that the satirist traditionally assigns himself, even though the folly that the husband sees is his own. But the folly that led him to invest in the mine is only a part of a more comprehensive failing that is much more in need of correction, and that failing is revealed in the portrait of the hypocrite that frames the account of the dream. The portrait is a satiric one, and as such it is highly selective. The husband focuses on all the evidence of hypocrisy and excludes everything else. Or nearly everything else. For the portrait is not a static one, but moves inexorably from the man himself to the type of hypocrite. It begins with the husband's account of his first meeting with the man, and his initial sense that he should not be trusted. 'But after, when I came / To know him more, I lost it, knew him less' (71–2). The paradox can easily obscure the more pervasive irony of this statement, for it is the satirist who types a man rather than trying to see him as an individual. Though the husband here condemns his sense of the hypocrite as an individual, that same sense which led him to invest his money will also be his salvation, so that his ruin and his renewal are fused in a mysteriously human way. But the husband steadily retreats from such understanding here. After his account of the dream, he focuses on the hypocrite's easy linking of loose accounts and religious faith (141–64), and then leaves the man altogether to give a picture of the type (180–93). This picture in style and image deliberately

suggests the satiric portraits of Restoration and eighteenth-century literature, particularly Dryden's Shimei, as Ricks points out (p 1101). The
portrait is there not just so that Tennyson can show off his skill with the
heroic couplet or his ability to imitate an older style. It also marks the
lowest point to which the husband descends. Gone is his sense of the man
as an individual and a contemporary; in its place is the picture of the
nameless type in a style that is old rather than immediate. In effect,
Tennyson is condemning the satirist, not because he is wrong in what he
attacks, but because his attacks reveal a temper of mind that excludes
some things that make us fully human.

The wife attempts to correct not the injury but the attitude. She constantly urges her husband to think of the man as an individual who is
perhaps silently racked with remorse. And when her husband asks her,
'How like you this old satire?' (194), she replies in words that are the key to
both the moral and literary concerns of the poem:

> 'I loathe it: he had never kindly heart,
> Nor ever cared to better his own kind,
> Who first wrote satire, with no pity in it.'   (195–7)

It is in this context that the wife recounts her dream. While the husband's dream tends toward allegory and ends with an explicit moral, the
wife's tends toward symbolism, and her reaction to it is one of awe. The
dream suggests the mysterious fusion of disparate things. The great wave
which destroys king, saint, or founder on the 'huge cathedral fronts of
every age' (211) moves not in a random fashion but in an orderly pattern
of swelling and retreat. And its noise is not wild but 'a low musical note'
(203). Similarly, the 'wildest wailings' of the people over the increasing
ruin and destruction are 'never out of tune / With that sweet note'
(224–5). The dream suggests that destruction and preservation are part
of the same orderly process, a continuum that cannot be explained but
only wondered at.

The dream suggests through symbolism the more comprehensive view
that the husband must come to, and it is a view that he must accept
emotionally as well as intellectually. Such a development is closely related
to the child who, in this as in other Tennyson poems, is the most important
of its figures, linking as she does the familiar and the mysterious, the
domestic and the heroic. The link is forged at the end of the wife's account
of her dream, when the cry of the Christ child 'mixt with little Margaret's'
(238). In one sense the link is simply an empirical account of the cause of

one particular part of the wife's dream; but in another sense, the dream reveals Margaret's divine form. In relation to her archetype, the child represents renewal and hope for the future. And the husband must become more like a child if he hopes to be saved; that is, he must see all events, creative and destructive, as the wonders and mysteries that they are. Throughout her husband's account of his dream, the wife treats him in effect as a child, offering as she does the familiar (the tide, the breaking of a glass) as an explanation for his bad dream. And she attempts to comfort him as one would comfort a child. When she fails to do so, she recounts her own mysterious dream, and when her husband refuses to believe that harmony and discord can be fused, she at last tells him that his enemy is dead. The moment is the turning point in the poem, and it is important that the husband's 'rough voice' (269) in reacting to the news should wake the child. To all appearances the husband remains unrepentant, but symbolically he has at last awakened the child within himself. This awakening is confirmed, paradoxically, by the lullaby which the mother sings to put the child to sleep. What in Theocritus would be an intercalary song is here intimately related to its context. The song, about a 'little birdie' not yet ready to fly from its nest, is about incomplete development. It applies in a familiar sense to Margaret and in a symbolic sense to the husband, who has not yet rid himself of hatred.

Yet he does forgive the man who has wronged him, and forgiveness and then sleep are the first steps in his renewal. The scene is a familiar one in Tennyson: a husband and wife reconciled above the cradle of their child. It is another appearance of that same picture of family life that is suggested in the song 'Sweet and low' in *The Princess*, and that appears explicitly in the song 'As through the land at eve we went' (also in *The Princess*). There, as here, it is a sacred image representing reconciliation, love, and peace. In this domestic context, the miracle of a change of heart takes place, and hatred dissolves in a love that is both common and divine.

The same concerns inform *Aylmer's Field*. It, too, is an attack on Mammonism, and it, too, makes use of some of the techniques of satire. But just as the husband's change of heart is crucial in *Sea Dreams*, so Averill's change of heart is crucial in *Aylmer's Field*. The story is twice removed from the actual events: it is told by Averill, now 'a grizzled cripple' (8), and then retold by the narrator to us. Averill's change of heart takes place during his sermon, which Tennyson gives word for word, and for which there is no parallel in Thomas Woolner's story, the source of the poem. Such a substantial expansion of the source should alert us to the importance of the sermon, though its importance is not what we might at first expect it to be. We expect the sermon to attack the Aylmers and to give the moral of the story. It does those things, but more important is what happens to Averill as he is speaking. He comes to feel sympathy and pity, and those feelings soften the satirist's traditional indignation and bitterness. Two attitudes shape the sermon: the satirist's anger, and the sympathy that depends upon feelings of common humanity. And these two attitudes shape the entire story, both as Averill tells it 'in rougher shape' (7) to the narrator and as the narrator tells it to us.

These two attitudes account for the shifts in tone that F.E.L. Priestley was the first to analyse. He points out that the narrator establishes two basic styles, 'scornful irony' for Sir Aylmer and his wife, and a 'high romantic style' for Leolin and Edith:

The two styles, one for Sir Aylmer, one for the young lovers, create a sense of two opposed worlds, two kinds of life, two sets of values, two kinds of persons. The one is the world of Mammon, seeking wealth and power, insensitive to beauty, guarded and circumspect; the other the world of Love, spontaneous, eager, full of beauty, taking 'joyful note of all things joyful', childlike in its charming openness and warmth. The one world is the world of the county, of the Baths, of Court; the other the world of the fresh countryside.[37]

The initial descriptions of Sir Aylmer and his wife are satiric portraits; he is 'that almighty man, / The county God' (13–14), and she is 'a faded beauty of the Baths, / Insipid as the Queen upon a card' (27–8). Contrasting with such satire is the romantic portrayal of the lovers, romantic not just because of the abundant 'allusions to the beauties of the natural world' (as Priestley points out, p 95) but because of the evocation of a fairy-tale world, especially that of the Sleeping Beauty story. The familiar pattern of that fairy tale appears again here, for the story is that of a beautiful maiden who will wake to love. She herself is young and inexperienced, and her surroundings change so little that they might almost be dormant. Indeed, the narrator tells us twice that the land was 'sleepy' (33, 45). And Edith's parents are metaphorically asleep, since they are blind to romance. Her parents, however, are more than just a part of the quiet landscape. They are also the deadly barrier around Sleeping Beauty, and the archetypal dragon guarding the hidden treasure is suggested by the fiery dragon, the 'blazing wyvern' (17), on Sir Aylmer's coat of arms. Given these suggestions, we are not surprised that the action should have a familiar shape: an approach to a maiden in a forbidden garden. As a boy Leolin is attracted to such heroic quests, and his 'boyish histories / Of battle, bold adventure' (97–8) both foreshadow the action of this poem and suggest its heroic type.

When one examines the setting carefully, other familiar images appear. There is much to suggest the Garden of Eden:

> so they wandered, hour by hour
> Gathered the blossom that rebloomed, and drank
> The magic cup that filled itself anew.   (141–3)

There is also much to suggest a fertile and settled land, a setting associated with Ruth, but more particularly with Demeter. Grain and poppies (Demeter's flower) mingle in a sleepy setting: 'A land of hops and poppy-mingled corn, / Little about it stirring save a brook!' (31–2). Demeter is associated not only with the ripeness and fertility of the land but with the peaceful arts of rural civilization. The narrator devotes a long passage (144–88) to a description of 'the labourers' homes, / A frequent haunt of Edith' (147–8), and indeed Edith is the presiding deity of these flower-covered homes, 'each a nest in bloom' (150): 'Her art, her hand, her counsel all had wrought / About them' (151–2). Edith is thus yet another appearance of a figure of some importance in Tennyson's idyls, and her mythical identity is suggested more explicitly in Averill's sermon: she is 'Fairer than Ruth among the fields of corn' (680).

The suggestions of the familiar figures of Ruth and Demeter are varied by suggestions of other Biblical figures that enrich our understanding of Edith and her situation. In the same part of the sermon I have just quoted from, Averill says also that Edith was 'Fairer than Rachel by the palmy well' (679). Here Rachel is similar to Ruth, for she is a desirable woman associated with water, which is in turn responsible for the fertility of the land. Moreover, Leolin's toiling to make a 'Name, fortune too' (395) so that he would be accepted by the Aylmers as eligible to marry Edith has its Biblical precedent in Jacob's toiling seven years for the hand of Rachel. Equally important is the simile in which Edith is described as 'Pale as the Jephtha's daughter' (280). The story from Judges makes itself felt again in the account of Edith's death, for though she declines slowly toward her end, her passing is described in terms of a human sacrifice in which the daughter of the house is placed upon an altar as a burnt offering. For she contracts 'some low fever' (569), and it

> found the girl
> And flung her down upon a couch of fire,
> Where careless of the household faces near,
> And crying upon the name of Leolin,
> She, and with her the race of Aylmer, past.   (573–7)

The relation of the Biblical story to this modern idyl must be defined carefully. Jephtha and Aylmer both sacrificed a daughter, but there the similarity between the two stories ends. Jephtha's vow, foolish as it was, was nonetheless an unselfish one, for it was made to the God of Israel for victory in battle. Aylmer's motive, however, is selfish devotion to Mammon. In the Bible, Jephtha's daughter quickly recognized the importance of her father's vow as well as her own duty, and, after bewailing her virginity, she willingly sacrificed herself. Edith knows how wrong her father is (though she has a lingering sense of duty and love which he occasionally merits), and remains loyal to Leolin. The reference to the Biblical story thus complements the satiric portrayal of Sir Aylmer, for that story provides us with a standard by which we may judge this modern Jephtha.

The narrator's treatment of Sir Aylmer is not, however, unrelievedly satiric. In the scene in which he loses his composure 'like a beast hard-ridden' (291) and breaks 'all bonds of courtesy' (323), the satiric style gives way to melodrama, and folly is transformed into the kind of demonic force that one expects of the antagonist in romance. In the earlier satiric portraits of Sir Aylmer, his folly (later personified, indeed deified, as 'This filthy marriage-hindering Mammon' 374) is presented, as one would expect in satire, as a failure to live up to the true duties and obligations of fatherhood. In this melodramatic scene, that failure is embodied in deformity, and presented in terms of a magic transformation. Sir Aylmer's is

> a hoary face
> Meet for the reverence of the hearth, but now,
> Beneath a pale and unimpassioned moon,
> Vext with unworthy madness, and deformed.   (332–5)

'Meet for the reverence of the hearth' – the phrase suggests everything Sir Aylmer should be and is not. Lines 481–91, the passage describing Sir Aylmer's activities in 'the woman-markets of the west, / Where our Caucasians let themselves be sold' (348–9), are heavily satiric, and the following

scene, the passage describing the discovery of the letter, is heavily melodramatic. The Aylmers are first objects of ironic attack ('worldly-wise
begetters' 482; 'those good parents' 483) and then dragons guarding the
'treasure-trove' (515, 531), the letters, and Edith herself. But Sir Aylmer is
not always a dragon, and the portrayal of him, whether as a satiric vice or a
romantic demon, is not unrelieved:

> once indeed,
> Warmed with his wines, or taking pride in her,
> She looked so sweet, he kissed her tenderly
> Not knowing what possessed him ...
> (553–6)

Such a passage is evidence of Averill's influence on the narrative, for it
forces us to see Sir Aylmer as not entirely a flat or one-dimensional
character. If Sir Aylmer is not 'Meet for the reverence of the hearth,' he is
at least meet for pity and sympathy. For how one views Sir Aylmer is as
important in this idyl as what Sir Aylmer himself does.

Averill's sermon, which bulks so largely in the idyl, is ostensibly about
the Aylmers, but is in fact about attitudes toward them. At first the sermon
is bitterly satiric: Averill 'dashed his angry heart / Against the desolations
of the world' (633–4). He attacks Mammonism in Biblical terms, by
contrasting the service of Baal with the service of the living God. From
that topic he passes on to eulogize Edith, and this part of the sermon is
quite different in tone. It is, as Priestley points out, 'filled, not with anger,
but with love and pity.'[38] At this point the narrator interrupts the sermon
to describe Edith's parents. 'This passage, short as it is, is of great importance in the structure at this point. For the first time in the poem, it
describes the Aylmers in direct, simple style, with no ironic tone, and with
no suggestion of their monstrosity. It emphasizes ordinary human feelings in them.'[39] The passage is evidence of Averill's change of heart, which
we now see happening in the continuation of the sermon. Averill abandons his initial intention, and speaks instead of the change in himself.
Initially he wanted revenge and retribution:

> 'I wished my voice
> A rushing tempest of the wrath of God
> To blow these sacrifices through the world –
> Sent like the twelve-divided concubine
> To inflame the tribes ...'
> (756–60)

In rejecting such an intention, Averill in effect rejects satire. He links the wrath of the satirist with the mad violence of the French revolution, and thereby suggests some characteristics of satire: it is subversive, revolutionary, and destructive. The contrasting attitude is charitable and Christian: 'O rather pray for those and pity them' (775). Averill appeals to what is earlier called 'the according hearts of men' (453), and such human sympathy is open rather than subversive, unifying rather than divisive, and constructive rather than destructive.

Averill's change of heart is central to the entire poem, as Priestley has shown. 'By implication, Tennyson, too, is rejecting anger and hate, and with it the bitter tone applied earlier to the Aylmers. The poem itself, like the sermon, is a progression, an illustration of the Christian way towards love.'[40] The change is confirmed by the final paragraph of the idyl, a superb example of Tennyson's fusion of varying tones. The prevailing tone is tragic, for the Averills destroy their home and themselves through their own folly. But there is a suggestion of the narrator's earlier irony in the wit of a line like 'Dead for two years before his death was he' (837), and satire reappears in 'the dark retinue reverencing death / At golden thresholds' (842–3). But there is also 'Pity, the violet on the tyrant's grave' (845). The image is crucial. The violet is a conventional symbol from the pastoral elegy, where it suggests resurrection and renewal. But the renewal here is in the minds and hearts of the beholders (and of those who listen to the story). Hence the conventional symbol is shifted to an attitude, and the shift confirms the poem's rejection of satire. Satire would correct, but Tennyson would correct satire itself. In thus rejecting satire, Tennyson recognized a deep truth of human psychology: that one can easily become what one attacks, at least in outlook if not in specific faults. The solution was another frame of reference entirely. Tennyson found that solution in the domestic ideal.

ENOCH ARDEN

To serve the domestic ideal does not mean that one rejects the work of the world, nor are all worldly pursuits to be seen as governed by Mammon. There is a right spirit as well as a wrong spirit with which to undertake those pursuits, and the right spirit is a spirit informed by the domestic ideal. When Tennyson deals with work which is undertaken in this spirit, he often sees that, however common or ordinary the work may be, it is nonetheless the realization of an ideal, and hence is heroic in the Carlylean sense. This sense of an ideal manifesting itself in everyday activities leads Tennyson to treat ordinary people as heroic. We have already seen how he does so in *Dora*, and that same concept of heroism is the basis of *Enoch Arden*.

Paul Turner has pointed out how Tennyson uses parallels with the *Odyssey* to suggest the heroic nature of Enoch's life,[41] and these parallels make us sense the heroic dimensions of domestic life in general. Enoch's goal is a home and all that goes with it: wife, family, and the joys and cares of family life. His motives are set in the play of the three children (play which also anticipates the shape of the story itself), and manifest themselves in virtues usually associated with the Protestant ethic: working hard, saving money, believing in a formal education, wanting to give his children a better life than his has been. But these things are never ends in themselves. The practical and business arrangements of Enoch's life symbolize the ideal he serves, and the profits of these arrangements he lays on the domestic altar.

I use the word 'altar' deliberately, for it is apparent enough that Enoch regards the home as a sacred place. The hearth is an altar, and its high priestess is Annie. Sacramental imagery appears very early in the poem, at the moment when Enoch proposes marriage:

> His large gray eyes and weather-beaten face
> All-kindled by a still and sacred fire,
> That burned as on an altar.   (70–2)

The image gives resonance to Enoch's charge at parting to Annie: 'Keep a clean hearth and a clear fire for me' (192). And it reappears in the dramatic scene when Enoch looks through the window of Philip's house, and sees a cosy domestic scene: 'For cups and silver on the burnished board / Sparkled and shone; so genial was the hearth' (738–9). The word 'genial,' in F.E.L. Priestley's words, 'suggests a household blessed by the gods, a holy place, just as the cups and silver shining on the board suggest not only comfort and prosperity but the sacramental.'[42] 'The warmth, the peace, the happiness' (757) that Enoch observes are thus not just familiar attributes of the home, but evidence of a divine harmony and a spiritual well-being.

It is in serving this ideal that Enoch destroys himself. In the classic pattern of tragedy, his exclusion from the family circle comes about, ironically, because of his devotion to it. And if one looks for a tragic flaw, one finds only virtue. The strength of Enoch's domestic affections, operating in conjunction with circumstances, makes Enoch's story tragic, and Enoch himself heroic. And indeed Tennyson treats him in just that way. He describes Enoch as a fisherman in an heroic style (92–100) and Enoch's catch, in the lines attacked by Bagehot as ornate, as 'ocean-spoil / In ocean-smelling osier' (93–4). He presents as an heroic struggle Enoch's silence and withdrawal after he has observed his family through the window of Philip's house. In tragedy, the catastrophe conventionally comes about through a discovery or a recognition of some sort. Tennyson varies the convention by having Enoch, who alone has the power of bringing about the discovery, deliberately prevent it. And while the discovery conventionally brings to the tragic hero a recognition of his responsibility for his own fate, Enoch needs no such understanding of himself and his actions. He holds by an ideal he has always adhered to, and deliberately chooses a course of action that sacrifices himself for the sake of others. The discovery takes place only after his death, and it is confirmed by the device of the lock of hair from Enoch's baby son. In romance or in comedy such a device would reveal the true hero, and make him eligible to marry the heroine and to form a better society. The lock has somewhat the same function here, for Enoch is revealed as the ideal family man. The notoriously expensive funeral is an offering to this heroic ideal, and it is offered in exactly the same spirit in which Enoch's hard work and commercial enterprises are offered to his marriage. In making such an offering the little port confirms the value of the ideal and honours the tragic hero who has sacrificed himself to preserve it.

The poem ends, then, not in the manner of a tragedy, with a sense of disintegration and isolation, but in the manner of a comedy, with a sense of social ideals confirmed and strengthened. The general pattern of the poem is in fact a familiar one: the establishment of a family unit, its break-up, and its re-establishment. It is the same pattern as in *Dora* and, as in the earlier poem, the pathos of the story comes about through an individual who is excluded from the marriage relationship. Not one individual is excluded here, however, but two: Philip at the beginning of the story, and Enoch at the end. Their contrasting fortunes complicate the three stages of the story. The first, up to the moment of Enoch's departure, deals essentially with the establishment and preservation of a family unit, and from this unit Philip is excluded. The second deals with the separation, tracing first Annie's fortunes, and then Enoch's. Here 'Philip gained / As Enoch lost' (351–2). The last presents the re-establishment of the family, but with Philip as its head. In preserving the family by refusing to reveal his identity, Enoch ironically fulfils the purpose of his return, and his willingness to sacrifice his own happiness for the sake of his family clearly makes him heroic. Hence his actions fall into a pattern one would expect to find in the epic, 'the mythic pattern,' in the words of Douglas C. Fricke, 'of voyage to an other world/underworld (Paradise-Hades), a symbolic death, and a subsequent rebirth.'[43]

Presiding over this action is a figure who, like Dora, is a type of Ruth or Demeter, though she does not further the plot in the same way that Dora does. That figure is, of course, Annie. Tennyson presents her not so much as the angel in the house (Annie herself applies that image to Philip at line 420) as the earth mother in the field. At two critical moments in the poem, Annie is pictured seated in a rural landscape. Those two moments are the two proposals of marriage, and, though Tennyson departs slightly from the pattern by making the setting a hill, 'Just where the prone edge of the wood began / To feather toward the hollow' (67–8 and 370–1), rather than a field of grain, and the activity nutting rather than the harvesting of grain, the significance of the scene remains the same. Annie is the fertility and vitality of nature, and in this idyl that energy manifests itself in her firm adherence to the ideal of family life. Like Demeter, she presides over both natural vitality and the arts of civilization, and since, in Tennyson's view, civilization depends upon family life, it is appropriate that the proposals of marriage should be treated in this way.

The realistic but somewhat unconventional setting in which Annie is described at these two critical points in the poem is part of a larger pattern in Tennyson's treatment of his characters' surroundings. Victorian readers and critics generally expected an idyl to present a pastoral landscape, a paradisal retreat that criticism has labelled the *locus amoenus* or 'the pleasance,' a landscape where living is easy and pleasure continuous. In *Enoch Arden* Tennyson makes ironic use of his readers' expectations. He has Enoch wrecked on an island that is, in most conventional ways, a paradise, and yet to Enoch it is a hellish prison. Tennyson refers to the island as 'this Eden of all plenteousness' (557), and his description of it (568–95) is rich and full. But, as F.E.L. Priestley has shown, the description modulates from the idyllic and the paradisal to the inhuman and the hellish.[44] What is missing are human relations. Hence for Enoch the *locus amoenus* is 'a darker isle beyond the line' (601), 'the sacred old familiar fields' (621), and in particular his own hearth.

Enoch Arden is a poem which has suffered more than most in the general reaction against Tennyson, partly because it was so popular, and because, for that reason, its fall from favour was all the more spectacular.

But if a modern critic will willingly suspend his disbelief in Tennyson's assumptions about domestic life, he may begin to see the poem as a skilful and effective combination of some of the recurring features of the idyls.

ROMANCE: *AUDLEY COURT*

When we turn to *Audley Court*, we discover an heroic dimension of the idyl quite different from that of *Enoch Arden*. Here the ideal manifests itself, not in the work of one's hands, but in the work of one's imagination, and in the Victorian age, the activity of the imagination is the basis of romance. For the imagination conceives a world better than our own, and romance presents the story of how that world is achieved. But the concept is prior to the action, and this idyl shows how the concept is formed by describing the discovery of its symbols.

'In form and mood,' writes Ricks, 'the poem is based on Theocritus's 7th Idyll, where Simichidas's song (ll. 96–127) resembles Francis's' (p. 704). Theocritus' seventh idyl is sometimes called *The Harvest-Home*. It describes the poet's journey from town to country to take part in a harvest festival, and includes an account of a meeting with a goatherd named Lycidas, the singing match with him, the arrival at the farm, and a rural picnic. The theme of both songs in the singing match is, as Gilbert Lawall points out, a wish to enter a world of quiet and contentment, a world where striving and effort are no longer necessary. Theocritus enhances this desire for *otium* with the picnic itself, which, though at first glance realistically enough described, comes to represent more than perfect rural contentment. Lawall argues that the 'idealized countryside finally becomes ... an inner landscape of the imagination' and 'an allegory of poetic inspiration.'[45] The key is the apostrophe to the 'Castalian Nymphs that dwell on Parnassus' height.' 'All the details in this final scene at Phrasidamus' farm – the grove and spring, the grotto of the nymphs, the pastoral symphony of birds and insects, the fruit gathered in, and the strong drink of wine and water – suggest an elaborate rhetoric of poetic imagination and creation which was beginning to develop in the Hellenistic Age.'[46] These two aspects of the Theocritean idyl – *otium* and an inner world of the imagination – Tennyson combines in his account of a rural picnic. But he presents both aspects in Victorian terms, and in doing so both sums up some themes and patterns we have been tracing, and anticipates some we have yet to explore.

The classical concept of *otium* finds its Victorian equivalent in these lines:

    and I, that having wherewithal,
And in the fallow leisure of my life
A rolling stone of here and everywhere,
Did what I would ...   (75–8)

The speaker of the idyl is describing his own attitude. He has 'wherewith-al,' and so is released from the common problem of earning a living. Leisure is possible only when one no longer has to worry about how to pay for it. He is 'in the fallow leisure of my life.' 'Fallow' refers to ground that is left uncropped for a year to maintain and improve its fertility. The word suggests a period of rest that is in fact a preparation for action that is productive. As an adjective, 'fallow' also means (in the words of the *Oxford English Dictionary*) 'of a pale brownish or reddish yellow colour.' Those are the colours of autumn, and, in the context of the cycle of the seasons, they anticipate the coming of spring. The sense of *otium* as an end in itself, then, is changed by Tennyson to a sense of potential, of leisure and contentment as a preparation for something else. That something else is work in the Carlylean sense, particularly as in *The Golden Year*, and the rural picnic here is the proper antecedent of the mountain climbing there. Activity is in fact present in this poem, but it lacks a sense of direction and purpose. Tennyson added the line 'A rolling stone of here and every-where' in 1855, and at first glance both the activity and the aphorism the words suggest (a rolling stone gathers no moss) seem inconsistent with 'fallow leisure.' But lack of direction was already suggested by the phrase 'Did what I would,' and the added line strengthens the sense of energy that needs only to be shaped and focused. The 'fallow leisure' is thus a complex state, a pleasure in itself and yet also a prelude to work. The specific kind of work which the idyl suggests is a life of heroic action, particularly in the forms it takes in chivalric romances. As in Theocritus, a realistic journey leads the poet to an idealized landscape, and that land-scape is described in such a way as to suggest the world of the imagination. If in Theocritus the description maps out or catalogues the Greek literary imagination, the description in Tennyson does the same for the nine-teenth century. Contemporary critics knew that the literary form which was primarily the product of the imagination was romance, and this actual picnic is pervaded with a sense of heroic action, as the shifts in style indicate.

The opening of the idyl is dramatic in form and colloquial in style. The familiar phrases of conversation – 'For love or money' (2), 'With all my heart' (7) – are appropriate to the brief description of a feast-day in town.

The outing of the speaker and Francis frames the account of the picnic: it is a retreat from the harbour and the town to Audley Court, and a return at the end of the poem. The harbour and town are crowded with people, and though 'Audley feast' is in progress, one is conscious of the fact that the feast is a commercial affair as well as a holiday. The two friends do not take part in it, or, rather, they celebrate it in their own way, just as Theocritus celebrated harvest-home in his own way, apart from the main festivities at the farm, none of which he even mentioned. The retreat begins as a withdrawal to 'the stillness of the beach' (9) as opposed to the noise and activity on the quay, continues as an ascent from the water to the meadows, and ends when the friends pass through the gates of Audley Court to the orchard. The pattern is a familiar one. It is the same penetration to a secret place we have seen in other idyls, and though this idyl differs in having no maiden at the centre of the retreat, the potential that the maiden represents is present in other ways, and indeed the sleeping maiden is herself the subject of one of the songs.

It is in the sentence describing the passage through the meadows to the gates that the style shifts from the familiar to the heroic:

> so by many a sweep
> Of meadow smooth from aftermath we reached
> The griffin-guarded gates, and passed through all
> The pillared dusk of sounding sycamores ...   (12–15)

The stately phrases, the inversions, the suspension of main subject and verb, all suggest the style of *Paradise Lost,* and indeed 'pillared dusk' echoes a Miltonic phrase, as Ricks points out in his notes (p 705). The shift in style suggests that the friends have entered a world that is the source of the heroic in action and character, a world which is associated with the imagination. That world is symbolized, not by the great house (for we are told in a matter-of-fact way that it is for rent, and that there has been a sale), but by the gardener's lodge, 'With all its casements bedded, and its walls / And chimneys muffled in the leafy vine' (17–18). For the friends, a common home is at the centre of Audley Court. Moreover, it is a home which is curiously dormant, as the words 'bedded' and 'muffled' indicate. This home takes the place of the maiden who is usually found sleeping in the garden, and its potential fruitfulness is indicated by its green covering. In terms of myth, the quester in the garden must release the energy lying dormant in this green thing, and so reveal the heroic aspects of domestic life.

In this revelation, the picnic is the chief event. Here the heroic style dominates (especially lines 19–27) but the effect is only partly mock-heroic. It is true that Tennyson uses an heroic style to describe the cloth and the pasty, and that style is (by eighteenth-century standards) inappropriate to a low subject. But the heroic style may aggrandize as well as diminish, and heightening is the primary effect here. The style compels us to see, in this actual picnic 'on a slope of orchard' (19), the fullness and richness of romance. The pasty becomes a treasure chest or jewel box, and the description of the treasures it contains fuses romance with nineteenth-century science. The 'damask napkin' is 'wrought with horse and hound' (20), and its function is similar to that of Achilles' shield in Homer or the cup in the first idyl of Theocritus: it pictures the aristocratic activities appropriate to Audley Court.

The style shifts again when Tennyson describes the conversation of the two friends. At first there seems to be nothing heroic about this discourse. The topics are everyday affairs of the neighbourhood, summarized so that the effect is rather comic, like that of a movie film speeded up. The verbs, however, suggest vigorous action: 'touched upon,' 'glancing thence,' 'struck,' 'split,' 'came again together.' There is a sense of a contest of some sort. In Theocritus it would be a singing match, with its boasting, challenging, and response, but though each sings a song here, there is no contest. In romance, the action would be a tournament, and in effect, through these verbs, Tennyson presents the conversation about contemporary matters as if it were jousting. The style, then, is appropriate to the action, and reveals in it an heroic dimension as surely as the more elaborate style in the description of the cloth and pasty.

The songs embody more variations in style, and the pair of singers present a contrast in both manner and matter – 'the one' (in Buckley's words) 'wittily disillusioned, eager to live free of dutiful entanglements, the other musing idly on dreams of sweet romance.'[4] But there is also a similarity in the songs which helps to explain the movement of the entire idyl. Francis' refrain, 'but let me live my life,' is in effect a plea for 'fallow leisure,' which he defines largely in terms of what he rejects: war, commerce, politics, and love, all of which he presents in their actual rather than ideal aspect. The speaker's song is also a plea for 'fallow leisure,' presented in terms of what is desired rather than what is rejected. The object of desire is a familiar one – a sleeping maiden – and the singer's relation with her falls into an equally familiar pattern: 'I go tonight: I come tomorrow morn' (69). A period of separation followed by a reunion, the separation associated with night and the reunion with dawn: the action of the Sleeping Beauty and Persephone myths, stripped to its bare essentials, is here. There is the sense, moreover, that Ellen embraces a mysterious world of imaginative vitality, which the singer will release on his return. The wish the singer expresses is a wish to control the mysteries of the imagination: 'I would I were / The pilot of the darkness and the dream' (70–1). The romance quest conventionally takes place in symbolic darkness, and its purpose is to realize the dream. This 'fallow leisure,' then, is very different from that of Francis.

The return from Audley Court takes place in the evening, and is described in such a way as to suggest that everything is waiting for dawn, waiting for some great thing to happen. The moon is a new moon and, as in Coleridge's simile, it transforms a familiar landscape, obscuring it mysteriously and yet making it extraordinarily rich: it 'dimly rained about the leaf / Twilights of airy silver' (80–1). The setting is pervaded with stillness, calmness, and darkness, and yet at the same time it seems full of latent energy. The sea, as so often in Tennyson, is the mysterious source and end of all life – a pattern suggested in this idyl by the fact that Francis arrives from the sea, and at the end the two friends return to it. The vitality in the sea is revealed by the 'one green sparkle' (87) of the harbour-buoy. Light is a traditional symbol for energy, and the colour of this light links it with the gardener's lodge, and through it with the whole pastoral-domestic retreat. One might argue that Tennyson is suggesting that life in a rural home is the true guide to heroic action. At the very least, the importance of the harbour-buoy is emphasized by the line Tennyson added in 1869 to describe it: 'Sole star of phosphorescence in the calm' (86). The image indicates a tiny point of light marking the place of vast but still distant energy. The energy is there, but it is not yet time to release it. For the time being it is enough to have glimpsed it. That is how the sense of well-being at the end of the poem ('we were glad at heart' 88) must be defined. When that energy is released, as we shall soon see, a rural idyl of this sort is transformed into a much more complex romance, and we have the *Idylls of the King*.

3

Romance: *The Princess*

When one concentrates on the recurring features of the stories of the idyls I have been dealing with, one discovers that the actions may be seen as symbolic variations of one basic action: death and rebirth. That action is the centre of romance, and hence all the idyls may be seen, in this sense, as versions of one of the most popular and enduring of all literary forms. What made romance popular? The answer is given again and again in Victorian criticism of prose fiction. While the novel depends upon the accurate and sympathetic observation of actual life, romance is a product of the imagination. As such, it is the projection of human desires and aversions, and its structure is governed by wish-fulfilment. Events symbolize inner events, and landscapes symbolize psychological states or points of view. The outer action of romance traditionally takes the form of a quest, involving a perilous journey, a crucial struggle, and a triumph of some sort.[1] When this action is internalized, we generally have what may best be described as a symbolic death and rebirth, the crucial struggle being the projection of this death, and the triumph the outward manifestation of the rebirth. In a work where outward events are less marvellous and more realistic, this symbolic death and rebirth often take the form of a conversion, a change of heart, or an education. The process involves a dying out of an unsatisfactory life and a birth into a new and better one.

If we examine the narrative aspects of the central myths which I defined in the last chapter in the light of these comments, we soon see that their essential shape is particularly suitable to romance. The stories of Ruth, Demeter and Persephone, and Sleeping Beauty are all, in essence, stories of a death and a rebirth, a pattern that takes various forms: the loss and regaining of a child, the break-up and re-establishment of a family, sleeping and waking, separation and reunion. The frequency with which Tennyson uses romance is an indication of the immense importance he attached to human desires. He comes close to affirming, as Browning does explicitly in *Saul*, that human desires are not illusions but witnesses of a divine plan. On this basis he affirms his belief in immortality and in the value of earthly life. But Tennyson's affirmation is generally more subtle and pervasive than Browning's, for Browning wrote nothing like *The Princess*, an elaborate treatment of the patterns I have been discussing.

The Princess consists of an ancient tale in a modern frame, and in this combination and in the action of the tale itself the poem resembles *The Day-Dream*, as John Killham has pointed out. *The Day-Dream*, he says, is a 'remarkable anticipation' of *The Princess*: 'One can easily see a resemblance to the central situation in *The Princess*, where the Prince enters the College garden at some peril to his life; his Princess is likewise reluctant to fulfil her role. Such a situation is part of the stock-in-trade of fairy tales and does not surprise us.'[2] He points to the same pattern in *Edwin Morris* and *Maud*, and in doing so identifies one of the essential actions of Tennysonian romance: the hero's approach to the heroine, and the awakening of vitality in her.

This action Tennyson treats in a way that is typical of the idyl; that is, by a mixture of styles and genres, so that, if one were required to give a short description of *The Princess*, it would not be inaccurate to call it an extended idyl. Tennyson's own word is 'A Medley,' which was confusing enough to early critics, but which becomes a good deal more understandable in the light of the mixtures examined in the last chapter. The nature and purpose of this particular mixture can be defined by looking at the relations between the frame and the story itself.

'It may be remarked,' Tennyson is quoted as saying, 'that there is scarcely anything in the story which is not prophetically glanced at in the prologue.'[3] The Prologue describes a rural picnic that is both an outing of the Mechanics' Institute and part of the vacation of a number of undergraduates. The description is a mixture of incongruities that reflects the age itself, as Aubrey de Vere and Charles Kingsley pointed out in their reviews of the poem. 'Sport / Went hand in hand with Science' (Prologue 79–80), the narrator tells us, and 'Strange was the sight and smacking of the time' (89):

> A Gothic ruin and a Grecian house,
> A talk of college and of ladies' rights,
> A feudal knight in silken masquerade,
> And, yonder, shrieks and strange experiments
> For which the good Sir Ralph had burnt them all –
> This *were* a medley! (Prologue 225–30)

Tennyson makes much of this mixture. In the Prologue, everything is brought together, like the collections, for instance, that Walter shows the narrator. There the natural and the artificial, the military and the peaceful, past and present lie side by side, a jumble representing a variety of human interests in which there is as yet no discernible pattern. An heroic past and a familiar present are juxtaposed in many ways. There is the chronicle, the 'hoard of tales that dealt with knights, / Half-legend, half-historic' (29–30), from which the narrator and his friend turn to the picnic where family and friends act in ways that are familiar, modern, and real. The picnic takes place on a lawn-like green inside a Gothic ruin that in effect serves as an heroic frame for the modern scene. Lilia's silk scarf clothes the statue of the old warrior, Sir Ralph, and even the familiar and colloquial style of the conversation is juxtaposed with the heroic style of the chronicle. The central story of the chronicle is about a lady,

> one that armed
> Her own fair head, and sallying through the gate,
> Had beat her foes with slaughter from her walls.　(Prologue 32–4)

Walter's question, 'Where ... lives there such a woman now?' (124, 126), turns their minds and ours to a consideration of a link between past and present, familiar and heroic. But his question, which starts the move toward the discovery of some pattern in this medley, only provokes a new division, this time between the sexes. Lilia's concept of herself is heroic: 'O I wish / That I were some great princess' (Prologue 133–4), while Walter's concept of her is determinedly familiar and domestic: 'The little hearth-flower Lilia' (165). The conversation leads directly to the romance which makes up the central part of the poem, and directly, too, to the stylistic problem that Tennyson faced. As I pointed out in analysing the relation between the frame and the story in *The Day-Dream*, the fairy tale reveals the essential and ideal pattern of the modern situation, and the romance here does the same for this medley of a picnic. In doing so, it develops fully the heroic hints and suggestions that we saw in the picnic in *Audley Court*, a picnic that also took place on a large country estate. But if an heroic ideal is fully developed here, it is also far more complex. In *The Day-Dream*, the fairy tale was a projection of one speaker's desires, but there are seven narrators here, the result of the game of telling 'a tale from mouth to mouth' (Prologue 189). Hence the tale is the projection of seven different dreams or points of view on the subject of women's rights. This situation results in the mixture of styles in the story, a problem that Tennyson discusses in the Conclusion.

When the narrator is asked to bring the seven parts of the narrative 'Together in one sheaf,' the chief problem is, 'What style could suit?' (9), for he realizes that the different styles are a manifestation of the wishes and desires of the different speakers:

> The men required that I should give throughout
> The sort of mock-heroic gigantesque,
> With which we bantered little Lilia first ...   (Conclusion 10–12)

The women want the 'true-heroic – true-sublime' (20). The narrator labels the two sides 'the mockers and the realists' (24) and describes his solution: 'I moved as in a strange diagonal' (27). The mixture of styles that is the result of this solution is a development of the mixture of forms and styles which we found to be typical of the idyl, but that mixture serves an especially complex purpose here.

In an important analysis of *The Princess*, F.E.L. Priestley points out that the poet himself has a didactic purpose in determining the precise nature of the mixture:

The subject with which the poem deals, the rights of women, and the place of women in society, was one which seemed to foster 'the falsehood of extremes'. To many men, the struggle for female emancipation was purely and simply comic: to many women, deeply and fiercely tragic. Both extremes, of facetiousness and of earnestness, made for tightly shut minds. As Tennyson knew, a comic treatment would delight the men, infuriate the women, and confirm both sets of prejudice; a solemn one would please the women and disgust the men. His difficult task is to persuade both sides, to write something which both sides will read and which will moderate both extremes. This task obviously confronts him with a very difficult aesthetic problem.[4]

The solution to this problem Tennyson describes in the image of the diagonal. Priestley points out that 'Tennyson's diagonal does not simply run from mock-heroic to heroic, from ridiculous to sublime; it operates in a delicate balance from the start.'[5] And he shows how Tennyson uses the styles of romance, comedy, tragedy, and lyric to achieve his purpose.

Priestley's analysis makes clear the fact that the mixture of styles is carefully managed, and that the linear continuity of the poem provides firm but delicate control of disparate things. The effect is one of order in variety, and it is an effect that soothes the sense of irritation that one feels at the jumble in the Prologue. Indeed, the conclusion even suggests, not just an ordering of the inconsistencies and incongruities of the Prologue, but a fusion of them. This falling into place of all things is symbolized, in the usual Tennysonian fashion, by the cycle of the day, and by the going out and the return that correspond to morning and evening. The poem ends with the line 'home well-pleased we went' (Conclusion 118), and the feeling is similar to that at the end of *Audley Court*: a day of leisure has released the imagination and given it the opportunity to reveal the essential patterns of seemingly unrelated human experiences. At the end of the poem there is a sense of rising to a point where those essential patterns are discernible, and this sense is apparent in a return that has two distinct stages. In the first,

> we climbed
> The slope to Vivian-place, and turning saw
> The happy valleys, half in light, and half
> Far-shadowing from the west, a land of peace ...(Conclusion 39–42)

Climbing to a height of course provides a broader perspective, but the action traditionally goes beyond that to suggest an approach to a moment of vision. What is seen here is an idyllic landscape where light and dark are fused, and that fusion evokes feelings of order and rest. 'The Tory member's elder son' (50), drawing on Gaunt's speech in *Richard II*, applies the metaphor of England as a garden, and contrasts its order, peace, and fruitfulness with the social and political upheavals in France. The narrator is not willing to see English society in such ideal terms, nor is he willing to make such a sharp contrast between the two societies at a moment when he senses that extremes are in fact part of a more comprehensive order. He tempers his friend's speech, then, and asserts his faith in moral and social progress. In suggesting that 'maybe wildest dreams / Are but the needful preludes of the truth' (73–4), he in effect defends romance by asserting the importance of the dreams and desires which are its basis. This first stage of the return culminates in a figure who combines the familiar and the heroic: Sir Walter, 'A great broad-shouldered genial Englishman' (85), who has various incongruous interests, most of them of the domestic and agricultural variety. Yet he is also heroic, and Tennyson describes the shout for him in heroic terms ('O, a shout / More joyful than the city-roar that hails / Premier or king!' 100–2). The account suggests that the future depends upon a man such as this, who fuses in his own person such disparate interests.

The second stage of the return is more symbolic, though it deals with the same themes:

But we went back to the Abbey, and sat on,
So much the gathering darkness charmed: we sat
But spoke not, rapt in nameless reverie,
Perchance upon the future man: the walls
Blackened about us, bats wheeled, and owls whooped,
And gradually the powers of the night,
That range above the region of the wind,
Deepening the courts of twilight broke them up
Through all the silent spaces of the worlds,
Beyond all thought into the Heaven of Heavens.

(Conclusion 106–15)

Light and dark are fused at twilight, but the description here goes beyond the fusion that has already been suggested in the first stage of the return. There is a suggestion of mysterious powers dissolving everything substantial, a sense of vast cosmic spaces opening up, and a glimpse of ultimate reality ('the Heaven of Heavens'). The two stages of the return correspond to the two results of the kiss in *The Day-Dream*: the world continues in its familiar round, and at the same time a vast and mysterious realm opens up. Here that vast and mysterious realm seems to inform our own little world, and Lilia's reaction, which combines thoughtfulness, purpose, and a sense of well-being, is the proper one for this double awareness.

This insight is evoked by the romance mode which is dominant in the story, and indeed the structure and characterization are as closely related to the wishes and desires of the characters in the frame as are the varying styles. Once the scheme is hit upon, Lilia's aunt provides in effect a licence for romance:

'As you will;
Heroic if you will, or what you will,
Or be yourself your hero if you will.'   (Prologue 214–16)

The references to *The Winter's Tale* both confirm the dominant mode as romance and suggest the flexibility that will allow a mixture of styles, unlikely and coincidental events, and stylization and exaggeration in character and event. The plot proceeds, as one would expect in romance, not according to the criteria of cause and effect, but according to human desires and aversions, and the linear continuity cannot disguise the coincidences: Melissa's overhearing of the meeting between Psyche and the three youths, the Princess's fall into the stream, the felling of the

Prince by Arac rather than another warrior. The characters tend to be types rather than individuals, with the exception of the Princess herself, who is portrayed with considerable psychological depth. The most heroic part of the story, as Priestley has already pointed out, is reserved for the account of the struggle within Ida herself. The struggle is a version of the romance pattern of death and rebirth, which in its more realistic guise takes the form of education. The conventional form of the outer action is thus complemented by the equally conventional form of the inner action. Outwardly there is a perilous journey, when the Prince and his two companions travel to Ida's college and enter its forbidden precincts; there is a crucial struggle, when warriors from the two nations engage in deadly combat; and there is a triumph when Prince and Princess move toward marriage. The chief interest in this narrative is discovery, and indeed the plot turns on a series of discoveries, as more and more of the women learn the identity of the maskers. This structural element merges with the theme of education, which in turn defines the shape of the inner action. Ida discovers the proper basis for the relation between men and women, and her education is complemented by the cessation of the Prince's seizures. His recovery from his near-fatal wound is the physical counterpart of the Princess's education, and both continue in a more desirable world as a result of their experiences.

Romance often manifests itself in neat patterns of opposites or threes, and such patterns are prominent in *The Princess*. We might begin with two groups of three: the Prince, and his two friends, Cyril and Florian; and the Princess, and her closest companions, Blanche and Psyche.[6] In each group, the Prince and Princess stand out as clearly superior and often heroic, though *vis-à-vis* each other they present a contrast, primarily of sex – the difference that is crucial in the poem – but also in such fairy-tale matters as colour of hair. The Prince has 'lengths of yellow ringlet, like a girl' (I, 3), while the Princess has 'long black hair' (IV, 257). This difference suggests that the Sleeping Beauty myth is submerged in the story, and the account of the sun god awakening the sleeping earth is here displaced in the account of the Prince bringing Ida to conceive properly of her role as woman. Each of the superior characters has a foolish or jealous friend, and each has a true friend. Cyril is 'given to starts and bursts / Of revel' (I, 53–4), and his thoughtlessness is the immediate cause of the disasters in the story. He is, however, a friend who is readily forgiven, and there is much to indicate that he is worthy of being the Prince's friend and of marrying Psyche. It is he who persuades Ida to return Psyche's child, and the Prince says of him after the unfortunate tavern song, 'These flashes on the surface are not he. / He has a solid base of temperament' (IV, 234–5).

Blanche is Cyril's counterpart in the other group. Her fault is not thoughtlessness but jealousy, primarily of Psyche, and she is a much more sinister figure than Cyril:

> Lady Blanche alone
> Of faded form and haughtiest lineaments,
> With all her autumn tresses falsely brown,
> Shot sidelong daggers at us, a tiger-cat
> In act to spring. (II, 424—8)

Nonetheless, Tennyson did soften the extremes of her portrait. In the edition of 1850 he got rid of the line, 'a double-rouged and treble-wrinkled Dame,' and he does indicate that she is worthy of Ida's love and affection. After all, she did raise Ida after the death of the queen, and her work in carrying out Ida's wishes in the college is important. She is essentially an autumnal figure, and what she once was is suggested by her daughter Melissa, who is a 'rosy blonde' (II, 302) and wears a gown 'That clad her like an April daffodilly / (Her mother's colour)' (II, 303—4). As the woman who nurtured Ida, the child who will usher in a brighter future for women, Blanche is a type of Demeter, though now grown old. The association is strengthened by the fact that the name Melissa was the name of the priestess of Demeter.[7]

Blanche contrasts with Psyche, just as the faithful Florian ('my other heart, / And almost my half-self' I, 54—5) contrasts with Cyril. Blanche is ugly, associated with autumn, and by part VI she has 'a wintry eye' (VI, 310). Psyche is beautiful, and is associated with fullness of summer:

> A quick brunette, well-moulded, falcon-eyed,
> And on the hither side, or so she looked,
> Of twenty summers. (II, 91—3)

The associations with the seasons are particularly important here, and help us define both likeness and difference in this very important pair. Blanche is autumn, Psyche is summer, and both have children. Both the children, Melissa and Aglaïa, are blonde: Melissa is a 'rosy blonde' (II, 302), and Aglaïa is 'headed like a star' (II, 94; Tennyson explained this simile as 'with bright golden hair'). Both are associated with April: Aglaïa is 'a double April old' (II, 95), and Melissa's yellow gown is 'like an April daffodilly' (II, 303). But the difference in the age of the children is important. Melissa is the spring, but Aglaïa is like the seed that has just come to life after a long winter. These four female figures thus provide us with the whole spectrum of the seasons: summer is the mother of winter from which new life springs; autumn is the mother of spring. The pairing of opposite seasons in a mother-daughter relationship suggests that they are part of a more comprehensive order bound together by human love, and that order is affirmed in the marriages at the end. Just as Psyche becomes Cyril's bride, so Melissa becomes Florian's, and, in this pairing off of the two groups of three, Melissa is a surrogate for her mother. The seasonal associations also help us to identify both Psyche and Blanche as types of Demeter. Each is separated from her daughter. Ida finally restores Aglaïa to Psyche, but Blanche leaves Melissa at court (VII, 41–2). Melissa will be restored to her mother only by becoming an autumnal figure herself. This pattern of separation and restoration is another version of the death and resurrection pattern that is the basis of romance.

Related to the pairing of the Prince and Ida is the contrast between north and south. The contrast is summed up in the Prince's song (IV, 75–98), where the south is characterized as 'bright and fierce and fickle' (IV, 79) and the north as 'dark and true and tender' (IV, 80). In part I of the poem there is a description of the south as 'a livelier land' (I, 109), a land where the vegetation is more luxuriant and the farms are more prosperous than in the north. It is worth noting that Ida's college is almost on the border between the two countries, and the setting foreshadows the union of north and south in the marriage at the end of the poem.

The two fathers are also paired, and present a superficial contrast. Gama is 'A little dry old man' (I, 116), effete and ineffectual (I, 113–65). The Prince's father is a rough man who doesn't think too much and relies on physical force. It is significant that 'He cared not for the affection of the house' (I, 26). He is essentially a military man whose solution to any problem, social or political, is 'a hundred thousand men' (I, 63) and 'iron gauntlets' (I, 88). In spite of this apparent contrast, the two are similar in their views of the relations between man and woman. The Prince's father holds the view that 'Man is the hunter; woman is his game' (V, 147), and argues for a sharp division of roles: 'Man for the field and woman for the hearth ... All else confusion' (V, 437, 441). The counterpart of this view of the 'lazy tolerance' (V, 433) of Gama, who lets Ida have her way but doesn't believe in what she is trying to do.

These views lead us to a consideration of the most important pair in the poem: man and woman. Their relationship is the principal theme of the poem. The popular view – the one expressed in its extreme form by the Prince's father – is that man and woman are opposites, with sharply defined roles. That view leads to a state of war between the sexes, and that is a state vigorously advocated by Ida, who characterizes women as slaves (IV, 110–14, 500). Though she opposes the division of roles, she conceives of woman's role as an imitation of man's, as the establishment of her college indicates. And the battle in part V is the military equivalent of the competition that Ida has already provided in her educational institution. Against this view the Prince argues (IV, 399–447). He uses the Platonic concept of man and woman as halves of one whole: 'half / Without you; with you, whole; and of those halves / You worthiest' (IV, 440–2). He expands this view in part VII (259–89), a view in which man and woman remain 'Distinct in individualities' (VII, 275) but grow into 'The single pure and perfect animal' (VII, 288). The marriages at the end, and particularly the marriage of the Prince and Ida, resolve the matter and realize the view expressed by the Prince.

The Prince's statement about the proper relation between man and woman includes these lines:

> 'Then comes the statelier Eden back to men:
> Then reign the world's great bridals, chaste and calm:
> Then springs the crowning race of humankind.'   (VII, 277–9)

The concept of 'the crowning race' gives immense importance to marriage and to children. The idea does not appear just at the end of the poem, but is implicit throughout in the figure of the child, who is in many ways the most important character in this romance. Hallam Tennyson quotes his father as writing, 'The child is the link thro' the parts as shown in the songs which are the best interpreters of the poem.'[8] Tennyson's comment needs some study, first of all through an examination of the child in the poem, and then the figure of the child in those songs that were added in the third edition (1850).

The child is used initially as an image for the subordinate, and indeed inferior, position of women. It is first introduced by Lilia in the Prologue, where she complains that men 'love to keep us children!' (133). The image reappears in Gama's reporting of Ida's feminist theories:

> they had but been, she thought,
> As children; they must lose the child, assume
> The woman ...   (I, 135–7)

And finally we hear it from Ida herself: 'Your language proves you still the child' (II, 44), she tells the Prince in reproving him for sounding 'the tinsel clink of compliment' (II, 41). The education she provides is to foster growth to woman (II, 71–80) – a purpose she reiterates at III, 205–8 and 279–80. The image reappears at IV, 128–9, where Ida describes men's view of women as 'pretty babes / To be dandled' and at V, 407–8: 'she / whose name is yoked with children's.' Tennyson thus anticipates Dickens' treatment of Dora in *David Copperfield* and his rendering of Bella's outburst in *Our Mutual Friend* against being 'the doll in the doll's house.'

Aside from these images, however, the child to which Tennyson refers is primarily Psyche's baby, Aglaïa. She is first introduced in part II:

> At her left, a child,
> In shining draperies, headed like a star,
> Her maiden babe, a double April old,
> Aglaïa slept. (II, 93–6)

The description is an interesting one. The child is associated with light and springtime, and her name (as Ricks points out in his notes, p 762) means Brightness. Her name is that of one of the Graces, who, among other things, were the companions of Aphrodite, and were associated with the fertility of gardens and fields, especially in the springtime. Hence light and flowers are Aglaïa's attributes. She is later described as 'The lily-shining child' (IV, 268); Ida addresses her as 'Pretty bud! / Lily of the vale! half opened bell of the woods!' (VI, 175–6), and Psyche calls her 'my flower' (V, 86) and 'my little blossom' (V, 97). The narrator tells us nothing of Aglaïa's father or of Psyche's marriage, so the child's origins are mysterious. The omission suggests the mythical quality of the child, an heroic figure come to guide mankind still closer to its goal. The child is the promise for the future and the prophet of it, and is a symbol of the love which makes such a future possible. Hence Aglaïa's male counterpart is Cupid, who is, metaphorically, also her father. It is perhaps no accident that Aglaïa's mother's name is Psyche, and that the chief interest in the legend of Cupid and Psyche – the union of earthly and heavenly, mortal and immortal – is suggested when Aglaïa is associated with light. For instance, in part VI, Aglaïa 'Half-lapt in glowing gauze and golden brede, / Lay like a new-fallen meteor on the grass' (VI, 118–19).

It is Cyril who refers explicitly to the legend:

'A thousand hearts lie fallow in these halls,
And round these halls a thousand baby loves
Fly twanging headless arrows at the hearts,
Whence follows many a vacant pang; but O
With me, Sir, entered in the bigger boy,
The Head of all the golden-shafted firm,
The long-limbed lad that had a Psyche too;
He cleft me through the stomacher ...'   (II, 378–85)

Cyril sets aside the figure of the mischievous boy and his 'baby loves' in favour of the 'long-limbed lad' and his mature love. The Prince does so too, as the device with which he seals his letter to Ida indicates:

The seal was Cupid bent above a scroll,
And o'er his head Uranian Venus hung,
And raised the blinding bandage from his eyes ...   (I, 238–40)

Uranian Venus is the higher heavenly love distinguished by Pausanias in Plato's *Symposium*, and her lifting of the blindfold symbolizes a move to love which is not fortuitous but purposeful, not blind but fully aware of its object. That object is 'the crowning race of humankind' (VII, 279), and hence these references to a Cupid who is not merely mischievous are particularly important. They, like other things in the poem, turn our attention to the means of producing 'the crowning race': marriage and a home.

Aglaïa represents the child that Ida must have if she is to achieve her purposes, but, while she is drawn to the child, she has not yet faced up to the relationship it represents. When the Prince in disguise woos Ida in part III, he asks her if she fears missing 'what every woman counts her due, / Love, children, happiness' (III, 228–9). Ida replies angrily, saying that 'children die' but 'great deeds cannot die' (III, 236–7), that children may turn out badly, and hence it is better to 'up and act' ourselves (III, 248). 'Yet will we say for children, would they grew / Like field-flowers everywhere!' (III, 234–5). She is instinctively drawn to children themselves, but doesn't want to think of their generation. And no wonder, when the prevailing male view is apparently that of the Prince's father:

'A lusty brace
Of twins may weed her of her folly. Boy,
The bearing and the training of a child
Is woman's wisdom.'   (V, 453–6)

Hence it is not surprising that, after the discovery, she should keep Aglaïa for herself. We have already seen how Aglaïa is associated with light and flowers; the Princess calls her 'this lost lamb' (IV, 342) and the image is repeated several lines later (IV, 372). The image links this central figure of the home with an older pastoral tradition, and introduces Aglaïa's principal function in the central part of the poem; she comforts Ida, and her love dissolves Ida's anger:

> 'indeed I think
> Our chiefest comfort is the little child
> Of one unworthy mother; which she left:
> She shall not have it back: the child shall grow
> To prize the authentic mother of her mind.
> I took it for an hour in mine own bed
> This morning: there the tender orphan hands
> Felt at my heart, and seemed to charm from thence
> The wrath I nursed against the world ...'   (v, 419–27)

It would be easy to dismiss this passage as Victorian sentimentality, but Tennyson is in fact presenting the child as a civilizing influence and the agent of human progress. The influence is not yet enough to lead Ida to stop the tournament, which she watches with Aglaïa in her arms (v, 501). It is only at the end of the tournament, when Ida sees the Prince's father mourning over his (apparently) dead son, and is shown the lock of hair which her mother cut, that 'Her iron will was broken in her mind; / Her noble heart was molten in her breast' (VI, 102–3). The scene is a version of a domestic scene: a father and a potential mother united above a son who embodies their hopes for the future:

> So those two foes above my fallen life,
> With brow to brow like night and evening mixt
> Their dark and gray ...   (VI, 114–16)

The fusion of light and darkness, hinted at here, foreshadows the human reunions and reconciliations that will soon take place. At Cyril's urging, Ida restores Aglaïa to her mother, and the two women are reconciled: 'Kiss and be friends, like children being chid!' (VI, 271). And Ida herself is soon to abandon her position, which Cyril describes as 'Orbed in ... isolation' (VI, 153) and accept married love and human ties. When she talks to Aglaïa just before restoring her to Psyche, she addresses her as

'Pledge of a love not to be mine' (VI, 180). The word 'pledge' is crucial here, and its figurative use – the child as 'token or evidence of mutual love and duty between parents' (OED.) – has special significance in the Victorian period. But Ida must undergo an heroic inner struggle before she can come to accept children in this sense. At the end of part VII, the Prince's statement of his view of the relation between men and women is in fact his pledge, which Ida accepts. Her acceptance is accompanied by a favourite Tennysonian image, which the Prince uses toward the end of his speech:

> 'all the past
> Melts mist-like into this bright hour, and this
> Is morn to more, and all the rich to-come
> Reels, as the golden Autumn woodland reels
> Athwart the smoke of burning weeds.'   (VII, 333–7)

An early Canadian critic of Tennyson, Samuel Edward Dawson of Montreal, realized clearly the central role of the child in this resolution. In his study of *The Princess*, first published in 1882, he wrote: 'Having thus reached the central thought of the poem [the influence of woman upon society], we must look for the hero or heroine of the story; that is, for the one person who comes triumphant out of the turmoil.'[9] Dawson reviews each of the leading characters in turn, and points out that they are 'all vanquished. All, save one – Psyche's baby – she is the conquering heroine of the epic.'[10]

Ridiculous in the lecture-room, the babe, in the poem, as in the songs, is made the central point upon which the plot turns; for the unconscious child is the concrete embodiment of Nature herself, clearing away all merely intellectual theories by her silent influence. Ida feels the power of the child. The postscript of the despatch sent to her brother in the height of her indignation, contains, as is fitting, the kernel of the matter. She says: [Dawson here quotes V, 424–7, among other lines, and comments on them.] Whenever the plot thickens the babe appears. It is with Ida on her judgment-seat. In the topmost height of the storm the wail of the 'lost lamb at her feet' reduces her eloquent anger into incoherence. She carries it when she sings her song of triumph. When she goes to tend her wounded brothers on the battle-field she carries it. Through it, and for it, Cyril pleads his successful suit, and wins it for the mother. For its sake the mother is pardoned. O fatal babe! more fatal to the hopes of woman than the doomful horse to the proud towers of Ilion – for through thee the walls of pride are breached, and all the conquering affections flock in.[11]

In a paragraph of Tennyson's letter to Dawson (dated 1882) which Hallam omitted when he reprinted the letter in the *Memoir*, the poet commended Dawson for recognizing the central role of the child, and explained to him the purpose of adding the songs in the third edition (1850): 'I may tell you that the songs were not an after-thought. Before the first edition came out I deliberated with myself whether I should put songs in between the separate divisions of the poem – again, I thought, the poem will explain itself, but the public did not see that the child, as you say, was the heroine of the piece, and at last I conquered my laziness and inserted them.'[12] The songs reinforce and elaborate the themes we have been tracing. 'As through the land at eve we went' has a ballad-like simplicity. It tells the story of a falling out between man and wife and a tearful reconciliation above the grave of their child. The lyric seems a prime example of Victorian sentimentality, and yet Dawson recognizes the way in which the child symbolizes the social order and hope for the future: 'An abiding influence, this, of the little one; reaching back from the grave.'[13] The second lyric, 'Sweet and low,' is a lullaby, and its theme is the same as the first: reunion of husband and wife for the sake of the child. Ricks suggests a comparison with the lullaby in the twenty-fourth idyl of Theocritus (p 772), but in Theocritus there is no mention of a reunion with the father. The key lines in Tennyson, as Dawson points out, are these: 'Rest, rest, on mother's breast, / Father will come to thee soon' (11–12). 'Sweet influence this of the babe,' Dawson writes, 'reaching far across the ocean, and uniting loving hearts!'[14] The third song, 'The splendour falls on castle walls,' seems at first to be a break with the themes we have been tracing, but again Dawson's comments are illuminating. He singles out the lines on which the poem turns, the analogy between the echoes in nature and human experience ('Our echoes roll from soul to soul, / And grow for ever and for ever' 15–16) and comments: 'The stress of meaning is in the word grow. The song is evidently one of married love, and the growing echoes reverberate from generation to generation, from grandparent to parent and grandchild. Once more it is unity through the family. In the first song a unity through the past, in the second a unity in the present, and in this a unity for the future. How important, then, does this relation of parentage seem to be.'[15] The next song, 'Thy voice is heard through rolling drums,' is 'a song of the influences of home and wedded love in nerving a man for the shocks and conflict of life.'[16] The next, 'Home they brought her warrior dead,' deals with the influence of the child on the widowed mother; the child brings about the release of tears and gives hope for the future (much as the family does at the end of *The Two Voices*). The alternative version of this lyric (which Ricks prints on p 1771) makes less of the child as the agent through which the mother accepts death and gains hope, and for that reason Tennyson may have rejected it. The final lyric, 'Ask me no more,' is the pledge of wife to husband, a pledge which, as we have seen, is symbolized by the child.

I have referred to an alternative version of one of the lyrics, and there are other versions, and indeed other lyrics altogether, which Tennyson considered using in *The Princess*. Of these the most interesting is *The Losing of the Child*, part of which is printed in the *Memoir*, and all of which is printed by Ricks (pp 848–9). In his letter to Dawson, Tennyson wrote:

You would be still more certain that the child was the true heroine if, instead of the first song as it now stands,

'As thro' the land at eve we went'

I had printed the first song which I wrote,

The losing of the child.

The child is sitting on the bank of a river, and playing with flowers – a flood comes down – a dam has been broken thro' – the child is borne down by the flood – the whole village distracted – after a time the flood has subsided – the child is thrown safe and sound again upon the bank and all the women are in raptures. I quite forget the words of the ballad but I think I may have it somewhere.[17]

The song is worth quoting in full:

> The child was sitting on the bank
>   Upon a stormy day.
> He loved the river's roaring sound;
> The river rose and burst his bound,
> Flooded fifty leagues around,
> Took the child from off the ground,
>   And bore the child away.
>
> O the child so meek and wise,
>   Who made us wise and mild!

All was strife at home about him,
Nothing could be done without him;
Father, mother, sister, brother,
All accusing one another;
   O to lose the child!

The river left the child unhurt,
   But far within the wild.
Then we brought him home again,
Peace and order come again,
The river sought his bound again,
The child was lost and found again,
   And we will keep the child.

The child as not just the symbol but the agent of 'Peace and order,' the child 'Who made us wise and mild,' is by now a familiar theme. Equally familiar, and very much a pattern of the poem, is the story of separation and reunion that is in fact a symbolic death and rebirth. This pattern brings us back to the romance which is the dominant mode of the poem. The myth of the mysterious death and rebirth of the hero, given here as a child carried away by a flood and then tossed up again by the water, anticipates the account of the coming of Arthur.

In *The Princess*, the pattern of separation and reunion is clearest in the story of Psyche and Aglaïa, the story which most closely resembles *The Losing of the Child*. Psyche, as I have pointed out, is a type of Demeter, and her child is constantly associated with light and flowers. Psyche herself is associated with fertility, as her youth, her vigour, and her immense personal attraction indicate. The mourning of Psyche for her lost child is like the mourning of Demeter for Persephone (v, 79–102). The theme of her lament is the bad influence others will have on her child, teaching her hardness and 'cold reverence' (v, 89) rather than love for her mother. The reunion is like the return of spring, and is associated with the renewal of human love and the advance of civilization.

This pattern reflects the larger pattern of the poem. Ida's actions lead to separation, from men and (as she comes to realize) from woman's proper role in human life. The motive of the Prince's quest is union, reconciliation, and love. In the course of the story each undergoes a symbolic death and rebirth. The Prince's ordeal is largely physical, a state of unconsciousness resulting from his near-fatal wound:

> but I
> Deeper than those weird doubts could reach me, lay
> Quite sundered from the moving Universe,
> Nor knew what eye was on me, nor the hand
> That nursed me, more than infants in their sleep.   (VII, 35–9)

But the Prince too is educated, as Winston Collins has pointed out, and awakes to a new sense of wisdom and purpose.[18] Moreover, his 'weird seizures,' which Tennyson added in the fourth edition of the poem (1851), apparently disappear. Presented initially as an inability to discriminate, to distinguish between shadow and substance, they are transformed, in the Prince's final speech in part VII, into the recognition that shadow and substance, light and dark, are in fact one, and that one is in a state of becoming. The Prince comes to accept incompleteness as a condition of man's growth.

The Princess's ordeal is less physical, and more psychological and spiritual. Symbolically she enters a waste land: 'So blackened all her world in secret, blank / And waste it seemed and vain' (VII, 27–8). In her there is an heroic struggle between love and duty; on the one hand there is her pride and her attachment to her ideals; on the other there is her gratitude and human sympathy. The turning point comes with the superb lyric 'Come down, O maid, from yonder mountain height' (VII, 177–207). In the story it is called 'a small / Sweet Idyl' (VII, 175–6), and its themes are familiar. 'Love is of the valley,' and it is associated with prosperity and fertility, 'Plenty in the maize,' domestic life, and children, whereas heights are associated with high ideals, and 'the splendour of the hills' is cold and remote. The pastoral and the domestic are linked when we find children and shepherds, homes and green fields, side by side. But there is also a suggestion that life in this pastoral-domestic setting is truly heroic, and the suggestion is contained in the epic description of the smoke drifting upwards from the fireplace: 'azure pillars of the hearth / Arise to thee.' The last three lines of the song fuse the domestic and the heroic in a particular way:

> 'Myriads of rivulets hurrying through the lawn,
> The moan of doves in immemorial elms,
> And murmuring of innumerable bees.'

The lines suggest both the innumerable particulars of the physical world and the common patterns that order all these particulars and give them their significance. The details are familiar, and the words 'myriads' and 'innumerable' point to an infinite number of individual things. But each action, 'hurrying,' 'moan,' and 'murmuring,' indicates a single common pattern that is unchanging and timeless, and the sense of something that transcends time and all the particulars within it is reinforced by the adjective 'immemorial.' Tennyson spoke of his interest in 'the abiding in the transient'[19] as it was expressed in 'Tears, idle Tears,' and the theme is equally apparent in this lyric. The same sense appears in the Prince's speech at the end of part VII, though less is made there of the numberless particulars of this world and more of the common pattern. Both the lyric and the speech suggest that the home is the proper beginning for progress into a golden future and ultimately into a spiritual eternity.

The semi-articulate Arac, whose tongue is given to occasionally felicitous turns, describes Ida at one point as 'the flower of womankind' (V, 277). The image sums up many of the patterns I have been tracing in the poem, but in particular the pattern of growth and development which produces this flower, this essence toward which change has been directing its energies. The image also suggests that Ida herself is the object of human desire. As such, she replaces the *locus amoenus*, the idealized rural landscape of the pastoral tradition, for that landscape is now not just around a female figure but inside her. The image of a bounded paradise takes the form of a woman's college in this poem, an ironic version of the more conventional enclosed garden. The quest involves the penetration of this forbidden place and the release of the energies that are dormant in it. Woven into this story is the story of the loss and regaining of a child, and the pattern common to both stories is a death and rebirth. It is a pattern that Tennyson works out in this poem with fertility of invention and admirable sureness in handling a variety of styles and a complicated narrative structure. The central myths were obviously congenial ones for him, and were rich in possibilities for a wide variety of treatments.

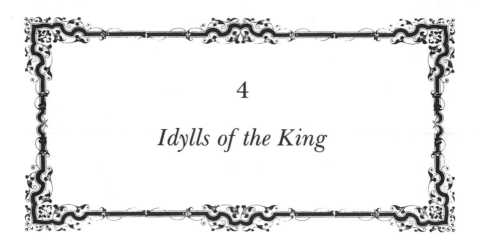

4

Idylls of the King

Tennyson's involvement with the stories of King Arthur and his knights, and the composition of his major poem itself, occupied him during most of his life, and it is not surprising, then, that the themes and patterns I have been examining should pervade the *Idylls*. But they are changed, modified, and transformed by Tennyson to suit the many-faceted character and complex purposes of his poem. One way of describing the *Idylls* is to say that they present an heroic treatment of domestic themes, images, and actions. The nature of this heroic treatment must, however, be defined carefully, for Tennyson was clearly not writing in the manner of older writers of epic and romance. Rather, truth must be given 'in the fashion of the day.'

THE FRAME: *THE EPIC, THE COMING OF ARTHUR,*
THE PASSING OF ARTHUR

The phrase, truth 'in the fashion of the day,' comes from the frame which Tennyson provided for the *Morte d'Arthur* in his volume of 1842, and which he called *The Epic*. The poet, Everard Hall, is reported to have said 'that a truth / Looks freshest in the fashion of the day,' and because his epic on King Arthur failed to present truth in this way, he burned most of it. The phrase neatly summarizes Tennyson's purposes and problems in dealing with the Arthurian material, and it is therefore a convenient place to begin a discussion of one major aspect of the 'fashion' in which Tennyson clothed his story. The Arthurian story was – and is – considered a romance; the 'fashion of the day' was the realism closely related to the empiricist philosophy which dominated popular thinking in the nineteenth century. Tennyson retained the essential romance character of his material,[1] but he made the improbable and the typical – the major characteristics of romance – suitable to his own age by exploring reactions to them that were realistic. Improbable events and characters; probable responses. That is the essential pattern here, and it is a pattern of considerable importance in the *Idylls* as a whole. That pattern is apparent when one examines the relation between the *Morte d'Arthur* and *The Epic*.

Tennyson's frames, as we have seen in *The Day-Dream* and *The Princess*, are never mere decoration, but are closely related to the central work. Though those relations vary, we notice a recurring pattern in these earlier examples. The central poem is an old form – a fairy tale in *The Day-Dream*, a romance in *The Princess* – but the frame is modern and realistic. So here. *The Epic* provides a realistic context for, and a modern response to, a fragment which, because of its fairly close reworking of Malory's text, is clearly archaic and romantic. It is the response which is crucial. The *Morte d'Arthur* narrates an event – a death full of suggestions of rebirth – which is unrealistic when judged by empirical criteria, and yet the possibility of such an event is something which the Victorians in general, and Tennyson in particular, wanted to believe in. This response is the expression of a desire to make the ideal actual, and that desire (or the lack of it) is, as we shall see, the central concern of the *Idylls*.

The way in which this pattern is worked out in the relations between *The Epic* and the *Morte d'Arthur* is particularly interesting. The links and parallels become apparent if one concentrates on the characteristics of the time that Tennyson has chosen for each.

The time in the *Morte d'Arthur* is clearly the end of a cycle: the Round Table has dissolved, Arthur's society is breaking up, and Arthur is fatally wounded. The cycle of the seasons is also coming to an end. It is well known that Tennyson changed the time of Arthur's death from early summer (as in Malory) to winter, and the scene from a down between Salisbury and the sea to Lyonnesse in the west, where the sun sets. For it is also the end of the cycle of the day. The battle is over, and it is evening. All these things suggest an end, with old ways and old values gone. But Tennyson treats this moment not just as an end but as a turning point. An end and a beginning are here fused and it is that fusion which attracts Tennyson's imagination. The appearance from the lake of the arm 'Clothed in white samite, mystic, wonderful' (144) provides a sense of the abiding in the transient, just as the three queens and the funeral barge suggest Providence operating through all the shocks and changes of human life. Arthur's speech about going to 'the island-valley of Avilion' (259) indicates a new beginning for him personally, while his famous speech, 'The old order changeth, yielding place to new' (240) affirms a universal order and a new civilization. The moment is a moment of both parting and reunion, for Arthur parts from the last of his knights, but is reunited with the three queens; and he leaves behind a defeated and despairing self, and is reunited with his better, eternal self.

In *The Epic*, too, it is winter, the end of the cycle of the year; and it is evening, the end of the cycle of the day. Moreover, as Everard Hall recites his poem, the fire is dying and almost goes out. The time suggests the decay of civilization, as the parallels between the conversation among the three friends, on the one hand, and the conversation between Arthur and Bedivere, on the other, make clear. When Bedivere disobeys Arthur, Arthur sees his disobedience as a sign of the times ('Authority forgets a dying king' 121) and accuses Bedivere of lying and of failing in his duty. The conversation among the three friends is also about decline and decay:

> How all the old honour had from Christmas gone,
> Or gone, or dwindled down to some odd games
> In some odd nooks like this ...   (7–9)

And then they turn to 'the general decay of faith / Right through the world' (18–19). The modern and familiar version of Arthur's mortal wound and desperate state is relaxation after strenuous exercise, Christmas games, good food, and wine – relaxation that, on the part of the speaker, settles into sleep while the burning questions of the day are being discussed.

But if the time suggests an end, it is also, clearly, a beginning, for it is Christmas Eve, and that time is as important here as it is in *In Memoriam*. There is much to suggest a new start: the crowing of the cock foretells dawn and suggests new vitality (282–3); night itself moves on toward dawn (290); and at the end it is Christmas morning and there is the peal of church bells. Moreover, there is the speaker's dream of Arthur returning 'like a modern gentleman / Of stateliest port' (294–5). Dreams in epics are often prophetic, but here the dream is more closely related to the human wishes that are the basis of romance. Here, as in Eliot's *The Waste Land*, the dream is a mixture of memory and desire, for it looks both backward and forward: back to an heroic age, forward to a new image of heroism. The mixing of memory and desire is appropriate for Christmas Eve; it is also an appropriate response to the reading of the fragment from Everard Hall's poem. Some of the listeners only lament the passing of an heroic age, but the speaker, to use Joseph Campbell's words, dreams the myth onwards.

For Everard Hall, the poem is clearly an end rather than a beginning. It is a fragment of a romance drawn from Malory, and stays close to the original. Hence Hall is reported to have thought of his poem 'that nothing new was said, or else / Something so said 'twas nothing':

> 'Why take the style of those heroic times?
> For nature brings not back the Mastodon,
> Nor we those times; and why should any man
> Remodel models? these twelve books of mine
> Were faint Homeric echoes, nothing-worth,
> Mere chaff and draff, much better burnt.'   (35–40)

Hall's comments are usually taken out of context, as a summary of Tennyson's views on the difficulties of treating the Arthurian material. But it is instructive to look at them in context. The attitude Hall expresses is an attitude consistent with the end of a cycle, and with the relaxation of purpose, decay, and dissolution evident in the imagery I have already mentioned. But the response of his friends suggests that the poem is not an end but a beginning. Francis Allen, the host, rescues one book from the fire, with the excuse that 'I hoard it as a sugar-plum for Holmes' (43). His real reason for his action is more substantial: 'keep a thing, its use will come' (42). Its use is almost immediately apparent in the reading. In this act, it quickly becomes evident that Hall's poem is by no means a failure. In fact, it evokes a response that suggests that the poem is as arresting as the Ancient Mariner's story is for the wedding guest:

> we
> Sat rapt: it was the tone with which he read –
> Perhaps some modern touches here and there
> Redeemed it from the charge of nothingness –
> Or else we loved the man, and prized his work ...   (276–80)

These attempts to explain the response are not to be ignored, for the response is a complex one. It is complete, however, only with the speaker's dream, which indicates that the response is primarily one of the imagination. The shape of the dream is the rhythm of going out and returning: going out with Malory's Arthur, 'To sail ... under looming shores, / Point after point' (289–90), but returning with Arthur 'like a modern gentle-man / Of stateliest port' (294–5). The rhythm of going out and returning suggests the essential shape of romance; that is, a quest outward into a darkness closely related to death, and a return closely related to rebirth. The shape of the dream is, therefore, governed by the fusion of memory and desire, Arthur's return representing the wish-fulfilment that some-times operates in dreams. Moreover, the figure in the dream is the figure of the hero, appearing not in his eternal form (as in a vision) but in a particular form (as in history). He comes back 'in the fashion of the day' (32). In the speaker's dream, one begins to discern the outlines of Ten-nyson's treatment of the Arthurian material: it is to remain a romance, but romance renewed and revitalized through a modern response to it. For Everard Hall, the *Morte d'Arthur* was an end; for the speaker, it is a beginning. It is perhaps worth pointing out that too much critical empha-sis has been placed on Hall's adverse comments on his own work, and too little on the speaker's response to the work itself. For in that response the characteristics of Tennyson's shaping of Malory are apparent.

Tennyson criticized Malory for 'very fine things ... all strung together without Art.'[2] However just that view of Malory, it was Tennyson's view, and it indicates that he intended to make the structure of his own poem much tighter than that of Malory's prose narrative. The way in which he was to do that was already implicit in the nineteenth-century view of romance, and hence I want to turn briefly to a theme of some importance in the literary history of the form: the progress of romance.

In choosing to write a romance, Tennyson chose the most popular and enduring of all literary forms – popular because it presented, not ordi-nary life, but life as shaped by human desires and aversions. In the popular view, romance must be full of wild and exciting adventures, have a setting remote in time and place, and present characters in whom particular traits and passions were larger than life. To this popular view of the form, critics added more precise accounts of its features. They iden-tified romance as a product of the imagination rather than of the observa-tion of men and events. Its characters tended to be types, and its actions tended to be fortuitous and coincidental when judged by the realistic criteria of probability, cause and effect, or the interaction of character and circumstance. Its limits were not the actual but the conceivable.

Though these were the enduring characteristics of romance, critics realized that it was by no means a static form. At a time when ideas of development and change were pervading every aspect of thought, it had for some time been common to talk about the progress of romance. James

Beattie, in his *On Fable and Romance* (1783), and Clara Reeve, in her *Progress of Romance* (1785), suggested a view of history in which an age of faith or credulity gradually gave way to an age of reason. This shift produced a corresponding change in romance. 'As a country became civilized,' wrote Clara Reeve, 'their narrations were methodized, and moderated to probability.'[3] Moderation to probability is a recurring theme in histories of romance from the late eighteenth and early nineteenth centuries. It appears in John Dunlop's *History of Fiction* (1814) and in an anonymous *Treatise on the Progress of Literature* (1834). Its most important appearance is in Scott's *Essay on Romance* (1824). As romance developed, he wrote, men began to demand 'some insight into nature, or at least into manners; some description of external scenery, and a greater regard to probability, both in respect of the characters which are introduced, and the events which are narrated.'[4] Scott himself suggests ways in which this greater degree of probability is to be achieved. Of these, the most important (for our purposes) appears in a review of *Frankenstein* which he wrote for *Blackwood's* in 1818:

In the class of fictitious narrations to which we allude, the author opens a sort of account-current with the reader; drawing upon him, in the first place, for credit to that degree of the marvellous which he proposes to employ; and becoming virtually bound, in consequence of this indulgence, that his personages shall conduct themselves, in the extraordinary circumstances in which they are placed, according to the rules of probability, and the nature of the human heart. In this view, the *probable* is far from being laid out of sight even amid the wildest freaks of imagination; on the contrary, we grant the extraordinary postulates which the author demands as the foundation of his narrative, only on condition of his deducing the consequences with logical precision.[5]

Scott is arguing that, if a figure or action or event in romance is improbable, the human response must be probable. That technique is central to Tennyson's treatment of the Arthurian material, and an understanding of it helps us to understand both the theme and the form of the *Idylls*. The theme is use; the form is romance, shaped in such a way that it is, paradoxically, both discontinuous and continuous.

The word 'use' neatly sums up the theme of the *Idylls*, and use may be seen as the heroic form of the domestic virtues. It involves a devotion to human civilization, and both the ability and the readiness to serve humanity. Though it is concerned with the shaping of the actual, use is informed by a sense of the ideal, and hence is most accurately defined as the human ability to respond to the ideal. In the *Idylls*, the ideal is represented verbally by the vows, personally by the king, and socially and politically by his marriage and the Order of the Round Table. Critics have sometimes complained that Arthur is not central to the action of the *Idylls*, because most of the stories are not about him at all, but about one or more of his knights. But Tennyson focuses on each individual's response to a king who, as Guinevere belatedly recognizes, is 'the highest and most human too' (*Guinevere* 644). In spite of Tennyson's attempts to emphasize Arthur's humanity – his final revision in 1891 added the line 'Ideal manhood closed in real man' (38) to *To the Queen* – Arthur remains improbable enough when judged by the criteria of realism. His ideal qualities are an essential part of Tennyson's plan. For he postulates a hero, and then shows probable human reactions to him. In these reactions, the knights find their use and assert their freedom.

The idea of freedom is closely related to the theme of use. Arthur does not impose his ideals upon his knights, nor do the vows bind them to him in such a way as to restrict their freedom (though in their fallen state they sometimes think of the vows in this way). Rather, they remain always free to choose, and their continuing and varying responses to the vows are the chief concern of the poem. But if they recognize the ideal for what it is, they must inevitably choose it, and in making such a choice they are asserting their freedom. This paradox is the subject of the conversation between Arthur and Lancelot at the end of *Lancelot and Elaine*. When Lancelot argues that, however ideal a love Elaine seemed to be, 'free love will not be bound' (1368), Arthur corrects him: '"Free love, so bound, were freëst," said the King. / "Let love be free; free love is for the best"' (1369–70). To paraphrase the *Book of Common Prayer*, the service of an ideal is perfect freedom. John R. Reed has best described the knights' situation: 'Their vows are the *recreation* of the ideal vision, which they actually behold within themselves, through their *own* imaginative powers. Arthur's vision is not imposed upon his followers' minds, it is born in them. It is their own creative act, sparked by the King's.'[6] When the knights first take the vows, they literally look like Arthur. 'I beheld,' says Bellicent to Leodogran in *The Coming of Arthur*, 'From eye to eye through all their Order flash / A momentary likeness of the King' (268–70). This likeness must constantly be renewed, and, as the *Idylls* proceed, it is renewed less and less frequently. One way of defining the tragic shape of the *Idylls* is to say that the knights' response to the ideal becomes less and less adequate.

Just as the idea of response to an ideal helps to define some of the main themes in the *Idylls*, so it helps, too, to define their form. *Idylls of the King* is not the story of a single hero like Ulysses or Aeneas, and hence its twelve parts do not have the narrative continuity of the *Odyssey* or the *Aeneid*.[7] Each idyll is a unit complete in itself, and each of the ten central idylls is about a person or persons around Arthur. These idylls each focus on a particular response or responses to Arthur's kingship, often as realized in the vows, more often as realized (or thought to be realized) in his marriage. There is, then, no continuous narrative line in the *Idylls* as a whole, but neither are the idylls wholly discrete. In a note quoted by his son in the Eversley Edition, Tennyson explained that 'I spelt my Idylls with two *l*'s mainly to divide them from the ordinary pastoral idyls usually spelt with one *l*. These idylls group themselves round one central figure.'[8] Tennyson, then, compensates for the narrative discontinuity of the *Idylls* by making each a response to Arthur. Hence the form of the *Idylls* is a romance that is both discontinuous and continuous.

Tennyson's concept of Arthur as 'the blameless king' apparently did not change during the long period of composition of the *Idylls*. His treatment of the ethical concerns of the poem provided the pattern for him to deal with the main events of Arthur's life, particularly the events that were, by the standards of realism, the most improbable: his birth, the quest for the Holy Grail, and his death. The narration of these events he assigned, for the most part, not to him 'who tells the tale' (sometimes Malory, sometimes the anonymous narrator of the four idylls of the 1859 volume), but to a character in the story who is clearly not Tennyson himself. To assign such events to the general narrator would make his account seem an assertion of truth, a telling of what actually happened; to assign such events to a character in the story shifts the question of truth from the events themselves to the make-up of the character narrating them. The pattern for such a practice is hinted at in 1859. In that volume, Tennyson generally avoided events that were obviously improbable. But he included in *Guinevere* an account of 'signs / And wonders ere the coming of the Queen' (230–1) – mermen, elves, spirits, and fairies that filled the land in the early days of Arthur. In his variorum edition of the *Idylls*, John Pfordresher points out that, in early drafts of *Guinevere*, these wonders 'are narrated in the first person,'[9] but in the published idyll they are described by the little nun. This small part of the 1859 idylls was the precedent for major parts of the volume of 1869 (dated 1870). There, Tennyson has Bellicent narrate the most improbable parts of *The Coming of Arthur*; Percivale narrates the story of *The Holy Grail*; and Bedivere gives the account of *The Passing of Arthur*.[10] In these idylls, then, we cannot take the story entirely at face value, but must constantly be aware of it as it is shaped, edited, and even distorted by the character who is telling it. Instead of a simple narrative of wonders for which the romancer would expect his readers willingly to suspend their disbelief, Tennyson presents the action in such a way that the narrator's shaping, amplifying, and explaining of the story reflect his character. Again we have the pattern that I have been tracing in a variety of forms: improbable events, probable responses. We can see how that pattern works in the idylls that provide the main framework for the poem: *The Coming of Arthur* and *The Passing of Arthur*.

In *The Coming of Arthur*, Tennyson has two main events to narrate: Arthur's birth, and his marriage. The marriage is a joyful event, but there is nothing marvellous about it, and Tennyson has his nearly anonymous narrator give the account of it. Arthur's origin, however, is full of mysteries. In telling of the mysterious birth of the hero, Tennyson must deal with a conventional feature of romance, but the birth is no less marvellous for being conventional. He presents the mystery, not as an independent truth, but as a truth which is apprehended in different ways by different characters. The question that Arthur's followers face is this: 'Who is he / That he should rule us?' (67–8). And Guinevere's father, Leodogran, must decide whether or not to consent to his daughter's marriage to a man whose claim to be king is shrouded in mystery. There are no final answers to these questions and doubts. Each character must respond according to his abilities, the test of each response being the extent to which it enables the character to act with purpose and a sense of use.

The responses of the knights and courtiers vary widely. The answer of the 'hoary chamberlain' (147) is an appeal to the authority of Merlin and Bleys, and the uncomplicated 'Ay' (172) of Ulfius and Brastias is, in J.M. Gray's words, 'the uncritical, popular assent to Arthur's leadership.'[11] It is Bedivere who gives the first of the extended accounts of Arthur's birth. Bedivere is a plain man, not much given to complexities of thought or flights of imagination. But he is also observant and honest. He is a good reporter, and he reports everything he knows of, just as in *The Passing of Arthur* he reports everything he hears and sees. He treats Arthur's birth rather as a realistic novelist would, and explains everything in terms of the interaction of character and circumstance. Hence his account (177–236) is almost entirely without mystery. J.M. Gray has pointed out that Tennyson, in having Bedivere retell the story from Malory, omits the chief marvel – that of 'Uther's shape-changing with Merlin's help whereby he accomplishes the begetting of Arthur in the guise of Gorloïs'[12] – and it is entirely appropriate to Bedivere's point of view that Tennyson should reject such a magic transformation. Bedivere gives a probable account of Arthur as Uther's son, and also explains why Arthur is associated with Gorloïs, Anton, and Bellicent. In spite of Bedivere's realistic bias, he is too honest to admit the one mystery he knows of – the curious fact that Arthur's birth coincided with Uther's death, and both took place 'the night of the new year' (208). He does point out that Arthur was born prematurely (210), but the explanation does not dispel our sense of mystery in the coincidence.

Bellicent's account is fuller and more varied than Bedivere's. Like Bedivere, she is a good reporter, and she gives a realistic account of what she has observed or experienced. Unlike Bedivere, she admits mysteries and marvels. She is both more knowledgeable than Bedivere, and less willing to suggest that everything can be explained in realistic terms. Hence, even when she tells of things that are part of her actual experience, she suggests that they are pervaded with mysteries. She witnessed the coronation and the establishment of the Round Table, and at the same time saw the knights transformed to 'A momentary likeness of the King' (270). She and Arthur grew up together as brother and sister, and yet Arthur's fairness, 'Beyond the race of Britons and of men' (330), is a mystery in the midst of a family that is dark. Bellicent, it is clear, is looking at Arthur, not just with her physical eye, but with the eye of the imagination. Hence her final narrative abandons realism altogether, a break that is marked by her curiously abrupt transition: 'But let me tell thee now another tale' (358). And she gives an account of Arthur's mysterious birth from the sea, on a ninth wave that is all aflame. For this account she does not claim truth. The story is neither true nor false, but rather a supposition, a symbolic narrative to which Leodogran must respond with as much insight as he can manage.

One way of describing *The Coming of Arthur* is to say that the idyll presents Leodogran's education, and his experience is a type of all the experiences of those who must respond to the mystery of Arthur. Leodogran's progress is clearly marked in his responses to the various witnesses who appear before him. For the chamberlain's appeal to authority Leodogran has only scathing irony (160–2). After Bedivere's account Leodogran is full of the kind of doubt and uncertainty that inconclusive empirical evidence evokes, and, more seriously, he finds that the evidence gives him little basis for a decision and no motive at all for acting. Leodogran's reactions to Bellicent's stories are quite different. At her description of the coronation, 'Leodogran rejoiced' (309). And again, after her account of her childhood experiences and Arthur's mysterious birth, 'Leodogran rejoiced' (424). His reactions are the proper ones to revelations of spiritual truth, and the question before him shifts from 'What is the truth?' to 'How shall I act?': 'Shall I answer yea or nay?' (425). With that question, he gives himself up to his dream. The dream is prophetic, for he sees a land ravaged by war, and a 'phantom king' (429) ineffectual in preventing the violence and destruction. But the dream is also revelatory:

> the solid earth became
> As nothing, but the King stood out in heaven,
> Crowned. (441–3)

The dream is a transcendentalist's dream of earthly things as insubstantial shadows and spiritual things as reality. It asserts the value and vitality of the ideal, even though this ideal is realized in imperfect ways. The dream is the final stage of Leodogran's education. It provides him with a motive for action, and he acts immediately in giving his consent to the marriage.

In *The Coming of Arthur*, there are many characters who respond to the king in a variety of ways. In *The Passing of Arthur* there is only one, Bedivere, and the idyll is, among other things, the account of his education. The idyll incorporates the *Morte d'Arthur* of 1842, the main change being the fact that Bedivere is made the narrator. The change is consistent with Tennyson's practice of putting a story full of marvels and wonders into the mouth of one of the characters. Bedivere is a particularly good choice. He is, as we have already seen in *The Coming of Arthur*, an accurate reporter who does not understand everything he observes, but has the unusual virtue of telling us everything whether he understands it or not. His reponse to Arthur takes the conventional form of the romance quest in which a knight arrives at the Chapel Perilous and there undergoes testing and initiation. The Chapel Perilous, here described as 'a chapel nigh the field, / A broken chancel with a broken cross' (176–7) is the place where the questing knight must face the horrors of physical and spiritual death, and in facing them learn that death may be the means to new life.

Bedivere's testing and initiation centre on the disposal of Excalibur, for in that act he confronts the problem of the abiding in the transient. As so often happens in romance, the test has three stages. In the first stage, Bedivere fails to obey Arthur's command because his senses are overcome by the dazzling richness of the sword. In the second, he fails to obey for a different reason: he deceives himself by his own arguments, and so his failure is an intellectual one. In the third stage, Bedivere acts swiftly, without looking at the sword and without thinking about it. His reward is a marvel, the recovery of the sword by the arm 'Clothed in white samite, mystic, wonderful' (312). In the first two tests he returned slowly to the king (233, 280); now he goes 'lightly' (315). But though he has passed the test, he has not yet been instructed in the significance of what he has seen and done. Such an initiation into mysteries is a major part of the final scene.

When Bedivere carries Arthur down to the shore, 'His own thought drove him like a goad' (353). His concern eventually emerges in his question ('whither shall I go?' 395) and in the lament that is like the lament of the faithful thane in Old English poetry: 'For now I see the true old times are dead' (397). It is typical of Bedivere not to be able to see beyond his immediate situation. The answer is Arthur's famous speech:

> 'The old order changeth, yielding place to new,
> And God fulfils himself in many ways,
> Lest one good custom should corrupt the world.'   (408–10)

Arthur affirms that spiritual ideals are constantly realizing themselves in many ways; that the one evil is a static rather than a constantly evolving universe; that the disappearance of a good is not evidence of its failure but of a divinely guided process.

The idyll ends with the description of Bedivere watching the funeral barge disappear in the distance. This is the final part of Bedivere's growth, and it too has three stages. For Bedivere climbs the crag to see the barge as long as possible, and an ascent of this sort traditionally suggests growing insight. On the shore, Bedivere remembers 'the weird rhyme' ('From the great deep to the great deep he goes' 445) without grasping its meaning. The mystery simply presents itself to him. On the 'last hard footstep of that iron crag' (447) he affirms that Arthur will come again, and wonders if the three dark queens are the same three queens he saw at Arthur's coronation. The affirmation and the question indicate that Bedivere is trying to make connections, to grasp patterns more comprehensive than any he has recognized before. His reward is something like a vision of the Heavenly City, which comes to him as 'Sounds, as if some fair city were one voice / Around a king returning from his wars' (460–1). Finally, at 'the highest he could climb' (463), Bedivere sees the sunrise 'bringing the new year' (469). What he sees, in short, is pure symbol. He is returning to a familiar world of sunrises, but also to a familiar world which he now sees as suffused with the spiritual energy which makes the sunrise a new beginning. Arthur has been associated with the sun throughout the *Idylls*, and the sunrise suggests his apotheosis as well as his reappearance. The end of the idyll thus fuses the real and the ideal in a way that has been represented throughout the poem by Arthur himself.

Improbable events and characters; probable responses. In that pattern some major aspects of both the form and theme of *Idylls of the King* are realized. The poem is primarily concerned with reactions to a king who is ideal and to events that are ultimately mysteries. These reactions allowed Tennyson to present his main themes – free will and use – and to moderate toward probability material of which all the essential features were romantic. His main concern was that romance be renewed, that its vitality and enduring appeal to the imagination be newly perceived. Its truth had to come alive in the mind and heart of every reader, just as Arthur's vows had to become living truth in each of the knights.

THE MYTH

'Use' – which Merlin defines as the desire and the ability 'to serve mankind' (*Merlin and Vivien* 487) – has as its typical action 'redressing human wrong' (*Dedication* 8), and as its typical institution marriage. The most important of all the marriages in the *Idylls* is, of course, the marriage of Arthur and Guinevere – important because it symbolizes (at least initially) the realization of Arthur's purposes, and because all other relations between men and women in the poem are, in one way or another, reactions to this marriage.

This marriage symbolizes a fruitful order that is analogous to the older concept of the Great Chain of Being. In that concept, man owed love and obedience to God, and had duties to perform and obligations to fulfil for his inferiors. Always there was a double perspective, up and down the scale. So here. Arthur, as the ideal, must work through the actual to carry out his purposes (Blake's proverb 'Eternity is in love with the productions of time' is again lurking in the background), and Guinevere must respond to the ideal and shape her life accordingly. A stooping to the actual; a reaching up to the ideal – that is what makes the marriage a dynamic relationship. It is not surprising, then, that Tennyson did not reject the allegorizing of the union as the wedding of Soul and Sense. The allegory at least makes clear the fact that Sense is the instrument of Soul, and that

the ideal must manifest itself in the things of this world. Arthur expresses
the idea in this way:

> 'For saving I be joined
> To her that is the fairest under heaven,
> I seem as nothing in the mighty world,
> And cannot will my will, nor work my work
> Wholly, nor make myself in mine own realm
> Victor and lord. But were I joined with her,
> Then might we live together as one life,
> And reigning with one will in everything
> Have power on this dark land to lighten it,
> And power on this dead world to make it live.'
>
> (*The Coming of Arthur* 84–93)

The qualifying adverb 'wholly' is important: it is ambiguous enough to
suggest that Arthur could accomplish some work without Guinevere, but
it also suggests that he himself is not whole without her.

This theme is embodied in a precise way in the typical action of the
poem: the approach of a questing knight to a lady in a secret or forbidden
place. The action is a version of the romance quest, its purpose is to release
spiritual and physical vitality, and its goal is marriage and family life. Each
of the ten central idylls makes use of this typical action, though with
variations appropriate to the place of the idyll in the larger structure of
the poem as a whole. Thus, Gareth undertakes a quest for Lyonors who is
imprisoned in the Castle Perilous, and is successful, though Tennyson
varies the pattern by having him marry Lynette. In *The Marriage of
Geraint*, Geraint releases Enid from her father's ruined castle just as, in
Geraint and Enid, he ultimately rescues her from Earl Doorm's hall, the
perilous place to which his own blindness has brought her. In *Balin and
Balan*, an ominous change appears in the pattern: Balin simply observes
Guinevere in her garden, and the disorder that he perceives is realized in
the meeting with Vivien in the forest. The meeting with Vivien in the
forest is repeated in the next idyll, though the protagonist is Merlin. Here
the pattern is inverted and reversed, for a woman pursues a man, rather
than the other way round, and the man is imprisoned rather than released. Thereafter, the typical action is usually a failure. Lancelot fails to
wed Elaine, and she is released from her father's house only by death. The
quest for the Holy Grail is a failure, and the Grail itself (traditionally a

feminine symbol and guarded by a maid or maidens) replaces the woman who is usually the object of the quest. Pelleas pursues Ettarre, and Tristram pursues Isolt, but both relationships are adulterous, and lead to madness and death. Finally, Arthur himself approaches Guinevere in the nunnery at Almesbury, an approach which brings to Guinevere both a conviction of sin and a sense (though chastened) of renewal. It is essential to the tragic shape of the poem that this action by the central pair be kept until the last.

The character of this typical action is not martial, as one would expect in epic and in some romances, and even Malory's descriptions of large encounters of thousands of men have no place in this poem. Rather, its character is essentially chivalric, and chivalry is both the code in which the ideal of 'use' realizes itself, and the heroic version of the domestic ideal of the *English Idyls*. The character of the action is best indicated by the time which the *Idylls* deals with. It is true that the poem presents the whole of Arthur's life, from his coming to his passing, but the actions of the ten central idylls all take place after Arthur's twelve great battles. These battles might have been the material of an epic, but Tennyson does not make them the main concern of his poem. At the point at which he might have described them fully he gives only the briefest of summaries. Arthur 'Fought, and in twelve great battles overcame / The heathen hordes, and made a realm and reigned' (*The Coming of Arthur* 517–18). Lancelot's account is the most detailed, and even it fills only thirty lines (*Lancelot and Elaine* 285–316). Elsewhere the twelve great battles are mentioned several times, but these references only strengthen the feeling that the twelve great battles are in the past.[13] The present time of the *Idylls* is essentially a time of 'gracious pastime' (*The Holy Grail* 324), a more active and heroic version of the 'fallow leisure' that characterizes the time of the *English Idyls*. It is more heroic because its chief formal actions are not country walks but tournaments, while its chief useful actions are not talks but 'noble deeds' (*The Holy Grail* 318) in righting wrongs. But this time is also less heroic than the time of the twelve great battles, for Lancelot refers to the jousts as 'our mimic wars' (*Lancelot and Elaine* 311). Related to this difference in periods is the important difference between Lancelot and Arthur themselves: 'For Lancelot was the first in Tournament, / But Arthur mightiest on the battle-field' (*Gareth and Lynette* 485–6). Arthur is sometimes thrown in jousting, but, as Lancelot tells us, 'in this heathen war the fire of God / Fills him: I never saw his like' (*Lancelot and Elaine* 314–15). It is, then, a time when Arthur's chief work is done, a time of relative stability and contentment which gradually gives way to decline and decay. On first thought, this period seems to be the opposite of 'fallow leisure,' for that was clearly a preparation for heroic actions, and this is clearly a time when heroic actions seem to be disappearing. But in fact, as Arthur's final speech indicates, the decline is, like the 'fallow leisure,' preparation for a new and higher order.

The character of the present time in the *Idylls* is related to Tennyson's concept of the heroic. The more traditional heroism that displays itself in military prowess, epic journeys, and the like does not figure largely in Tennyson's poem, though it has clearly characterized Arthur's early experience. Tennyson focuses instead on heroism of a more common sort: the struggle to live up to ideals in everyday life and ordinary activities. And this kind of heroism manifests itself, not so much in one central figure, but in the many different figures grouped around him. Hence Tennyson explained the moral purpose of his poem: 'I tried in my "Idylls" to teach men the need of the ideal.'[14] This ideal is embodied in the vows, and heroism, as Tennyson conceived it in the *Idylls*, was each man's response to those words.[15]

As the poem proceeds, that response becomes less and less adequate. Hence, when the individual idylls are seen as part of a larger structure, the shape of that larger structure is the shape of tragedy. But just as Tennyson avoided the traditional epic or heroism, so he avoided the concept of tragedy which we have inherited from the Greeks. Malory made the cause of Arthur's downfall his incestuous union with his sister and his begetting of Modred, and Swinburne thought that Tennyson ought to have retained the incest, so that, after the Greek pattern, 'from the sin of Arthur's youth proceeds the ruin of his reign and realm through the falsehood of his wife, a wife unloving and unloved.'[16] But the failure of Camelot is not a failure in Arthur but a failure in the knights' response to Arthur. They define their response in terms of Guinevere's purity, or the lack of it, and hence it would be easy to see the adulterous relation of Guinevere and Lancelot as the cause of the tragedy; it is, in fact, not the cause but the symptom of it. The late confirmation of the truth of the rumours only emphasizes the varying responses that individuals make to what they think is the truth. Arthur's subjects, then, bring about their own downfall, and Arthur's increasing age and ineffectiveness simply reflect the condition of his society.

The central figure in the tragedy is not Arthur but Guinevere, and it is possible to see all other responses to Arthur as types of Guinevere's response. Like the knights, she takes vows which wed her to the ideal. But the complexity of human nature is such that she is attracted to Lancelot;

and she later rationalizes that attraction by arguing that Arthur's ideal is humanly impossible. Her actions lead directly to her downfall, and her last meeting with Arthur at Almesbury is a moment of tragic insight, when she realizes that Arthur is 'the highest and most human too' (*Guinevere* 644).

The tragic shape of the poem affects its typical action – the approach of a questing knight to a lady in a secret or a forbidden place. This action, as we have seen, is appropriate to romance, but when it is treated as a tragedy some new aspects of the myth begin to appear. These aspects can be seen most clearly in some of the major patterns of imagery in the poem. The most obvious pattern is the cycle of the seasons, and Tennyson himself has pointed out how the chief events of Arthur's life correspond to the cycle of a single year.[17] That cycle supports the tragic pattern, since, in its downward movement, it is characterized by decay and dissolution, just as the coming of the New Year is the beginning of renewal and revitalization. Closely related to the seasonal imagery is a pattern that has not been much explored, but which pervades the whole poem. Its chief recurring images are a flood, and a boat containing the seeds of new life.

This pattern of imagery Tennyson apparently derived from the mythological studies that provided the context for his early reading of the Arthurian material. From the eighteenth century he inherited a tradition which identified the Druid bards with the Old Testament patriarchs and prophets, so that priest, prophet, and poet were seen as united in one figure, and the Israelites and the Celts as united in history. This tradition was extended to include the figures of Arthur and his knights, and one book in particular – Edward Davies' *The Mythology and Rites of the British Druids* (1809) – is of special importance for the *Idylls*, for it was in Tennyson's library,[18] and the morphology of symbolism which Davies describes is analogous to the pattern in the *Idylls*. Tennyson may, of course, have derived the pattern from elsewhere, since it appears in the work of a number of mythologists. W.D. Paden has argued that the structure of images in George Stanley Faber's *The Origin of Pagan Idolatry* (1816) is the source of some of the images in the *Idylls*, and certainly Faber's work is related to that of Davies, just as it is related to the work of an earlier scholar, Jacob Bryant, who, in *A New System, or, an Analysis of Ancient Mythology* (1774–6), sets out the same pattern and, like Davies, relates it to Arthur. Whatever Tennyson's particular source, however, these mythological studies are similar enough to Tennyson's poem to suggest that Tennyson is making poetic use of a way of dealing with myth that was immensely influential in the early nineteenth century.

The pattern is based on a feature of myths and rituals which was inescapable: the resemblances among myths from widely different parts of the world, the similarities of rituals among different peoples, and the recurrence of symbols in the myths and rites of nations that had no apparent connection with one another. Mythologists speculated that such resemblances and recurrences could be explained if all were derived from a common source. But what was that source? The answer to that question grew out of the Christian context within which myth was studied, and it was no accident that Davies and Faber were both clergymen. The Christian myth was derived from the Old Testament, and Christ himself instructed his followers in a typological reading of the scriptures (Luke 24: 25–7 and 44–8). If the Christian myth represented the highest development of the book of 'Moses and all the prophets' to which Christ refers, pagan myths would seem to represent the corruption and debasement of those same traditions. The common source of all myths – the 'key to all mythologies' – was the story of Noah. This is the story of the destruction of the world by a flood (a destruction brought upon mankind by its own wickedness) and the renewal of the world through one family, which emerged safe and sound from a boat. It is the story of a death and a rebirth, in which water is the chief element, since it destroys the old civilization and preserves on its surface the seeds of the new one. God's covenant with Noah leads on to the covenant with Moses and to the events of Exodus; but outside this convenant were all the peoples left after the dispersion from Babel. They, too, remembered this great event in human history, and in their myths and rituals, however corrupt, continued to commemorate it. 'All the rites and mysteries of the Gentiles,' wrote Jacob Bryant, 'were only so many memorials of their principal ancestors; and of the great occurrences, to which they had been witnesses. Among these memorials the chief were the ruin of mankind by a flood; and the renewal of the world in one family.'[19] Davies pays particular attention to the similarities between the Eleusinian mysteries and the rites of the Druids, and finds in the Welsh triads a Celtic version of the Noah story. Later nineteenth-century scholars were to discredit much of this kind of work, but, however unsatisfactory it was from a scholarly point of view, it was especially productive for a poet like Tennyson. For it suggested to him a treatment of Arthur, not as a figure of local or national interest, but as an archetypal hero; and it further suggested a treatment of the events of Arthur's life not only as particular and unique but also as typical and recurring. It was Faber who stated the typical patterns most clearly. Noah, he wrote, was the second Adam, who ushered in a second Golden Age and was the father of all men as well as the type of all kings, rulers, and heroes. He was identified with the sun. Just as all the gods and heroes of pagan antiquity are derived from Noah, so 'all the goddesses of paganism will be found ultimately to melt together into a single person, who is at once acknowledged to be the great mother and the Earth.'[20] She is identified with the ark which preserved the seeds of new life on the face of the waters, and the emergence of Noah and his family from the side of the ark is described as a rebirth. Davies and Faber both deal with the story of Arthur as a version of this archetypal story, and the pattern of imagery of this myth pervades Tennyson's poem.

Tennyson was receptive to such a pattern, not just because he was fascinated with the Arthurian material, and read everything about Arthur that he could put his hands on, but because the images fitted so well with interests he already had and with patterns already apparent in his poetry. His son's *Memoir* records his fascination with the sea, not only on the Lincolnshire coast, but off Cornwall and Devon and the west coast of Ireland. At many times and in many places he comments on the sea, describing its appearance and its characteristics. 'From his boyhood,' Hallam Tennyson writes, 'my father had a passion for the sea, and especially for the North Sea in wild weather.'[21] It is apparent that the sea stirred his deepest feelings and excited his imagination. His reading in the old mythologists confirmed his fascination with the sea, and hence it is not surprising that it should be so central an image in the *Idylls*. Similarly, the Sleeping Beauty pattern that is so central to the *English Idyls* and other early poems is related to the story of the Great Mother, and Sleeping Beauty's garden or castle is analogous to the ark. If Paden is right in relating Faber to the *Morte d'Arthur*, Tennyson may in fact have been aware of such a pattern in the works of the mythologists from a very early stage in his career, but it is just as likely that he was aware of such a pattern in his own reading of myths and fairy tales, and found in the mythologists material enriching a pattern that had already excited his imagination. What is clear is that a major pattern in the *Idylls* – the one most closely related to its structure and theme – clearly has its context in late eighteenth- and early nineteenth-century understandings of myth.[22]

The flood is the chief image of destruction in the *Idylls*. The image first becomes prominent in *Merlin and Vivien*, and that is appropriate enough, for it is in this idyll that Arthur's civilization clearly makes a downward turn. Vivien is the 'little rat that borest in the dyke' (110), and releases the flood to which Merlin refers specifically:

'You seemed that wave about to break upon me
And sweep me from my hold upon the world,
My use and name and fame.'   (300–2)

The flood is not only an external threat but an internal one, and hence it is
not only associated with the heathen (to whom Arthur refers in *The Last
Tournament* as 'that ever-climbing wave' 92) but with Arthur's civilization
gone awry. The chief formal expression of his civilization is the tournament, and when the wave image is first used to describe the jousts (as it is in
Gareth and Lynette), it seems innocent enough, though ominous in retrospect: Gareth 'saw the knights / Clash like the coming and retiring wave'
(511–12). In *Lancelot and Elaine*, the image is far more threatening, for
Lancelot's 'kith and kin' move against him

> as a wild wave in the wide North-sea,
> Green-glimmering toward the summit, bears, with all
> Its stormy crests that smoke against the skies,
> Down on a bark, and overbears the bark,
> And him that helms it ...   (480–4)

The epic expansion of the earlier simile suggests that the flood that will
destroy Arthur's civilization is Arthur's own subjects, and this suggestion
becomes the actual state of affairs in *The Last Tournament*. The wet wind
parallels the wetness (both actual and metaphorical) of the action. Though
the epic simile of the wave in this idyll is used to describe the fall of the Red
Knight (461–6), it is Arthur's knights who are clearly the destructive
force, as the context of the epic simile indicates. Hence, in *The Passing of
Arthur*, the last great battle takes place on the sea shore, and when the
armies have destroyed each other, the tide comes in:

> only the wan wave
> Beats in among dead faces, to and fro
> Swaying the helpless hands, and up and down
> Tumbling the hollow helmets of the fallen ...   (129–32)

Related to the flood are images of storm, rain, and mist. They too appear
in the idylls dealing with a happier time, and they too foreshadow the
tragic action to follow. The tempest in Geraint's mind (*Geraint and Enid*
11) and the image of slander as a storm (*The Marriage of Geraint* 27) look

forward to the storm, both inner and outer, that breaks over Merlin, and to the storms that pervade *The Holy Grail*. Similarly, the 'happy mist' that comes over Enid's eyes (*Geraint and Enid* 768) gives way to the mist in which Guinevere sees Arthur disappear after he leaves her at Almesbury, and to the 'deathwhite mist' (*The Passing of Arthur* 95) that makes the last battle such a confused one. The sea-wave and the mist represent two stages of the cycle of water, and hence it is not surprising that the middle stage, the stream, should be used as well in this pattern of imagery. A stream in flood appears very early in the poem, at the beginning of *Gareth and Lynette*, when Gareth watches a 'spate' sweep away a pine, and associates it (happily for him but ominously for the outcome of the *Idylls*) with the action of a knight. His three battles are also close by or in a stream, and the stream washes away his second opponent, Noonday Sun. Balin and Balan are associated with the source of a stream, a fountain, but the poem as a whole makes more of streams in relation to the sea than it does to their source. Elaine is carried away upon a stream, and sea journeys recur again and again in the *Idylls*. There is the fatal journey of Merlin and Vivien to Brittany, Galahad's disappearance out at sea, Lancelot's journey to Carbonek, and Tristram's journey from Brittany. And finally, in *The Passing of Arthur*, the sea claims all the combatants.

Or almost all. For the sea does not always represent destruction and the end of things. It may, as in *De Profundis*, be the mysterious source as well as the end of all things, and it may be both physical and spiritual. Tennyson's term for the sea in this more comprehensive sense is 'the great deep.' Arthur is apparently born from the sea, and certainly at his passing he disappears out to sea. And even when the wave imagery is at its most destructive there are reminders that we are to understand the sea in a broader sense. The 'wan wave' that covers Arthur's last battlefield, for instance, is heard 'rolling far along the gloomy shores / The voice of days of old and days to be' (*The Passing of Arthur* 134–5). Tennyson thus makes the flood image a far more complex symbol than the flood we find described in the mythologists whom he may have read, and in doing so he tempers our sense of tragedy with a sense of the ultimate unity of all things.

In the tragic action of the poem itself, however, the archetypal image of renewal is a boat containing the seeds of new life. The image is a commonplace in nineteenth-century poetry, and it is not surprising that in the *Idylls* it should appear in a variety of forms. There is the dragon-winged ship that brings the infant Arthur to shore, and the barge with the three queens that carries the aged and mortally wounded Arthur away at the end (thus preserving him so that he may come again). Galahad is apparently carried off in a boat, 'If boat it were' (*The Holy Grail* 514–15), and there are other journeys by boat that are related to the archetype but vary its meaning and sometimes reverse it, like Lancelot's journey to Carbonek or Merlin's to Brittany. Also related to the boat are things like the eagle's egg and the helmet that opens to reveal a blooming boy in *Gareth and Lynette*, and the oak in which Merlin is enclosed. More typically, the boat, in whatever form it takes, encloses a female figure or is associated with the female, like Elaine's funeral barge, or the eagle's nest with the maiden babe in it in *The Last Tournament*. The Grail itself is traditionally a female symbol, since it nourishes body and soul, and it is present in the *Idylls* (as Arthur knows, though most of his knights do not) in the related symbol of the Round Table, which with its meats and drinks nourishes the body, and with the vows of which it is the emblem nourishes the soul. A major part of this symbolic pattern is the great number of enclosures about a female figure: gardens, bowers, groves, woods, and castles. There is Lyonors in the Castle Perilous, Enid in Doorm's castle, Vivien in the woods, Guinevere in her garden, and so on. The approach to the female figure is as likely to bring about destruction as it is renewal, but whatever the result, the pattern remains constant. All of these enclosures are types of one symbol which seems to sum up all the rest: the barge containing the three queens who were present at Arthur's coronation and appear again at his passing. Their significance requires some explanation.

We have already seen how, in making the wave imagery but one aspect of 'the great deep,' Tennyson greatly extended the significance of the flood. The same extension and enrichment are apparent in his treatment of the boat. In myth, the boat contains the seeds of new life; in Tennyson it contains not only the seeds of new life but the forces that destroy life, the Viviens as well as the Enids. In short, it contains life and death, and implies their ultimate unity. Tennyson does not, however, present this concept by means of abstractions. The three queens are, I think, related to the Welsh tradition of three Guineveres, a tradition described by Tom Peete Cross and more recently in Gerhard Joseph's excellent work.[23] Tennyson's early notes for the *Idylls* indicate his familiarity with this tradition,[24] and one can see that the religious allegory in these notes represents woman in her triple role as mother, wife, and destroyer. Aside from Bellicent, mothers do not figure largely in the *Idylls*, or at least are important by their absence, since our attention is drawn to the fact that Guinevere has no children. But faithful wives like Enid, and potentially faithful wives like Elaine, are of considerable importance, as are the women who betray, like Vivien and Ettarre. Woman as mother, wife, and destroyer represents the whole pattern of human life, which T.S. Eliot defined in starker terms as birth, copulation, and death. The approach to woman both releases this pattern and realizes it. Tennyson's Guinevere acts out two of woman's roles (wife and destroyer) but it is the Lady of the Lake who sums up all three roles. Though she is 'of the Lake,' she is not overwhelmed by it, but rather 'Hath power to walk the waters like our Lord' (*The Coming of Arthur* 293), and even the keystone of the gate of Camelot on which her statue stands is 'lined / And rippled like an ever-fleeting wave' (*Gareth and Lynette* 210–11). She carries the symbols of her triple role: the fish which, among other things, represents both the physical and spiritual nourishment one would expect from a Great Mother, the censer which suggests the pervasive work of the spirit through matter, and the sword which destroys. All three symbols carry a weight of Biblical meaning as well, and may be remnants of the religious allegory into which Tennyson first shaped the Arthurian material. In addition, 'drops of water fell from either hand' (*Gareth and Lynette* 216), and her dress 'Wept from her sides as water flowing away' (213). When we stand back a little from this remarkably complex figure, we begin to see that she is both the boat containing the whole pattern of human life and the water itself. She is, in short, a figure who contains everything else. Her type is the poet who contains the pattern of the whole poem, and the reader who re-creates within himself the poet's vision.

That may be done by standing back and trying to see some of the patterns of the whole poem, but we must also move forward and look closely at the central idylls.

VERSIONS OF ROMANCE: *GARETH AND LYNETTE, THE MARRIAGE OF GERAINT, GERAINT AND ENID*

Critics have often pointed out that *Gareth and Lynette* is the one idyll where events are given in a strictly chronological sequence, so that it seems to have, as James R. Kincaid says, 'the simplest and clearest form of any of the idylls.'[25] It also seems to be the most loosely constructed. But when one examines the poem in terms of the idyll's typical mixture of narrative, dramatic, and descriptive, patterns begin to emerge that are considerably more subtle and complex than would at first appear. Tennyson uses narrative to give an account of Gareth's actions. The pattern of this account is essentially the romance pattern of the quest, consisting of a journey, a crucial struggle, and an outcome in which the hero is rewarded in some way. The action of the poem in fact falls into two such quests. In the first, Gareth journeys to Camelot, undergoes the test of the kitchen, and is rewarded by Arthur with the task of rescuing Lynette's sister; in the second, Gareth journeys to the Castle Perilous, fights four battles, and is rewarded with a name and a bride. The first quest has the tone of a fairy tale, and indeed Gareth himself refers to the Cinderella story when he mentions her 'who lay / Among the ashes and wedded the King's son' (881–2). The second quest Tennyson treats allegorically. In allegory, the reader ought to be able, to use Tennyson's own words, 'to say, "*This* means *that*,"'[26] and certainly the names of Gareth's four antagonists indicate that the poet is presenting 'The war of Time against the soul of man' (1168). The first quest anticipates the second, and indeed is not completed until it is complete, so that the fairy tale develops into allegory and is ultimately fused with it.

The four knights are not, however, Gareth's only opposition. His course of action is opposed by his mother, Bellicent, and by the 'damsel of high lineage' (574), Lynette – the one in the name of love, the other in the name of rank and courtesy. Lyonors, the lady who might inspire Gareth (and who is likely to become his bride, if the expectations aroused by the romance tradition still have any force) is remote and unknown, so that woman presents Gareth with a subtler and more complex difficulty. The three female figures are, like the three queens, related to the three Guineveres, and suggest the triple role of woman: Bellicent is Gareth's mother, Lyonors his intended bride, and Lynette his destroyer. But Tennyson varies this pattern so that the would-be destroyer undergoes a change of heart or conversion and becomes the bride of the hero. For Gareth's relations with female figures Tennyson uses the dramatic aspects of the idyll and, though there are dialogues with other characters as well, Gareth's dialogues with Bellicent and Lynette are crucial, especially since he brings about a change of heart in both of them.

With this fact in mind, we begin to see that the interweaving of narration and drama is not as simple as it first appears. The narrative is like a fairy tale and lends itself to allegorical treatment, while the dramatic presents characters reacting to one another in a psychologically realistic way. It is easy enough to link a fairy tale and allegory; it is much more difficult to understand Tennyson's linking of a realistic dialogue with symbolism. Yet Gareth's relations with women are pervaded with a comprehensive pattern of symbols, which appear in that third aspect of the idyll form, description. The idyll is a long one, and it is made so in part by descriptions (particularly of Camelot) which seem at first glance to have only a loose connection with the concerns of the poem. But the descriptions are all closely related to the pattern of symbols that Tennyson derived, directly or indirectly, from the mythological studies of Bryant, Davies, and Faber. In this pattern, as we have seen, human beings constantly fear death by water (a death of which the type is the flood in the Noah story), and seek to preserve life in an enclosed space that will float (a space of which the type is the ark). Woman is identified with this enclosed space, an identification which is familiar enough in the *hortus conclusus* image in the Song of Songs, but which is perhaps less familiar when the images of a city, a castle, a helmet, or an egg are used, as they are in this idyll. Allegory and symbol converge in the description of the hermit's cave, where the enclosed space contains the type of all human endeavour. Presiding over the symbolic aspects of the idyll is the figure of the Lady of the Lake, who unites within herself the three aspects of woman, and carries the symbols of her triple role.

By interweaving the narrative, dramatic, and descriptive, Tennyson thus writes an increasingly complex idyll, the subtleties of which can best be appreciated by a more detailed analysis.

The idyll begins with an image – the 'spate' or river in flood – which will reappear in a more tranquil form as the stream over which or in which Gareth fights his first three battles. The image introduces a more comprehensive symbol, water, which appears here as an agent of destruction: 'A slender-shafted Pine / Lost footing, fell, and so was whirled away' (3–4). The description is not overtly symbolic, but Gareth's response invests it with meaning. His initial response is allegorical as he identifies himself with the stream: '"How he went down," said Gareth, "as a false knight / Or evil king before my lance"' (5–6). His second response is more complex, and anticipates one of the major themes of Victorian thought: that nature does not provide a model for human conduct. The cataract is 'senseless' (7), but Gareth is blessed with consciousness, so that he may think and choose, and he has 'strength and wit' (12) so that he may act, and act intelligently. But having made this distinction between himself and the stream, Gareth also insists on a parallel: both he and it work God's will. The distinction and the affirmation are the grounds of Gareth's actions. God guides all things, though his purpose may be dark; man, with his limited perspective, must choose a course of action that applies his intuitions of God's purposes. In Gareth's case, that course of action is to work Arthur's will. The symbolic form of that action is the release of fertility and vitality from an enclosure or prison, and hence Gareth's actions all involve relations with female figures.

The first such figure is his mother, Bellicent. The vitality that must be
released is Gareth's own 'strength and wit' (12), and the prison (a word
which Tennyson uses as a verb in line 14) is 'my good mother's hall' (12).
The action takes the form of a dialogue between Gareth and Bellicent,
and in this dialogue allegory and symbol are fused. For Gareth tells two
stories – the story of the 'lusty youth' (48) who was prevented from
reaching the eagle's egg, and the story of the prince and the two brides –
and the allegory is immediately apparent: Gareth is the 'lusty youth' in the
first story and the prince in the second; the eagle's egg is knighthood, and
the two brides, Gareth himself says, are Fame and Shame. Bellicent attempts to deal with the allegorical thrust of the stories, first by appealing
to her own loneliness, and then by raising questions about Arthur's claim
to be king. But the dialogue is pervaded with symbols to which Gareth is
more alive than she. For it is from Bellicent herself that Gareth's vitality
must be released. Her hall is to him a prison (14) or a cage (20); related to
this enclosure is the eagle's nest containing the mysterious egg, an egg
which is itself another symbol of the vitality Gareth is trying to grasp.
The beautiful bride who must be won by force is the human form of this
egg.

Allegory and symbol are thus fused in this dialogue, which has a
pattern of challenge and response. It is Gareth who challenges by telling
stories; Bellicent responds, and her response ultimately becomes the
means by which Gareth frees himself. For he sees the condition which she
imposes to keep him with her as a test of obedience in which, paradoxically, he will find freedom.

With the journey to Arthur's court, the dialogue gives way to narration
and description. Description, in fact, dominates, and we have a detailed
account of the appearance of Camelot from the plain (184–93), and of
the richly ornamented gateway (209–26). One must ask why Tennyson
chooses to expand the story here by such descriptions. At first glance, they
seem to have only a loose connection with the account of Gareth's journey
to Camelot, for while they give what he would see at this point, they seem
to have a function that is chiefly ornamental. But when the descriptions
are looked at in the context of the idyll's structure of symbols, their close
organic relation with the rest of the poem becomes apparent. For both
descriptions give versions of the female symbol of which the ark bearing
the forms of new life is the type. Gareth and his companions see Camelot
as a shining city floating above the mist and sometimes disappearing in it.
The mist is another version of the flood which threatens to sweep away
human civilization, while the city itself contains the forms and patterns of

life to which Gareth aspires. In the description of the gateway the dominant figure is the Lady of the Lake. Like the city, she sometimes floats on the water, and, again like the city, she contains the forms of life, specifically the pattern of human life as it is suggested by the censer, the sword, and the fish. This pattern appears explicitly in the portrayal of Arthur's wars in the spaces on either side of the central figure, but the portrayal is such as to remind the viewer that the pattern manifests itself in time and yet is by its very recurrence timeless: 'New things and old co-twisted, as if Time / Were nothing' (222–3).

Though Gareth and his companions are disguised as 'tillers of the soil' (178), their appearance is in one sense no disguise at all, for Gareth has not yet made his name, and hence anything that he is called does not yet name the true self that is to be. Merlin's question 'Who be ye, my sons?' (237) is crucial, and the dialogue between Gareth and Merlin dramatizes the jumble of ambiguities and paradoxes to which Gareth must give shape and purpose. The dialogue is pervaded with irony. Gareth lies about himself but asks for the truth about Camelot; Merlin 'made answer playing on him' (248), beginning with fiction, but then, after mentioning the king (261), mingling fiction and truth in a series of paradoxes that culminate in the enigmatic

> 'the city is built
> To music, therefore never built at all,
> And therefore built for ever.'   (272–4)

Paradoxes such as this are the verbal form of the mist in which Camelot floats, and we begin to understand that, in this idyll, dialogue is a sea which both threatens and preserves the forms of vitality with which Gareth is so much concerned.

With the account of Gareth's entry into Arthur's hall, the focus of narrative interest shifts from Gareth himself to what he observes. And what he observes is Arthur dispensing justice. Tennyson gives this scene in considerable detail. There are, as one would expect in romance, three suppliants, and their speeches and Arthur's replies are given in full. Again one must ask why the poet includes such a scene when it is so loosely linked to the story of Gareth, and when it is likely to make the idyll appear episodic. And again the answer lies in the pattern of symbols which pervades the poem. There are three suppliants, and they present Arthur with increasingly complex political and moral issues. There is the widow whose land has been taken from her by force, the widow who wants her son's death avenged, and the messenger with Mark's request that he be made a knight. The three suppliants suggest, in an oblique way, the triple role of woman. The first widow is of Uther's generation, and chooses land over money; hence she is linked with nurturing, and may be associated with motherhood. The second widow is also a mother, but Arthur grants her request partly because 'The woman loves her lord' (364), and hence treats her primarily as a wife. Mark is associated with destruction; Tristram is his cousin, and he is the match of Vivien, who is never mentioned by name, but whose destruction of Merlin is perhaps foreshadowed in a detail it would be easy to pass over: the oak-tree smouldering on the hearth (394) where Arthur burns Mark's gift. The scene, then, presents through a picture of Arthur as judge the same pattern that the Lady of the Lake presented symbolically. It will also be the pattern of Gareth's experience, though with some important variations.

The variations come about when the triple role of woman is fused with the romance pattern of the story. Man's experience of woman as mother, wife, and destroyer is, in that order at least, a tragic pattern, in which man is born, fulfils his desires in marriage, and then discovers that the object of his desires is also his fate. Romance reverses the order of this experience. Man pursues his desires by means of a quest in which he undergoes a death of some sort, but that death turns out to be the means to new life. Destruction thus leads to renewal, and that triumph is often symbolized in a marriage. The pattern of romance dominates this idyll, though one is constantly aware of a potential tragedy that will be realized in the *Idylls* as a whole.

Thus the first stage of Gareth's life is essentially a romance. He undertakes the journey to Camelot; he descends into an ironic underworld ('So Gareth all for glory underwent / The sooty yoke of kitchen-vassalage' 468–9); and he emerges to be rewarded by Arthur. Gareth's own comment on his release suggests the pattern of romance: 'Out of the smoke, at once / I leap from Satan's foot to Peter's knee' (527–8). The dominant female figure in this part of the story is Bellicent, and though she is literally Gareth's mother, she is potentially his destroyer in her attempt to imprison him at home. But, like the youth in Blake's *The Mental Traveller*, Gareth bursts the bonds, and the waning power of woman as guardian of the prison house is suggested in another detail which, again, it would be easy to overlook. For the time when Bellicent looses Gareth from his vow is 'Between the in-crescent and de-crescent moon' (519), and the moon is yet another symbol that Davies and Faber associated with woman.

The second stage of Gareth's experience is also, in its main outlines, a romance, as a summary of the action which is recounted in the narrative sections of the idyll indicates. The quest begins with the journey to the Castle Perilous, and with the preliminary adventure in which Gareth rescues one of Arthur's barons from the six rogues. The crucial struggle falls into four parts. The battles with Morning-Star, Noonday Sun, and Evening-Star are battles that are increasingly difficult, and the descent into an underworld is symbolized by the coming of night. The last battle, with Death, promises to be the most difficult of all, but turns out to be the easiest. It takes place just before dawn, and Gareth's success coincides with the sunrise: 'Then sprang the happier day from underground' (1386). Gareth's triumph is celebrated 'with dance / And revel and song' (1387–8), and should culminate in his marriage to Lyonors. Tennyson does not entirely dismiss such an outcome: 'And he that told the tale in older times / Says that Sir Gareth wedded Lyonors' (1392–3). Tennyson himself, however, has some other concerns in telling the story: 'But he, that told it later, says Lynette' (1394). His alternative draws attention to a pattern fused with the romance pattern, and presented largely in the dialogue between Lynette and Gareth.

This pattern is the change in Lynette from potential destroyer to beloved bride. The symbolic significance of Lynette's conversion is not immediately apparent, because Tennyson uses the dramatic sections of the idyll to present it, and the dialogue gives Lynette's change of heart a deceptively realistic air. The stages of her conversion are psychologically probable. When she first appears at Arthur's court, she is proud and presumptuous, and her readiness to instruct the king in his duties mars her beauty and nobility. All that she demands is based on her notions of rank and courtesy, and since Lancelot is the best of Arthur's knights, the quest must be given to him. Hence she feels shame (though we recognize it as a false shame) when Arthur gives the quest to Gareth, and her scorn of him as a kitchen-knavè smelling of grease appears again and again in the dialogue. But as the quest progresses, this motif appears in new contexts that indicate Lynette's reconsideration of her words. This process begins soon after the pair leaves Camelot, when Lynette realizes that, whatever her feelings about Gareth, she is now dependent on him. As the quest progresses, she faces increasing evidence of a knight proved by his works, but it is evidence that she is not yet willing to accept. When he rescues the baron, she discounts the difficulty of the task, and will not eat at the same table. But when he faces Morning-Star, she allows him for an hour (870) and confesses that 'Some ruth is mine for thee' (873) when he must inevitably be killed. Throughout the battles, considerations of rank and

courtesy struggle in her with the indisputable evidence of Gareth's prowess. After the first battle her scorn momentarily subsides but soon
reappears. Gareth's second victory she dismisses as chance or luck, but her
curiosity is aroused, as is indicated by the phrase 'What knowest thou ...?'
that she uses repeatedly in response to Gareth's song. She actually encourages Gareth in the fight against Evening-Star, and afterwards accepts
Gareth as her equal: 'I lead no longer; ride thou at my side' (1128).
Curiosity gives way to wonder, for Gareth as kitchen-knave has, she says,
'mazed my wit: I marvel what thou art' (1141). But this sense of wonder is
not an unmixed response, for, as she confesses to Lancelot, she has
suspicions that she is being made a fool. Her pride has not entirely
disappeared:

> 'I gloried in my knave,
> Who being still rebuked, would answer still
> Courteous as any knight – but now, if knight,
> The marvel dies, and leaves me fooled and tricked,
> And only wondering wherefore played upon:
> And doubtful whether I and mine be scorned.' (1217–22)

Lancelot tells Lynette the story of Gareth, and at last she realizes that the
fault lies within herself: 'worse than being fooled / Of others, is to fool
one's self' (1242–3). And so as she watches Gareth sleeping, she falls
unreservedly in love with him.

All of this Tennyson presents dramatically, so that the symbolic significance of Lynette's conversion tends to be submerged. But the fact is
that Lynette has changed from potential destroyer to potential bride, so
that she usurps the role that is conventionally reserved for Lyonors. Such
realistic treatment is consistent with Tennyson's interest, as we shall see
in his portrayal of inner experience in the following idylls. Moreover,
Lynette's conversion makes more vivid and believable the strength of
Gareth's character as it manifests itself in unfailing courtesy and obedience. Most important, however, it presents in realistic terms a symbolic
pattern that pervades the idyll.

This pattern concerns the dispelling of the threat of a flood by releas-
ing the seeds of new life from the place in which they have been imprisoned. The flood appears literally at the beginning of the idyll with the
spate that Gareth watches; it appears in an ominously still form as the
mere in which thieves are drowned and above which their spirits 'flicker-
ing in a grimly light / Dance' (806–7); it appears again in a more ordinary

form in the river whose three loops enclose the Castle Perilous – more ordinary but equally ominous, since the narrator refers to it as 'the serpent river' (884). Gareth's first three battles are closely associated with the water, and his role as preserver is indicated by the fact that the battles take place either above or just barely in the stream. He fights Morning-Star on a bridge; he fights Noonday Sun on a ford in the river, and when his antagonist's horse slips, 'the stream / Descended, and the Sun was washed away' (1020–1) – an event that suggests the romance convention whereby the forces of nature are slightly suspended in the hero's favour. The battle with Evening-Star takes place on 'a bridge of treble bow' (1060), and Gareth ultimately wins by throwing his opponent into the river. One way of describing these first three battles is to say that Gareth clears and makes safe a passage over the water; it only remains for him to release the new life whose way he has prepared. This he accomplishes when he cleaves Death's helmet and discovers 'the bright face of a blooming boy / Fresh as a flower new-born' (1373–4). Though the narrator gives a realistic reason for this incident, the symbolic import of it cannot be missed. The helmet is yet another feminine symbol, like the Castle Perilous itself, and from both Gareth releases in human form the vitality that will form a new social unit. In retrospect it may be seen that Gareth does exactly the same thing with Lynette, though the action is presented in dramatic and psychologically realistic terms. For his steadfastness leads Lynette to free herself from the bonds of pride, so that she is in effect born again, and fit to become the bride of the hero to whose character she owes her moral awakening.

The triple role of woman in the idyll is complemented by the three male figures who preside over Gareth's quest: Kay, Lancelot, and Arthur. Tennyson accounts for the presence of the first two with reasons that are acceptable enough when judged by the criteria of realism, but it is difficult to get round the thought, after first reading, that Kay's foolish attempt to stop Gareth and Lancelot's sudden appearance when Gareth and Lynette reach the cavern are not absolutely necessary events. They seem to interrupt the flow of the narrative and to be less than integral to the action. Nonetheless, a Tennyson who criticized Malory for a want of art is not likely to have included these incidents without a purpose. That purpose becomes evident when we examine these three figures in the context of the idyll's symbolic pattern. Kay, the seneschal, the 'master of the meats and drinks' (442), is Gareth's accuser and potential destroyer. He is the male counterpart of the Bellicent who would keep Gareth enthralled at home, and of the Lynette who first appears at Arthur's court, full of concerns about rank and ready to detect presumption in others though blind to pride in herself. Gareth quickly disposes of the physical threat that Kay poses for him, but it takes him the whole quest to dispel Kay's faults in Lynette. Lancelot is charged by Arthur to be Gareth's protector, and his actions make him the male counterpart of the mother. By a remarkable coincidence (remarkable in realistic fiction but not in romance) he appears just when Gareth has entered the womb-like cavern. When he overthrows Gareth, Gareth at last reveals his identity, and the resumption of his name is like a birth. Moreover, it is Lancelot who tells Lynette the story of Gareth, and brings about her final change of heart. Lancelot thus presides over the appearance of new life in both Gareth and Lynette, and as such he is the male counterpart of the Bellicent who gave birth to Gareth and nourished and protected him. Arthur's relations with Gareth are, it would seem at first, difficult to fit into this symbolic pattern, but a little reflection reveals that Arthur is the male equivalent of Gareth's bride. Gareth, after all, is wedded to the ideal that Arthur represents, and the vows

> 'Of utter hardihood, utter gentleness,
> And, loving, utter faithfulness in love,
> And uttermost obedience to the King'   (542–4)

are like marriage vows. The vows themselves make explicit the close relationship between the ideal of knighthood and the ideals of marriage and domestic life.

The cavern to which Gareth and Lynette retire after the third battle sums up nearly every aspect of the pattern of symbolism that I have been exploring. It is the enclosed space that protects something vital, symbolized by the 'bread and baken meats and good red wine' (1160) which Lyonors has sent to refresh Gareth. It is the place where Gareth, with Lancelot's help, regains his identity, and where Lynette's change of heart is completed. It is a feminine symbol, a womb from which Gareth and Lynette are reborn. But equally interesting is the allegory portrayed on the rock, 'The war of Time against the soul of man' (1168). The five figures are morning, noon, evening, night, and death, and so they represent the shape of human life. The study of such shapes in the cavern is analogous to embryology, for what Gareth sees here is both the pattern of his personal experience and the recurring form of human life. It is Gareth's task to release that form by realizing it in his own life, and so serve its continuing vitality. But there is a danger in doing this, and this danger lies in the possibility that the pattern may be seen as something outside the individual, determining the course of his life, rather than something that the individual learns to shape and use. Gareth avoids that danger. The strength of his arm conquers death and the strength of his character conquers those aspects of woman that would destroy him.

The idyll is thus a remarkably complex one, in which Tennyson has mingled narrative, drama, and description, allegory and symbolism, realism and romance. The apparent simplicity of Tennyson's verse is deceptive, like the apparent obscurity of Browning's. For Tennyson is far more subtle and complex than his contemporary, as an idyll of this kind, considered thoughtfully, indicates.

Though Tennyson uses the mixture of forms that is characteristic of the idyll in *The Marriage of Geraint* and *Geraint and Enid*, it is narrative that is dominant in these two poems. As such, the story of Geraint and Enid is very different in character from the story of Merlin and Vivien, the idyll with which these idylls were first linked. There, the dramatic dominates the major portion of the poem. Here, it is the shape of the narrative itself that Tennyson concentrates on, and his technique of beginning in the middle of the story, going back to the beginning, and then proceeding to the end gave him the opportunity of presenting two actions – a quest in the past and a quest in the present – which, through parallels and differences, illuminate one another. *The Marriage of Geraint* presents a complete quest as a flashback; and *Geraint and Enid* presents a second complete quest which is linked to the first in all sorts of ways, and yet is radically different from it. The first is largely a story of outward actions and events, while the second is largely a story of an inner psychological crisis and its resolution. That the two central characters in both quests are the same suggests that the second quest is both a repetition and the completion of the first.

Because *The Marriage of Geraint* deals primarily with outward actions and events, it is the more conventional of the two quests. Convention in romance often takes the form of neat patterns, and these patterns are often governed by the figure three. Characters are grouped in threes, actions take place in a sequence of three, three antagonists appear, and so on. In many of the details of this idyll this pattern is apparent. In the tournament alone, for instance, there are three clashes on horseback and three on foot, of which the third is the decisive blow. (In this Tennyson tidies up his source in *The Mabinogion*, where the battle between Geraint and Edeyrn is a good deal less stylized and a good deal messier.) But the pattern of threes governs not only many of the details of the idyll but the general pattern of the quest as well. The events take up three days, and the sequence is a good example of the recurring shape of romance. The first day is the day of the hunt, and of Geraint's journey to Edyrn's town. Even at this early stage the shape of the action is apparent in Geraint's promise to the queen:

> 'I will track this vermin to their earths:
> For though I ride unarmed, I do not doubt
> To find, at some place I shall come at, arms
> On loan, or else for pledge; and, being found,
> Then will I fight him, and will break his pride,
> And on the third day will again be here,
> So that I be not fallen in fight.'   (217–23)

Following the journey, whose dangers lie mainly in the hostile atmosphere of the town, is the tournament, which takes place on the second day. The tournament is the crucial struggle, and from it Geraint emerges victorious, with his enemy conquered and his maiden won. The return to Arthur's court takes place 'the third day from the hunting-morn' (597) – Tennyson takes care to remind us of the sequence of time – and it is followed by the wedding of Geraint and Enid. This three-day pattern is the controlling shape of the story, and it is not too difficult to see that this particular treatment of it is another version of the myth that informs so much of Tennysonian romance, the tale of Sleeping Beauty. The idyll is, after all, the story of a prince in bright colours who frees a maiden in drab colours from a ruined palace. My sentence has already revealed the clue to Tennyson's treatment: his constant emphasis on dress and armour and on all the coverings that come under the heading of clothes. A concern with clothing is pervasive in the idyll, and clothing is the chief symbol. Tennyson's long account of Enid's concern with her dress is an elaboration at considerable length of one of the details in his source. The other point at which Tennyson greatly expands upon the story of *Geraint the Son of Erbin* in *The Mabinogion* is Geraint's first approach to Enid. These two expansions can, I believe, best be accounted for by the central place which the pattern of the Sleeping Beauty fairy tale held in Tennyson's poetic imagination. In examining the idyll in more detail, I concentrate both on the appropriateness with which Tennyson presents each stage of the quest so that the symbolic overtones of each of the three days are clear, and on the expansion of and changes in his source that bring his story closer to its type.

The first day is characterized by varying degrees of discomfort, irritability, and division. Guinevere is late for the hunt because she has overslept, dreaming of Lancelot. Geraint is also late, and misses the hunt entirely. The surliness of the dwarf who accompanies the unknown knight and lady is matched by the irritability of Geraint himself, for though he is quick to avenge the insult to the queen, he is also 'A little vext at losing of the hunt, / A little at the vile occasion' (234–5). And he undertakes the quest without armour and in dress that is totally inappropriate from a realistic point of view. But his 'summer suit and silks of holiday' (173) are symbolically apt, as his appearance in Edyrn's town soon confirms. The description of the town is changed considerably from *The Mabinogion*, and both Herbert G. Wright and J. Philip Eggers have analysed these changes.[27] In both the Welsh and modern versions, the inhabitants are preparing for the tournament, but, in Eggers' words, 'the spirit of their activity has changed from cheerful anticipation to a surly absorption in their labour.'[28] Tennyson in effect describes the town as a waste land, a place where humane values have almost disappeared, and where human activities serve the interests of a totalitarian ruler rather than enhancing the quality of individual lives. Vitality has been perverted to mindless power, and the new fortress – 'White from the mason's hand' (244), a detail not in *The Mabinogion* – suggests the ascendancy of brute force. Opposite the fortress are 'a castle in decay' (245) and 'a dry ravine' (246), and there is a cacophonous noise from the whole town. In older stories the town would be an underworld or hell to which the hero must descend. This town is not such an absolute, but it has lost, or at least is asleep to, the higher human values represented by Geraint. That these values are present but dormant is suggested in the armourer who directs Geraint to Yniol. In *The Mabinogion*, Geraint simply happens to see 'an old palace in ruins' (II, 76),[29] and makes toward it. But in Tennyson the armourer who directs Geraint is amazed at 'seeing one so gay in purple silks' (284), and the vitality in Geraint's appearance is a quality to which the armourer responds. Tennyson thus replaces coincidence with a thematic connection, for it is at the ruined palace that the seeds of a new life, in their most attractive form, await Geraint's coming.

The importance of dress in this whole passage is already apparent. The fallen nature of the town is defined largely in terms of armour and drab clothing, as the long section (lines 251–93) that is Tennyson's own addition to the story indicates. *The Mabinogion* gives a brief account of the dress of Yniol, his wife, and Enid, and Tennyson makes use of all these details (though not without modification) in his expanded version of Geraint's arrival at Yniol's castle. Yniol himself wears 'a suit of frayed magnificence, / Once fit for feasts of ceremony' (296–7); his wife wears 'dim brocade' (363), and Enid is 'all in faded silk' (366). The clothes represent a fall, which is literally usurpation and symbolically the decline of fertility and vitality in winter. Geraint is the sun god come to reawaken that life; he wears the bright colours of summer, and, though Tennyson does not give the colour of his hair, *The Mabinogion* tells us that he was 'a fair-haired youth' (II, 72).

Tennyson greatly expands upon his source in describing Geraint's first approach to Enid. The poet is clearly interested in suggesting all the symbolic dimensions of this action, and his treatment of it brings it closer in character to the Sleeping Beauty story. Yniol's castle is in ruins, and the tangle of stone and natural growth that Tennyson describes in some detail (lines 312–25) is a less sinister version of Sleeping Beauty's perilous hedge: it 'looked / A knot, beneath, of snakes, aloft, a grove' (324–5). None of this is in *The Mabinogion*. Similarly, the account of Enid's song is original with Tennyson. Geraint hears the sweet song emerging from the ruined castle, and its importance is emphasized by the fact that Tennyson uses not one but two extended similes to describe it. The first simile (lines 329–34) indicates how the song evokes curiosity and desire in Geraint, and hence its function is to explain the change of direction in Geraint's motives. The song plays the same role here that the 'Magic Music' played for the Prince in *The Day-Dream*, but its effect is more complex. The sound of Enid's voice and, later, the sight of her arouse in Geraint a sense of purpose that is unalloyed by doubts or conflicting emotions; his immediate reaction is, 'Here by God's rood is the one maid for me' (368). Firm and steady, this sense differs from his intention of avenging the insult to the queen, readily undertaken but mingled, as I have already pointed out, with contrary feelings. The second simile (lines 335–44) deals with the return of the nightingale as the harbinger of spring. Its function is proleptic, since it anticipates one of the symbolic dimensions of the successful outcome of Geraint's quest. Together, the similes indicate the motivation of the hero and the shape of the action.

Though the action is heroic, its goal is firmly domestic in character. Geraint's new purpose is, of course, to marry Enid, but the marriage will simply make formal his commitment to an ideal he has already discovered. Though Yniol's castle is in ruins, it still shelters a way of life that has apparently disappeared from the rest of the town. It is a hidden place that protects the ideal of family life from a hostile society, and preserves the means by which that society may ultimately be transformed. This tiny family unit cherishes human values that are quite different from the Sparrow-hawk's power politics. Enid's song defines the difference. She sings about the wheel of Fortune, to which the Sparrow-hawks of this world are subject, but her theme is not, as one would expect from her subject, determinism or fatalism. The vicissitudes of Fortune cannot touch the essential part of family life: 'Thy wheel and thee we neither love nor hate' (349). Fortune is concerned with the political and business arrangements of life, but the values of the family are human and timeless: 'Our hoard is little, but our hearts are great' (352). From this point of view, 'man is man and master of his fate' (355). The last stanza of the song suggests that the turning of Fortune's wheel is a shadow of the phenomenal world, whereas, by implication, the family is devoted to spiritual reality. But this spiritual reality manifests itself in common things, and Geraint is attracted to Enid performing her domestic tasks as he is to Enid singing her song. Tennyson retains from *The Mabinogion* all the details of Enid's household duties, and to these he adds Geraint's reactions. She appears to him 'sweet and serviceable' (393), and the second adjective embodies the same ideal of 'use' to which Arthur, Merlin, and the knights of the Round Table are devoted. The domestic ideal, then, gives immense significance to common tasks, and gives direction and purpose to the more conventional heroism of romance.

The second day of the quest is the day of the tournament, and it is the crucial struggle for Geraint. Again, the pattern of romance makes itself evident in dress. Geraint exchanges the bright colours of his 'summer suit' for Yniol's old and rusty armour, and the change is an indication of his descent into this underworld and even suggests a kind of death. The battle with Edyrn Tennyson narrates with considerable economy. The event moves along quickly. Many of the actions are conflated and summarized. Geraint fulfils his initial purpose when Edyrn asks for Guinevere's pardon, and that, as well as Edyrn's change of heart and the whole of his subsequent career, are summarized in only a few lines. The brevity of the treatment suggests that the crucial struggle is largely a physical effort. In this *The Marriage of Geraint* contrasts with *Geraint and Enid*, where the crucial struggle is an inward one, and takes up nearly the whole of the idyll.

After thus speeding up and summarizing the crucial struggle, Tennyson devotes the final 250 lines of the idyll to Enid's clothes, a considerable elaboration of a topic to which *The Mabinogion* devotes only a few sentences. Clearly he wants to round out the quest by giving a full account of its final stage, the return to Arthur's court. But it seems curious that he should focus on a most unheroic matter, and treat it in such detail. The treatment is, however, consistent with the generally realistic treatment of the first four idylls published in 1859, for it excludes the marvellous and the improbable, and focuses on human reactions and concerns that are both familiar and predictable. Enid's girlish fears of the court and her concern for her appearance strike us as probable, as matters that would be expected of a novelist (as opposed to a romancer). But the realism of Tennyson's treatment is not in itself enough to account for the length of this section. He was, I think, equally interested in rounding out the romance pattern of his story, and in suggesting some of its symbolic significance. The story of the dress is particularly appropriate for these purposes, because the putting off of the 'faded silk' and the donning of the dress 'All branched and flowered with gold' (631) suggest a rebirth, and in particular the pattern of spring emerging from winter. Enid is linked with springtime largely by her association with flowers. A flower simile ('like a blossom vermeil-white' 364) is one of the first images applied to her, and it is picked up when her mother likens her to two legendary figures: 'that maiden in the tale, / Whom Gwydion made by glamour out of flowers' (742–3), and 'Flur, for whose love the Roman Caesar first / Invaded Britain' (745–6). The flower images suggest the myth that underlies this section and gives it its vitality: the story of Demeter and Persephone, with Guinevere as Demeter and Enid as Persephone. And the putting on of the new dress is a realistic version of Persephone's return to Demeter in the springtime. The awkwardness created by the presence of Enid's real mother Tennyson gets round by having Geraint give reasons for his request (and, incidentally, introducing the test motif that becomes important in *Geraint and Enid*) and by treating the gathering together of the family's possessions (including the dress) in a rather comic fashion. But the meeting of Enid and Guinevere, and the subsequent marriage of Geraint and Enid, are treated in romance fashion, as the fulfilment of the highest human desires. The pattern is confirmed by the season, Whitsuntide. Originally an agricultural festival celebrating the wheat harvest, it now commemorates the descent of the Holy Spirit, and is a favourite time for baptism. It is an appropriate time, then, for Geraint and Enid to enter upon a new life.

Narrative, rather than drama or description, dominates *The Marriage of Geraint*, and it dominates *Geraint and Enid* as well. The arrangement of this second idyll is linear, and the narrator traces the course of events in their actual chronological sequence. In terms of outward actions, the story tends to be loose and episodic. There are many coincidences, such as the chance meetings with various villains, or Geraint's becoming conscious at just the right time. Yet, in spite of all this apparent looseness, the structure of the story is far tighter and the pattern far neater than in *The Mabinogion*. There, Geraint fights three battles on the first day of his quest, with four, three, and five horsemen respectively; on the second day there is the adventure with Earl Dwrm and on the third the battle with Gwiffert Petit; there is an interlude while Arthur holds court in the wood and Geraint is healed of his first serious wound, the result of senseless battles with Kai and Gwalchmai; then follow the meetings with Limours and Owain, and the final crucial struggle within the hedge of mist. Tennyson omits some of these incidents, and arranges the rest in a pattern of threes. Geraint fights three battles of increasing difficulty, and in each of the first two he has three opponents. Out of a variety of characters Tennyson chose Dwrm and Limours as important for his story, and, while retaining their essential actions, switched their names, as G.C. Macaulay long ago pointed out.[30] Such changes and such obvious patterning clearly indicate that Tennyson had a theme and a shape in mind, and that he saw possibilities in his Welsh source that he wanted to develop.

Those possibilities lay primarily in the romance mode of the story. Romance tends to be episodic and full of coincidences. But Tennyson, like Dickens and Scott, knew that the abandoning of the realistic criteria of probability, verisimilitude, and cause and effect did not mean that events were arbitrary or fortuitous from other points of view. Dickens knew that apparent coincidences and a seemingly loose sequence of events might reflect inner psychological experience. *Geraint and Enid* is an excellent example of Tennyson's mastery of this function of romance. He shaped the events so that they reflect what is going on in Geraint himself, and hence Geraint's dreams and anxieties govern the structure of the story. The outward journey is really an inner quest and, like Browning's 'Childe Roland to the Dark Tower Came' and Conrad's *Heart of Darkness*, it is a descent into the horrors of the knight's own soul. This quest falls into a shape we should expect in romance – a symbolic death and rebirth – and it is this shape that informs Tennyson's treatment of the Welsh story.

The story of the quest begins in the first 144 lines of *The Marriage of Geraint*. There, there is little indication that we are to be shown inner events, for the narrator simply tells us what happened without analysing Geraint's character and motives. There is the rumour about the queen and Lancelot, and 'Not less Geraint believed it' (28); there is his manufactured plea to the king to 'cleanse this common sewer of all his realm' (39) of criminals and lawless men; and there is Geraint's increasing uxoriousness and effeminacy. The incident in which he awakes and hears some of Enid's words – particularly her fear that 'I am no true wife' (108) – makes Geraint 'lonely and miserable' (123), we are told. In none of these matters are we taken into Geraint's mind. Nonetheless, these events all impress themselves upon Geraint, and each will reappear, in a different guise, in the quest itself.

The real nature of the quest is indicated by the confusion of Geraint's motives. At first he acts decisively, as when he leaves Arthur's court to prevent Enid from associating with the queen. After overhearing Enid, he and she ride forth into the wilderness, and Geraint's purpose is not nearly so clear. He does not tell her, as he earlier told Arthur, that he wants to set his lands in order. Nor does he make any mention of testing her, though his insistence that she ride on before him suggests a test of some sort. He defines his purpose vaguely in terms of winning his spurs (*The Marriage of Geraint* 128), but this is not much of an explanation. His very vagueness makes clear the fact the quest is primarily a function of his loneliness and misery. Though he seems to be testing her, he is in fact testing himself. What is apparent in his speeches is a need to prove himself to her, as when he flings away his gold:

> 'Effeminate as I am,
> I will not fight my way with gilded arms,
> All shall be iron ...'
> (*Geraint and Enid* 20–2)

And he tells her, 'Yourself shall see my vigour is not lost' (82). Moreover, the isolation which he imposes on her symbolizes his own isolation. Tennyson, James Knowles tells us, 'was fond of saying, "*every man imputes himself*,"'[31] and this insight into human psychology is the clue to Tennyson's treatment of romance in this idyll.

The quest begins with a descent into a waste land:

> they past
> The marches, and by bandit-haunted holds,
> Gray swamps and pools, waste places of the hern,
> And wildernesses, perilous paths, they rode ...
> (29–32)

It is a commonplace of criticism to point out that the waste land symbolizes an inner state, and that the events that take place there symbolize inner events. In dealing with this idyll, Lawrence Poston III has written that 'the journey through progressively more difficult combats symbolizes the corrosive growth of despair and jealousy within [Geraint].'[32] I want to argue that the battles are tied more precisely to things Geraint has already experienced, and must now confront and deal with if he is to regain his mental and spiritual health.

The first two battles are relatively easy ones, since they make demands on Geraint's physical strength. It is easy for him to dispose of the three knights who would kill to have his horse, his armour, and his damsel, and of the three horsemen who attack for the same purpose. But it is worth noting that in the second battle Geraint is tired, and he defeats his antagonists as much with 'his terrible war-cry' (170) as with sheer physical strength. The move away from physical force suggests that the crucial battle is to be fought with other means (mainly words, which, as slander, become more dangerous as the *Idylls* proceed). Moreover, though Geraint has got rid of the six 'wolves' – that is the image applied to his opponents – he has not yet rid himself of the lawlessness they represent. They regarded Enid simply as an object to be possessed, and that is how Geraint, consumed with jealousy, regards her too. That is why Geraint must still undergo the crucial struggle at the hall of Earl Doorm. Doorm symbolizes the same lawlessness, and poses the same threat to Enid, as the six wolves, and it is only when Geraint discovers that the value of Enid's love lies in her free choice to be faithful to him that he finally frees himself of all that the wolves represent.

Though Tennyson narrates Geraint's first two battles briefly, he presents the meeting with Limours at much greater length. It is clearly an important episode in Geraint's mental journey. Tennyson's characterization of Limours is the key to this episode. Limours has been Enid's suitor, and he is 'Femininely fair and dissolutely pale' (275). 'The all-amorous Earl' (360) boasts of keeping 'a touch of sweet civility / Here in the heart of waste and wilderness' (312–13), and that boast suggests that he is a fallen version of the courtly lover. This characterization may explain why Tennyson transposed the names of Limours and Doorm in using his source. J.M. Gray has suggested that 'the French-sounding name Limours, approximating the term *amours* close enough to be a pun, might have helped to give rise to the effeminate philanderer.'[33] It is appropriate that Geraint should meet Limours at this stage of the quest: after all, Geraint himself has been just this kind of person when he returned to Devon:

> He compassed her with sweet observances
> And worship, never leaving her, and grew
> Forgetful of his promise to the King,
> Forgetful of the falcon and the hunt,
> Forgetful of the tilt and tournament,
> Forgetful of his glory and his name,
> Forgetful of his princedom and its cares.
>
> (*The Marriage of Geraint* 48–54)

People said that his 'manhood was all gone, / And molten down in mere uxoriousness' (59–60), and Enid quotes men as 'saying all his force / Is melted into mere effeminacy' (106–7). In Limours, then, Geraint comes face to face with one aspect of himself, and with the embodiment of one stage of his life. This is clearly a greater threat than sheer physical force. Moreover, Limours and Geraint are host and guest. There was no such relation with Geraint's first two sets of opponents, and the socializing indicates the extent to which Limours' effeminacy is a part of Geraint's character, and Limours himself the double of the questing knight (Tennyson here uses the *Doppelgänger* technique of romance to good effect). Geraint can dispose of Limours by physical action and feats of arms, but he cannot dispose so easily of what Limours represents, as his hidden wound indicates.

Coupled with the meeting with Limours is the episode in the meadow outside the town. The episode is in *The Mabinogion*, and Tennyson retains it, though it seems at first glance to be a digression. But he treats it in such a way that it picks up some principal themes and images; and he carefully relates it both to Geraint's present situation and to the outcome of the quest. The theme of the episode is appetite, and it is presented in a psychologically realistic way. Geraint feels remorse, just as he did after his first battle, but that feeling is quickly caught up in physical hunger. His effort to provide food for Enid quickly becomes a matter of feeding himself, and he says afterwards, 'I never ate with angrier appetite' (233). His greedy eating is an outward manifestation of his being eaten within by jealousy, and so we have the consumer being consumed – part of the irony that pervades the episode. The irony is created by Geraint's blindness, his 'taking true for false, or false for true' (4), as the moral at the beginning of the idyll indicates. In this episode he is blind to the significance of everything around him. All about him is the means for physical and spiritual well-being. The setting is a fertile meadow rather than a wild wood. The fair-haired youth is not upset at Geraint's eating of all the food, but is ready to return at once with more. And the mowers are not concerned but go on working. The point seems to be that there is plenty of food for all human needs, that nature is bountiful and work a matter of human service. At the centre of the episode is the picture of Enid sitting on the grass. The study of Tennyson's other idyls has taught us to recognize her type, for she is like Ruth or Demeter, and as such is associated with fertility and well-being. The occasion, however, makes the picture an ironic one. Enid thinks not of the harvest but of her 'old ruined hall' (254), and her weaving and unweaving of grasses and her marriage ring are empty gestures though the interweaving of the two is potentially a symbol of fertility. For Geraint, all is potential. He confronts a lovely woman in a meadow and a youth who bears food. Though he is blind to this as anything other than an occasion to satisfy an angry appetite, though this garden is for him a waste land, it nonetheless anticipates the paradise he will gain at the end of the quest.

When Geraint heard Enid saying, or apparently saying, that she was no true wife, he suffers what Tennyson calls a 'pang':

> Then though he loved and reverenced her too much
> To dream she could be guilty of foul act,
> Right through his manful breast darted the pang
> That makes.a man, in the sweet face of her
> Whom he loves most, lonely and miserable.
>
> (*The Marriage of Geraint* 119–23)

In *Geraint and Enid*, this 'pang' becomes the secret wound with which Geraint is left after the episode with Limours. Geraint treats his wound exactly like the pang. He 'rode on, nor told his gentle wife / What ailed him, hardly knowing it himself' (503–4). He falls, as Lawrence Poston III has pointed out, 'from a self-inflicted wound.'[34] Literally dealt by another, the wound is symbolically inflicted by Geraint himself.

Geraint's lapse into unconsciousness is a symbolic death, and it takes place in 'the waste earldom of another earl, / Doorm' (438–9). 'That realm of lawless turbulence' (521) is a projection of Geraint's inner state throughout the quest. It is here that the crucial struggle takes place, for it is the Doorm in him that Geraint must face up to and conquer. And it is here that Tennyson's patterning of the idyll becomes most precise, for the sequence of events in Geraint's recovery carefully parallels his fall. The immediate occasion of the fall was his overhearing Enid while he was supposedly asleep; the immediate cause of his recovery is his overhearing her while he is supposedly unconscious. In previous episodes, he watched her closely, not so much for proof of her fidelity as for evidence of her unfaithfulness, or (to put it another way), for proof of his fears rather than proof of his desires. It is a symptom of his fallen state that he seems to find what he seeks, as when he 'looked and was not satisfied' (435). Now at last he has proof of his desires, though it is proof that grows out of self-pity. The symbolic healing of Geraint's wound thus parallels the inflicting of it.

Though recovered in spirit, Geraint still has Doorm to deal with, but he does not do so until after the feast in Doorm's hall. The delay seems hardly necessary, and even more curious is Tennyson's considerable expansion of the part of the story where Doorm (Limours in *The Mabinogion*) converses with Enid and commands her to eat and drink and to clothe herself in other garments. With such a keen sense of the shape of a poem, Tennyson was not likely to expand haphazardly upon his source. It is relatively easy, of course, to see that Doorm symbolizes an aspect of Geraint, and hence it is appropriate that his character should be given in some detail before he is slain. But this section does more than that. It also balances the episode with the fair-haired youth and the mowers, and it does so by treating the same theme, appetite. The most memorable part of this section is the description of Doorm and his men eating:

> And men brought in whole hogs and quarter beeves,
> And all the hall was dim with steam of flesh:
> And none spake word, but all sat down at once,
> And ate with tumult in the naked hall,
> Feeding like horses when you hear them feed ... (601–5)

This action, and Doorm's greedy feeding of himself, parallel Geraint's eating with angry appetite. Contrasting with such appetite is Enid's attention to her lord's spiritual well being as well as his physical satisfaction. In the earlier scene she

> took a little delicately,
> Less having stomach for it than desire
> To close with her lord's pleasure ... (212–14)

Here she will not eat, and her reactions to Doorm's peremptory commands have sacramental overtones:

> 'I will not eat
> Till yonder man upon the bier arise,
> And eat with me.' (655–7)

> 'I will not drink
> Till my dear lord arise and bid me do it,
> And drink with me ...' (663–5)

Literally Enid refers to Geraint's return to consciousness and then physical health; symbolically she suggests a death and resurrection: the return of Geraint's mental health and his sense of spiritual purpose. That can happen only when Geraint faces up to the evil within himself. That evil is embodied in the figure of Doorm, and Doorm's insistence that 'I compel all creatures to my will' (628) is a projection of the demonic forces behind Geraint's will. In Doorm Geraint meets the figure of his own worst self, and there can be no recovery for him until he has slain this demon. The moment when Doorm strikes Enid – something Geraint has never done – is the moment when Geraint acts in Enid's defence.

Doorm's death marks the moment of Geraint's rebirth. He and Enid leave the hall by riding together on one horse, an act which symbolizes in an obvious way their new unity. Tennyson compares their reunion to the regaining of Paradise (762–70). Enid does not weep,

> But o'er her meek eyes came a happy mist
> Like that which kept the heart of Eden green
> Before the useful trouble of the rain ...   (768–70)

The key word in the simile is 'useful.' Without this adjective, the rain would represent simply a fall; with it, the fall has a purpose. The simile suggests development and growth, but it is largely inner growth. Outward circumstances remain the same. Doorm's land is still a waste land, 'a hollow land' (820), where 'huddled here and there on mound and knoll, / Were men and women staring and aghast' (802–3). For them a social order has broken up; but for Geraint an inner order has been established, and it is very close to Milton's 'paradise within thee, happier far.'

The last part of the idyll concentrates on this change of heart. The two hundred lines with which the idyll ends (762–969) are Tennyson's own, and are not derived from his source in *The Mabinogion*. This addition parallels his expansion of the passage dealing with Enid's dress in *The Marriage of Geraint*, but it is a parallel with an important difference. The first passage concentrates on outward things, while the second deals with inner renewal. Enid's change of dress is highly symbolic, but it can now be seen as foreshadowing the more important change in the second idyll. There her change of dress is mentioned in only one line (947), but the change of heart – Edyrn's, mainly – is described in detail. In the first idyll Edyrn's conversion is summarized in four lines (593–6), but in the second his renewal is discussed at length. All of this is a careful piece of patterning that supports the emphasis on inner psychological experience in the second idyll.

Edyrn describes his change in terms of ironic contrasts:

> 'For once, when I was up so high in pride
> That I was halfway down the slope to Hell,
> By overthrowing me you threw me higher.'   (789–91)

Edyrn plays on language by comparing high and low, throwing and overthrowing, in terms of physical force, on the one hand, and moral growth, on the other. What he defines here in witty summary he gives in more detail in his long speech to Enid (823–72), though throughout this speech is the sense of a redeeming paradox ('There was I broken down; there was I saved' 850). One way of describing this paradox is to say that it represents the ethical advance of the nineteenth century over the medieval concept of tragedy. Edyrn's is the typical fall of a person of high estate, but to that fall he now applies a moral standard which recognizes the pride in his high position and the value of obedience and inner discipline in his new role as a knight of Arthur's court.

Edyrn's enlightenment is indeed typical of Tennyson's modern treatment of the whole story. In selecting and shaping his material from *The Mabinogion*, he carefully avoids actions that are obviously improbable, such as Geraint's disposing singlehandedly of fourscore knights of Earl Dwrm. Without such actions, the general impression of Tennyson's idyll is a realistic one. But in fact he has shifted the improbable and the miraculous from events to character. Arthur's speech (887–918) describes the shift, and in doing so defines the treatment of the story:

> 'His very face with change of heart is changed.
> The world will not believe a man repents:
> And this wise world of ours is mainly right.
> Full seldom doth a man repent, or use
> Both grace and will to pick the vicious quitch
> Of blood and custom wholly out of him,
> And make all clean, and plant himself afresh.
> Edyrn has done it, weeding all his heart ...'   (898–905)

This change Arthur twice describes as 'great and wonderful' (897, 913), as more of a miracle than great and improbable feats of arms. He contrasts such a change of heart with the kind of action found in *The Mabinogion*, a knight making 'an onslaught single on a realm / Of robbers' (916–17), and makes it clear that the change of heart is more desirable. Tennyson thus succeeds in giving a modern treatment to the old story, by shifting the interest from sheer adventure and excitement to moral concerns. The flexibility of romance made such a shift possible, for Tennyson retained the patterns of romance while changing their function and significance.

The ending of the idyll is a combination of the heroic and the domestic. Geraint continues to act out Arthur's purposes; he and Enid have children, and he eventually falls 'In battle, fighting for the blameless King' (969). In *The Marriage of Geraint*, Geraint mentions the possibility of children as a way of comforting Enid's mother: 'another gift of the high God, / Which, maybe, shall have learned to lisp you thanks' (821–2). In *Geraint and Enid*, the children actually appear, 'Enids and Geraints / Of times to be' (964–5). It is a suitable ending, for the idyll as a whole suggests that Geraint's strength in battle depends upon the moral and spiritual strength of his marriage.

DIVISION AND REVERSAL: *BALIN AND BALAN* AND *MERLIN AND VIVIEN*

Merlin and Vivien was the first of the idylls that Tennyson completed, and *Balin and Balan* was the last. Yet his sense of the structure of the whole poem was so sure that the two serve brilliantly as the turning point or pivot. They do so by extending or reversing or parodying the patterns in the three idylls we have just been examining. In each of those three there was a quest, an approach to a woman in a secret or forbidden place, and in each the quest was successful and released spiritual and physical vitality. In *Merlin and Vivien* that pattern is reversed, for there a woman pursues a man, and by defeating him she imprisons the shaping forces of civilization. In the two Geraint idylls, Geraint kept meeting figures who represented aspects of himself. That pattern is extended in *Balin and Balan*, where Tennyson uses the device of the *Doppelgänger*. The device indicates that a separation is beginning to take place: body begins to manifest less of spirit; words which unify (the vows) give way to words that divide (slander); integration gives way to division. The *Doppelgänger* is a brilliant technique to suggest the beginning of this process, and Tennyson uses it with considerable complexity.

To begin with, there are not one but two plots in this idyll, one giving an account of Arthur extracting tribute from Pellam, and the other narrating the quest of Balin and Balan. The plots are complementary. The central characters in each are twins – a literal description of Balin and Balan (in Malory, as J.M. Gray has pointed out, they are simply brothers),[35] and a symbolic description of Arthur and Pellam. In some ways the pairs are alike. Balan, like Arthur, represents civilization; both devote themselves to the maintenance of order, and both realize that the price of such order is constant readiness to deal with all threats and challenges. Balin and Pellam represent such threats, though they take the form of thoughtless action in one and asceticism in the other. While the similarities are revealing, the distinction between the pairs is crucial. Pellam represents an outward threat. His castle is a parody of Camelot, and his ideals are a perversion of Arthur's vows. Pellam's asceticism has no counterpart in Arthur himself, for to deny the body is not a part of the King's nature. Balan calls such threats as Pellam 'outer fiends' (138), and would like Balin's moods to be 'outer fiends' also. But, as critics have long recognized, Balin and Balan are two sides of one personality, so that each is an aspect of the other. Balin's 'heats and violences' (186) are a part of Balan, as is apparent in his rash and blind attack on (what he thinks is) the wood demon. And though Balin is labelled 'the Savage,' his brother's control and restraint are enough a part of his nature that for a time 'he felt his being move / In music with his Order, and the King' (207–8). Because Pellam is a threat from without, Arthur may deal with him with relative ease. Balan's task is by no means so easy, for he is dealing with a part of himself, and ultimately he destroys himself. Yet his fate foreshadows Arthur's. For Pellam's asceticism needs only to be inverted to become the Red Knight's licentiousness, and that demonic Round Table, we realize in *The Last Tournament*, is not the opposite of Arthur's, but a precise reflection of it. The outer threat becomes the inner nature. In the twins, then, Tennyson prefigures the fall of Camelot. By placing their story in the context of that of Arthur and Pellam, Tennyson suggests in a particularly striking way that the threat from without is in fact a threat from within. The idyll is open-ended, for Arthur does not destroy Pellam or put an end to his way of life. By line 116, Arthur has extracted tribute from Garlon, and the story of his relations with Pellam ends there. Nonetheless, that story is an important part of the structure of this idyll. For the poem begins with Arthur sending to Pellam for tribute, and the story of the reinstatement of Balin and Balan is framed by the going and coming of Arthur's ambassadors. The success of that journey coincides with the period when Balin and Balan are valuable members of the Round Table. Pellam's castle does not appear again until after the brothers separate, and then it is the scene of an action-filled part of Balin's mad quest. Beyond that, the castle does not figure in the action, nor indeed is any further use made of the lesser of the two plots. But the context has been established, and it makes an important contribution to the idyll.

In the story of Balin and Balan themselves, Tennyson makes use of patterns he has used elsewhere, though with important variations. One way of describing the plot is to say that it is an account of a family unit which, as in *Dora*, is broken up and then reunited. But Tennyson gives that pattern tragic treatment here. In *Dora* the union represented a release of spiritual vitality. Here the reunion is a reunion in death, and it represents the exhaustion of warring elements: primal energies, on the one hand, and discipline and self-control on the other. As in *Dora*, Tennyson works out his pattern by describing or suggesting relations with female figures.

When we first hear of the brothers, they are described as

> 'two strange knights
> Who sit near Camelot at a fountain-side,
> A mile beneath the forest, challenging
> And overthrowing every knight who comes.'   (9–12)

And Tennyson goes on to give a detailed description of the brothers 'sitting statuelike' (22) beside the spring. A spring or fountain is the source of life-giving water, and hence may be associated with woman as mother, an association strengthened by the 'plume of lady-fern' (24) from beneath which the water flows. The 'statuelike' appearance of the brothers symbolizes the fruitlessness of their actions by the fountain, and from these meaningless demonstrations of prowess Arthur rescues them by overthrowing them. The king thus presides at their rebirth, and by accepting them as knights enlists their abilities in the service of civilization. The passage describing Balin's entrance into Arthur's hall (77–87) combines suggestions of the parable of the Prodigal Son with the account of the one sinner whose repentance caused more joy in heaven than the presence of ninety and nine just persons. If rebirth is suggested by Balin's taking of the vows, a metaphor of marriage lurks beneath his loyalty to them, and it is suggested in particular by the new emblem on Balin's shield – the crown – and by his devotion to the person it symbolizes – the queen. The queen represents for Balin the highest in Arthur's civilization, and he is symbolically wedded to her. But woman as wife eventually gives way to woman as destroyer. The queen's crown replaced an emblem that Balin was never able to discard entirely, a 'rough beast ... / Langued gules, and toothed with grinning savagery' (192–3). The red tongue of the heraldic beast symbolizes both the slander to which Balin is so susceptible, and the violence that is the result of it. This slander is personified by the last woman with whom Balin comes in contact, Vivien, and she presides over his destruction. The tri-natured woman is, then, as central to this idyll as to the others. And we begin to realize that the pattern of the action – an approach to a woman in a secret or forbidden place – is a familiar one. But as always Tennyson varies the pattern, and to understand those variations we must examine how he uses the romance quest that is the dominant feature of the plot.

On first reading, the critic is likely to think that there are two quests, for the brothers go off separately, and their reasons for going, and the ways in which they go, are very different. But as the idyll proceeds, we begin to realize that the two quests are in fact one, and the brothers are seeking each other.

Balan's departure is wholly characteristic of him. He claims the quest for the demon of the woods with the single word 'I!' (134), and his verbal reticence suggests his self-confidence, his self-control, his assurance, and his readiness to undertake the task. And in his farewell speech he urges these same qualities on his brother. But there are psychological forces at work here that Balan is unaware of, or but dimly aware of. It is true that he claims the quest in the same way that any knight of Arthur would, but this quest has a special meaning for him, a meaning beyond the vows which he obeys. For the demon of the woods was 'once a man' who, 'driven by evil tongues' (122), became a fiend. The demon is thus closely associated with slander, and his dwelling in the deep woods suggests his identification with the dark forces of the subconscious. Balin's chief flaw is susceptibility to slander, and his three years' exile came about because he assaulted a thrall, 'for I heard / He had spoken evil of me' (55–6). Moreover, Balin's 'heats and violences' (186) are linked with the deep woods, where men are attacked blindly, or from behind. In undertaking the quest, then, Balan is, like Geraint before him, seeking the other half, the dark side, of himself. In psychological terms, his is a search for an integrated personality. In his understanding, however, the demon is to be destroyed rather than trans-formed and integrated, and his advice to Balin about keeping his moods 'outer fiends' (138) is an indication of his inability to cope with such forces. For Balan speaks to Balin in terms of restraint rather than harmony, and one has a sense of control imposed from without rather than order freely chosen from within.

The idea of such order, nonetheless, is not lacking in this idyll, and it is particularly apparent in Balin. Where Balan was unconsciously drawn to the dark side of his character, Balin consciously seeks the bright side of his. His quest begins as soon as he is accepted again at Arthur's court, and its direction becomes explicit as soon as Balan has departed. Balin

> now would strictlier set himself
> To learn what Arthur meant by courtesy,
> Manhood, and knighthood ... (154–6)

His model is Lancelot, and his struggle is given through dialogue and lengthy soliloquies. The fact that so much of the direct speech in the idyll is given to Balin is important, for words may symbolize both integration and disintegration. Through words Balin struggles for the one, and through words he falls prey to the other. The highest form of the word is the vow Balin has made to Arthur; it symbolizes integration, and is a fruitful thing, since it is related to the Word that stands for creation as described by St John in the New Testament. The word in its demonic form is slander, and it divides and destroys as much as the vows unite and create. Music in this idyll is analogous to the word. It symbolizes integration, as when Balin 'felt his being move / In music with his Order, and the King' (207–8). Its demonic form is Vivien's 'warbling' (432), which foreshadows her words and the destruction they will cause.

Balin's quest, to which the narrative of this idyll is chiefly devoted, takes a familiar form: an approach to a maiden in a secluded place. This action occurs three times (with variations) in a sequence that seems loose and episodic. For Balin 'chanced' (235) to observe the meeting of Lancelot and Guinevere, and the meeting with Vivien is pure chance as well. Equally coincidental is Balin's arrival at Pellam's castle. But if these three episodes seem unlikely when judged by the criteria of realism, they appear as essential when judged by the more complex criteria of romance. For the three episodes are stages in Balin's inner life, and they reveal a psychological process that is as real as the outer events whose probability the episodes apparently ignore.

Balin chooses as his model for conduct Lancelot, and as his inspiration the queen, whose crown on his shield is the 'golden earnest of a gentler life!' (204). In terms of fairy tale, Guinevere is Balin's Sleeping Beauty, and his approach to her symbolizes all that he would awaken in himself. The scene in which he happens to observe Lancelot and Guinevere in the queen's garden is a version of this fairy tale, but it is an ironic version. What Balin sees awakens in him suspicion and distrust, of himself as much as of the queen: 'Queen? subject? but I see not what I see. / Damsel and lover? hear not what I hear' (276–7). What he sees and hears is a pattern of divided opposites that is analogous to his own relations with his brother, opposites that ought to complement one another. The roses and lilies, with their contrasting colours of red and white, suggest body and spirit, sensuality and purity. The walk of roses and the walk of lilies cross each other at right angles, and there is no suggestion that the two may be intermingled. The actions and words of Lancelot and Guinevere reinforce the division. Lancelot turns aside from the queen and walks among the lilies. He tells of a dream of a maiden saint associated with a spiritual lily, while she states a preference for the rose, 'Deep-hued and many-folded!' (265). Balin's actions, too, indicate division. Where the questing knight in the fairy tale pressed on into the garden, he dashes away, 'mad for strange adventure' (284).

The second stage of his quest also involves a penetration to a forbidden place. 'He took the selfsame track as Balan' (285) and descends into the forest: 'down the long glades he rode' (306). There he fails to see the symbolic manifestation of the very thing he fears and is trying to escape from: the 'cavern-chasm' (307), which is traditionally associated with the mouth of Hell (an association that Tennyson makes explicit in lines 311–12), and which here symbolizes slander. (We can also see the cavern as a parody of the cavern in *Gareth and Lynette*.) Balin rides eastward from the setting sun into the darkness, and there discovers the second of the secluded places on his quest, Pellam's castle. The castle is the extreme form of the queen's garden. There is the same separation of body and spirit, sensuality and purity, but a separation carried to its logical conclusion in Pellam's asceticism. For Pellam will let only the pure enter his castle, and, as Arthur's ambassador reports,

> Hath pushed aside his faithful wife, nor lets
> Or dame or damsel enter at his gates
> Lest he should be polluted. (103–5)

Here, then, is a secluded place, without Sleeping Beauty at the centre of it. What Balin would like to find is the pure maiden; what he does encounter is slander in the form of Garlon. At this stage Balin is able to reject Garlon's attack on the queen's purity as 'Felon talk!' (375), and to strike down Garlon himself, even though to do so means a loss of self-control. The passage describing his escape from the castle is full of rapid and exciting action, and the dominance of narrative at this point indicates that Balin's struggle is largely a physical one.

Though he is fit for physical action, he is ill prepared for the third and most difficult stage of his quest. After the escape from Pellam's castle, he penetrates farther than ever into the forest, and there encounters Vivien and her squire. Vivien is slander in a form that Balin is least prepared to

cope with: that of a beautiful and desirable woman. Her song, 'The fire of
Heaven is not the flame of Hell,' continues the pattern of separation
established in the first two stages of Balin's quest. In it she denies that Hell
may serve the purposes of Heaven, while at the same time she makes the
fire of Heaven an amoral natural force ('This old sun-worship' 451) that is
opposed to the Christianity of Arthur's civilization. Her song ends with a
prophecy of division and destruction:

> 'This fire of Heaven,
> This old sun-worship, boy, will rise again,
> And beat the cross to earth, and break the King
> And all his Table.' (450–3)

Her slandering of Lancelot and the queen is the first step toward such
destruction, and Balin believes what she says. In terms of the Sleeping
Beauty fairy tale, he has entered the hidden place and discovered the
maiden there; in psychological terms, he has fully awakened the worst
within himself. He has found what he feared to find, and his quest is over.
He has been destroyed by slander, and has become in fact the demon of
the woods that his brother is seeking. In terms of realism, the presence of
Balan is pure coincidence and the blind attack improbable. But in terms of
romance the battle completes the major pattern of the idyll. Balan tried to
destroy dark, unknown forces, and ended up destroying himself. Balin
sought the order and self-control that were so much a part of his brother's
character and, when he failed to achieve them, was destroyed by them.

It is Balan who makes clear the pattern of Balin's quest by linking
Pellam, Vivien, and the cave mouth:

> 'this good knight
> Told me, that twice a wanton damsel came,
> And sought for Garlon at the castle-gates,
> Whom Pellam drove away with holy heat.
> I well believe this damsel, and the one
> Who stood beside thee even now, the same.
> "She dwells among the woods" he said "and meets
> And dallies with him in the Mouth of Hell."
> Foul are their lives; foul are their lips; they lied.
> Pure as our own true Mother is our Queen.' (597–606)

Thus Balan makes a close connection among episodes that seem only loosely linked, and indicates that his own quest has paralleled Balin's at least in part. The dialogue at the end of the idyll bears witness to a union never before so strong (it is only at this point, significantly, that we learn that Balin and Balan are twins) and, though both questers die, there is a sense of triumph. Yet there is also a foreboding note, and this note sounds more loudly in the next idyll, *Merlin and Vivien*.

The time in this second idyll is one we are familiar with from the earlier domestic idyls, 'a time of golden rest' (140), a time 'While all the heathen lay at Arthur's feet, / And no quest came, but all was joust and play' (142–3). In the earlier idylls that time would be a preparation for further heroic deeds; here there is a sense of a process completed, of a society established and settled, and about to decline. Vivien represents a deterioration that will soon become widespread. She is the type of the lowest in man, just as Arthur is the type of the highest. The contrast is an obvious one, but Tennyson qualifies the difference in an unexpected and revealing way. The leavening metaphor in the passage from which I have already quoted parts carries the burden of the complexity:

> then as Arthur in the highest
> Leavened the world, so Vivien in the lowest,
> Arriving at a time of golden rest,
> And sowing one ill hint from ear to ear,
> ...
> Leavened his hall. (138–44)

The use of the superlatives 'highest' and 'lowest' indicates a contrast, but the verb 'leaven' which is used to describe the actions of both indicates a parallel. The verb is appropriate enough in describing Arthur's deeds, because the metaphor is one of growth and of organic process; it is appropriate, too, in its figurative sense of producing 'profound change by progressive inward operation' (the words are those of the *Oxford English Dictionary*). It seems strange that the same metaphor of growth should be applied to Vivien's actions when she is bent on destruction. But there is a parallel with Arthur that Tennyson wants to draw attention to. Certainly Vivien produces 'profound change by progressive inward operation,' but the point Tennyson seems to be making is that this ferment is also to be seen as growth. From a far wider perspective, Vivien's destructiveness is another stage in the advance of the world, and we sense in this passage a long-range view of man's prospects that is the Tennysonian equivalent of Milton's constant reminders that Satan is an agent of God's permissive will. The parallel with Satan is not far-fetched, for the image that the narrator most consistently applies to Vivien is the snake, but the parallel with Arthur is, on first consideration, unexpected and startling.*

The single action of the idyll – Vivien's seduction of Merlin – is thus not a simple one, though it seems possible to reduce it to an allegory of sense conquering soul, of sensuality and materialism overcoming the intellect and imagination. The complexity of the action becomes apparent when we look at Tennyson's skilful use of the mixed form of the idyll. There are narrative, dramatic, and descriptive sections, and an intercalary song as well. The way in which Tennyson mixes and arranges these forms is important. The idyll begins *in medias res*, with Merlin and Vivien already in the woods in Brittany; the opening lines describe the scene. The idyll proceeds with a flashback (lines 6–216) which is predominantly narrative. The seduction itself is given largely in terms of long speeches, and here the dominant form is the drama. The dialogue includes Vivien's song, and the speeches themselves include little stories which are used for ironic purposes. It is important to note that so long as Merlin speaks – that is, so long as the dramatic is dominant – he does not give in to Vivien. At the end, when he does give in, narrative once again is used; we are told about his fall rather than shown it. The failure of the word is thus reflected in the structure of the idyll itself.

The idyll begins with five lines of description, but they are important lines, for they introduce the main features of the setting: the woods with the oak that is so soon to be Merlin's prison, and the oncoming storm. There is an ominous sense of impending disaster, for the woods here, like the woods in *Balin and Balan*, will swallow up this quester.

The flashback is largely narrative, and it proceeds by weaving a web of ironies. It juxtaposes Mark's court and Arthur's court, the one a parody of the other. The link between the two is Vivien, and the common theme is fame, a theme particularly well suited to ironic treatment. Mark and Vivien assume that there must be a discrepancy between what an individ-

---

* A similar point about Vivien's role could be made by noting that she is clothed in much the same way as the Lady of the Lake (219–23). Indeed, J.M. Gray argues that 'Tennyson's Lady of the Lake and Vivien, polar opposites in every respect, originate in a single ambiguous character in Malory, Nimuë, chief Lady of the Lake' whom Tennyson has separated into two forms, one good and one evil ('Two Transcendental Ladies of Tennyson's *Idylls*: The Lady of the Lake and Vivien,' *Tennyson Research Bulletin* 1 (November 1970) 104). The common origin of the figures suggests they are both part of a divine plan.

ual is known to be, or what he appears to be, and what he really is. They are both materialists, and materialism undermines all human thoughts and human values by reducing them to a function of matter. Vivien seeks out 'That old true filth, and bottom of the well, / Where Truth is hidden' (47–8); her goddess is 'Great Nature' (50), nature not as ordered and bountiful but as amoral and governed by chance. She and Mark both assume that appearances in Arthur's court are simply a 'mask of pure' (35), and hence they assume that they can get behind the mask and make individuals writhe at the discrepancies thus exposed. In this assumption they are both right and wrong. They are wrong in assuming that the bond of the Round Table is an ideal so high that it is humanly impossible; but they are right in assuming that not all will live up to the ideal. They go further, however, and assume that none will live up to the ideal. Thus, they become the romantic exaggeration (or, more precisely, distortion) of a real problem in Arthur's court. Mark and Vivien are not simply outsiders; rather, they embody faults in the court itself. It is not just courtesy that lets Vivien remain at Camelot. She is a part of Camelot, and a very dangerous one.

These aspects of Vivien's role, however, are only hinted at. The narrative, instead, concentrates on ironies of a much more obvious kind, and Vivien is portrayed primarily as a dissembler and deceiver. There is the discrepancy between Vivien's meek and humble appearance and her actual contempt; there is the discrepancy between what Vivien says to the queen ('stainless bride of stainless King' 80) and what she really thinks of her; and there is the discrepancy between what Vivien observes as the queen and Lancelot go hawking, and what really happens. In all of these encounters the narrative exposes Vivien for what she is, but it is only in the last episode that the narrative tips the balance clearly in favour of the queen and Lancelot. Their adulterous relation is a rumour at the beginning of the idyll, and it has spread widely. The queen's appearance when Vivien appeals to her – 'All glittering like May sunshine on May leaves / In green and gold' (86–7) – does not clearly dispel the rumour, though the queen's colours are those of youth and innocence. It is the juxtaposition of two points of view that finally dispels the rumour, at least for the time being. Here the narrative and the dramatic serve Tennyson well. Vivien's view is given in a monologue (101–20) which is full of sentence fragments and of phrases linked only by association. She is 'muttering broken-wise' (98), as the narrator tells us, and the language is that of self-deception. (The effect here is very different from that of her speech to the queen (70–83), where the fragments are wrought into a piece meant to deceive someone else.) Juxtaposed with this revealing monologue is the narrator's account of the queen and Lancelot hawking. Dialogue is given; actions are reported; and the effect is that of objectivity. We seem to be seeing things as they really are.

Vivien's initial relations with Merlin are described in a passage where the narrative is unbroken by speeches or dialogue. Throughout this account Vivien's purpose remains unchanged, but Merlin changes, and this summary of the stages in his downfall is psychologically plausible. At first he is amused by Vivien, 'As those that watch a kitten' (175). 'Thus he grew / Tolerant of what he half disdained' (175–6). Such tolerance is dangerous when it is linked with his susceptibility to flattery, and there are times when he would 'half believe her true' (184). In spite of the plausibility of Merlin's reactions, the chief factor in his downfall has no immediate relation to Vivien's blandishments: 'Then fell on Merlin a great melancholy' (187). This melancholy is related to *accidia*, a sense of the loss of purpose and meaning, but it takes the particular form here of a sense of impending doom, 'World-war of dying flesh against the life, / Death in all life and lying in all love' (191–2). What he senses is the decay of a society and a civilization, and from this point of view Vivien is not the cause of the fall but the symptom of it. This double role of Vivien is an indication of the different literary techniques that Tennyson combines so skilfully. On the one hand, he uses the techniques of the realistic novelist by showing characters acting and reacting, growing and deteriorating, influencing one another for better or worse; on the other, he uses the techniques of the romancer by making his characters types of general social states and conditions.

Merlin and Vivien each tell a sequence of stories, and each comments on the other's. Since the stories are part of the debate on fame, Tennyson might have had the speakers tell the stories alternately, and had each story comment on its opposite. But instead he has each speaker present a series of stories, and the two sequences provide him with a richer opportunity to suggest both likenesses and differences. Each sequence moves toward the central situation in the *Idylls*, the relations of Arthur, Guinevere, and Lancelot, but each does so in a different way and for different purposes.

Merlin's three stories illustrate three aspects of fame, and suggest the moral progress that makes Arthur's civilization great. The first story is about the hunting of 'the hart with golden horns' (407). The motive for the hunt is 'fire for fame' (415), and fame here seems to be the desire for personal glory in a romantic adventure. It is significant that the hunt diverts the company from its discussion of the founding of the Round

Table. The time of the action indicates that Merlin is dealing with fame in a pagan or primitive sense. The second story, about Merlin's meeting with the 'fair young squire' (470), illustrates fame as it is understood at Arthur's court. This is fame as 'use,' and the change in the blazon from 'an Eagle rising or' (473) to 'a Gardener putting in a graff' (477) indicates a considerable advance on the primitive understanding of fame. Merlin's third story differs from the other two in being (apparently) a 'legend' (552) rather than history, but it turns out to be an account of how Merlin came by his book with its deadly charm. The story has to do with a beautiful queen, a jealous king, and the wizard who enabled the king to charm his lady for himself alone. Fame here is not glory or 'use' but something mysterious, magic, and dangerous. The queen's fame saps the strength and purpose of the whole kingdom: youths 'sickened; councils thinned, / And armies waned' (570–1). The wizard's fame leads to the charm which stops the queen: 'she lay as dead, / And lost all use of life' (642–3). The story's implications are double-edged. On the one hand, Merlin is criticizing Vivien for reaching for fame beyond 'use,' and hence his middle story and the speech on fame that follows it define the proper goal of life on earth. On the other, Merlin is glancing obliquely at the influence of Guinevere and the way in which she will undermine 'use.' The function of the story is thus a complex one. It seems to be a fairy tale, but it is in fact an account of the origin of Merlin's work; it seems to be a legend from the past, but it is in fact an oblique account of the actual situation at Arthur's court.

Vivien's sequence of four stories also moves toward the actual situation at court, but hers is very different in character from Merlin's. Her stories are based on gossip, and each slanders a knight of the Round Table. At first it is easy enough for Merlin to correct her, but as she proceeds the discrepancy between her words and the truth grows less and less. Her stories all deal with illicit love. It is not difficult for Merlin to point out her distortions of the truth in the stories of Sir Valence and Sir Sagramore, for he knows the facts in each case. The story of Percivale is not so easy to deal with. Merlin does not know whether or not Percivale has sinned, and defends him rather on the basis of his knowledge of the moral consequences of sin and repentance. For the story about Lancelot and the queen Merlin has no answer other than 'let them be' (775).

The two sequences of stories are ultimately ironic in their effect. In this story of temptation and seduction, the sequences defeat Vivien's purpose and confirm Merlin's resistance, as his monologue (807–36) indicates. He clearly sees Vivien for what she is, and remains firmly committed to the

Arthurian ideal. But the sequences also foreshadow in an ironic way his downfall. Both lead to the central situation in the *Idylls*, and that situation will ultimately destroy the Round Table. Vivien is the type of that situation – indeed, she represents half of Guinevere, as the picture of her sitting with the queen and Enid in the garden indicates (*Guinevere* 27–9) – and she will ultimately prevail.

The last part of the idyll, where narrative is again dominant, describes Vivien's triumph. She has no new ways to tempt Merlin. She simply starts in again, asserting her love and his cruelty, and excusing her slander as an attempt to elevate Merlin by comparison. And Merlin is soon back to his state of mind at the beginning of the idyll:

> his anger slowly died
> Within him, till he let his wisdom go
> For ease of heart, and half believed her true ... (889–91)

This state of mind is the mental equivalent of the 'time of golden rest' (140) that prevails in Arthur's society, and the 'joust and play' (143) of that time are mirrored here in Merlin's dallying with Vivien. The threatening nature of such pastimes is revealed by the storm. It does not, as one might expect, symbolize a tempest in Merlin's mind, where all is slackening, slowing down, and dissolving. Rather, it is the destruction that follows such a loss of purpose, and is associated here with sexual passion.

When one steps back a bit from the idyll, it is possible to see it as an ironic reversal of the Sleeping Beauty fairy tale. Instead of the release of energy and vitality by a kiss, energy and vitality are imprisoned by a kiss. The active figure here is female, and she is a villain rather than a heroine; the passive figure is male. Tennyson changes, or at least ignores, Malory on this point. In Malory, Merlin pursues Nimuë: 'he was so sore assotted upon her, that he might not be from her ... And always Merlin lay about the lady, for to have her maidenhead' (IV, i). But in Tennyson Vivien is the pursuer. The setting is the same as Perrault's version of the fairy tale – a wood – and the charm itself, 'Of woven paces and of waving hands' (966), imitates in physical movement the thicket that closes around the oak. The tree is not unlike Sleeping Beauty's castle: 'It looked a tower of ivied masonwork' (4). To the charmed man inside, it is 'the four walls of a hollow tower' (207), and there he 'lay as dead' (211) – not actually dead but, like Sleeping Beauty, 'lost to life and use and name and fame' (212). This fall is to be repeated again and again as Arthur's society dissolves.

IRONIC VARIATIONS: *LANCELOT AND ELAINE, THE HOLY GRAIL, PELLEAS AND ETTARRE, THE LAST TOURNAMENT*

Once the 'time of golden rest' gives way to decline, the quest that is the typical action of each of the *Idylls* is a failure, and Tennyson often treats it ironically. The irony, which often makes the action a parody of the romance quest, varies considerably. In *Lancelot and Elaine*, each stage of the quest is characterized in a way that is just the opposite of what we should expect. In *The Holy Grail*, the irony arises from the use of a narrator with limited understanding, for here and in the next two idylls the central character comes to no such understanding as Lancelot achieves at the end of the seventh idyll. Hence, the quest in *Pelleas and Ettarre* ironically releases a demon rather than a true knight. Here Tennyson uses (and condemns) the conventions of courtly love, which he fuses ironically with the romance quest. Finally, there are two quests in *The Last Tournament*, and the abrupt transitions suggest the confusion of values that characterizes the autumn of the Round Table. Moreover, the quests are framed by the account of Dagonet the fool, and in him we see the mingling of memory and desire that is the basis of the idyll's irony.

If we were to reduce *Lancelot and Elaine* to its bare essentials, we would have the improbable story of a beautiful maiden who dies because of unrequited love. In spite of the idyll's realistic details, it is not an actual picture of unrequited love but an ideal one; that is, it is what we imagine unrequited love should be, or fear that it might be, rather than what it actually is. Benjamin Jowett defined the romance accurately when he wrote to Tennyson: "There are hundreds and hundreds of all ages (and men as well as women) who, although they have not died for love (have no intention of doing so), will find there a sort of ideal consolation of their own troubles and remembrances."[36]

Although the story is clearly a romance, our knowledge of Tennyson's treatment of this mode leads us to expect that he will not present us with the improbable for its own sake. Rather, he is likely to treat it in such a way as to make the action explicable in terms of inner psychological experience. But when we examine the idyll in terms of Elaine's inner life, we do not find a great deal beyond the information that the narrator explicitly gives us. And so we begin to suspect that Elaine is a figure in somebody else's inner life, and that the story is (from this point of view) not about Elaine at all. That somebody else is Lancelot.

Lancelot is a central figure of the *Idylls*, and it could be argued that this poem, like *Paradise Lost*, has a double hero. Arthur sets the standard of heroism in this poem, as Christ does in Milton's epic, while Lancelot, like Adam, falls but is ultimately redeemed. This idyll explores the nature of that fall. Its central subject is the love triangle of Lancelot, Guinevere, and Arthur, and its central concern is the conflict within Lancelot himself. This conflict is given through the conventional action of romance – a journey, a struggle, and an exaltation – but Tennyson treats this action ironically. The journey is not so much perilous as it is aimless; the crucial struggle has no clear heroes or villains, but is a chaos of confused identities; and the exaltation Lancelot expects turns out to be a bitter disappointment. The outer action conventionally corresponds to the inner action – a symbolic death and rebirth – and Tennyson treats that ironically also. For though Lancelot undergoes a symbolic death, it is his old self rather than a new one that is resurrected. This action Tennyson works out through a narrative structure he often uses: he begins in the middle of the story, goes back to the beginning, and then goes forward to the end. This structure draws attention to Elaine, and helps give the impression that the idyll is about her. It is only when we start examining the nature of her experience that we begin to realize that the idyll is really about Lancelot.

The poem begins with a description of how Elaine guarded Lancelot's shield. It is a realistic account of a young girl's love longings and the fantasies in which they embody themselves. But the description also suggests an emblem. The scene might be allegorized as purity and innocence supporting a shield representing the virtues of Arthur's court. If we step a bit farther back, we begin to sense that the shield and the figure supporting it are identical, that Lancelot's armour is the purity and chastity to which he is bound by his knightly vows. The type of this kind of allegory is St Paul's advice to the Ephesians to 'put on the whole armour of God.' Lancelot has left this kind of armour behind him, and with it the certainty of the standards and ideals for which he struggles. Without it, he is in a world of moral confusion. This opening, then, foreshadows both the nature of Lancelot's quest and the role of Elaine in his inner life.

The flashback confirms the ideas that are suggested, somewhat elliptically, in the opening picture, and in giving an account of events leading up to Lancelot's quest explores the complex ramifications of his moral confusion. There is, first of all, the story of the diamonds themselves. They once ornamented a crown brought down by fratricide, and, as such, they both symbolize a period of civil strife and foreshadow a time when Lancelot, who is in spirit though not in fact Arthur's brother, will be Arthur's enemy. These same diamonds are both the prize in tournaments and a gift to the queen, a pledge to her of Lancelot's loyalty in love.

Confusion is evident not only in a symbol of this sort but in a dramatic scene such as the one that follows. The three central figures, Arthur, Guinevere, and Lancelot, are all present, and in their speeches weave a tangle of cross purposes and mistaken imputations. The confusion is here worked out in terms of another literary technique, dramatic irony. There is the obvious irony that arises from Arthur's lack of knowledge of the adulterous affair. But there are ironies of other sorts as well. There is the kind of irony that lies in the discrepancy between intention and actual outcome. Lancelot's motivating force, 'a heart / Love-loyal to the least wish of the Queen' (88–9), drives him 'to speak against the truth' (92), and then he discovers that he has misread the queen's feelings. Trying to please her, he gains only bitter criticism. There is also the kind of irony that lies in the discrepancy between an ideal and an individual's understanding of it. Guinevere speaks scornfully of the king as 'faultless': 'He is all fault who hath no fault at all' (132); he is 'A moral child without the craft to rule, / Else had he not lost me' (145–6). Later in the *Idylls*, scorn is condemned as deformity of mind (*Guinevere* 39–45). Lancelot does not condemn it as such here, and that failure indicates his own fallen state as much as his words, which echo those of the fallen Eve who is ready to deceive Adam: 'But to Adam in what sort / Shall I appear?' (*Paradise Lost* IX, 816–17):

> 'And with what face, after my pretext made,
> Shall I appear, O Queen, at Camelot, I
> Before a King who honours his own word,
> As if it were his God's?' (141–4)

The deception is the other half of the dramatic irony involved in Arthur's lack of knowledge, and is another aspect of the confusion that is basically moral. Lancelot feels such confusion keenly, and that feeling raises questions about himself and his own role at Arthur's court.

Lancelot's sudden riding out from court is an attempt to escape *from* this complex situation rather than a quest *for* something. At least that is how his journey appears initially. But the aimlessness and coincidences of his journey should alert us to the fact that we are dealing with romance, where happenstance and lack of direction serve other functions. The pattern of Lancelot's journey is in fact an outward symbol of his inner desires and anxieties, and his turning away from the court is a turning into himself:

> Not willing to be known,
> He left the barren-beaten thoroughfare,
> Chose the green path that showed the rarer foot,
> And there among the solitary downs,
> Full often lost in fancy, lost his way ... (159–63)

'Lost in fancy' – that phrase is the key to Lancelot's state, and indicates his way of coping with the complexities at court. He was lost there, too, and now he turns to an inner world of the imagination. In that world he discovers 'a faintly-shadowed track' (164) across a green landscape, and the effect of the discovery is like that of a pastoral retreat. It promises rest, ease of mind, and a relatively simple way of life. Such a fancy is like being lost from the point of view of ordinary life, but it is in fact an entry into another order of being. Finding Astolat and Elaine is a coincidence, by realistic criteria, but the place and the maid are what Lancelot wants to find. 'That his fancy should lead him to Astolat and the pure Elaine,' John Reed quite properly writes, 'might suggest something about the nature of his fancies.'[37]

The meeting with Elaine and her family Tennyson treats in a realistic way. Hers is a male-dominated household, characterized by rough kindliness and jesting. Her father is plain-speaking, practical, and courteous. Torre, the elder son, is several times described as 'plain,' and is overly quick in neither wits nor body. Lavaine, the younger son, is 'full of lustihood' (202); he is a 'childe' in the chivalric sense. About Elaine we learn a surprising thing. We expect a maiden who is to die of unrequited love to be utterly passive and helpless; instead we learn that she is wilful. Tennyson in fact gives her determination and fortitude, and so establishes her as a character in her own right. Throughout the narrative he fuses our sense of Elaine as a person with our sense of Elaine as a function of Lancelot's fancies. A good example is the moment when Elaine falls in love with Lancelot (241–59). That passage describes the reaction of a young girl to a mighty hero. But the passage also describes Lancelot's inner state and the marring of his appearance by his fiend-like mood. Elaine does not see such marks, and the fact that she sees what Lancelot wishes her to see – 'the goodliest man / That ever among ladies ate in hall, / And noblest' (253–5) – indicates that she is also a creature of his imagination. From this point of view the problem of hypocrisy simply does not apply to this situation. Elaine sees Lancelot as he wishes he were, not as he is, and hence she is a figure of romance, and a projection of Lancelot's 'fancy.'

When Lancelot returns to Camelot wearing Elaine's colours, 'A red sleeve / Broidered with pearls' (370–1), his journey now has direction and purpose. Outwardly his behaviour suggests all the complexity Lancelot has been trying to escape, because all the arrangements are designed to deceive the court and, less explicitly, Elaine. Inwardly, it is simple and straightforward, for Lancelot is wearing the colours of the ideal to which his fancies are true, and for which the quest and the crucial struggle are undertaken. The discrepancies between conscious intention and unconscious attention, between what appears to be and what actually is, creates irony, which pervades the tournament itself. It works in many ways. Lancelot in disguise fights against Arthur's knights, and that action both symbolizes what he is actually doing in another way at court, and foreshadows the time when he will be Arthur's open enemy. Lancelot puts on his disguise so that his reputation will have no bearing on the outcome of the tournament, and yet, ironically, he is overthrown by his reputation, which his 'kith and kin' are determined to uphold. The wound, like Geraint's, is really self-inflicted. His reputation as a hero can wound him only when he is not what he appears to be. Hence, though he wins the tournament, he thinks that his prize is death. And his retreat to the hermit's cave is in fact a kind of death, much closer to actual death than such a symbolic experience often comes.

At this point Tennyson shifts the narrative away from Lancelot, and gives instead an account of the search for him. The effect of this shift is an increasing emphasis on Elaine as a character in her own right, loyal, determined, courageous, and resourceful. Her firm dealing with Gawain (whose quest is made to parallel Lancelot's initial ride, though it is very different in character and result) and her successful completion of Gawain's quest are ample evidence of the determination which her father called wilfulness. And her nursing of Lancelot is for her a crucial struggle that requires heroic qualities as much as the tournament.

The reference to the repair of 'man's first fall' (854) and the possibility of making 'that other world / Another world' (868–9) for Lancelot suggest a rebirth to primal innocence. But Lancelot's awakening is ironic:

> The shackles of an old love straitened him,
> His honour rooted in dishonour stood,
> And faith unfaithful kept him falsely true. (870–2)

We have, not a new world and a new man, but the old world and the old man.

The irony in this awakening makes itself felt in lines 873–98, the account of Lancelot's convalescence. The passage is a good example of Tennyson's method in this idyll. He simply describes the conflict in the knight's soul (whereas Browning would re-create it in dramatic terms) and then gives an account of Elaine's growing realization that Lancelot does not love her. But the passage is more subtle than it at first seems. There are two contrasting movements: as Lancelot gradually regains his physical strength, Elaine gradually loses hers. We begin to realize that those contrasting movements symbolize what is taking place in Lancelot himself. As his old self waxes, his new and better self wanes. Elaine's physical decline has no good physical cause, but it is a precise symbol for Lancelot's sense of what his relationship with her must be.

The result is yet another inversion of the Sleeping Beauty story. The Prince, instead of coming to the maiden in the enclosure, rides away from her. Elaine's dwindling vitality after Lancelot's departure leaves her shut up alone in her tower, and her arrangements for the funeral barge, with its 'chariot-bier' (1114) covered in black, are similar to the arrangements by which Sleeping Beauty was laid out in her death-like slumber. It is, of course, a coincidence that the funeral barge should appear at Camelot just at the height of a crisis in the relations of Lancelot and Guinevere, but the coincidence is explicable in terms of romance, for at this moment Lancelot's sense of what might have been is keenest. Lancelot has had the opportunity to enjoy the fertility and vitality represented by Sleeping Beauty, and now the embodiment of those desirable things returns to haunt him. The moral of this version of the Sleeping Beauty story is given in the dialogue between Arthur and Lancelot, a dialogue which is the ethical centre of the idyll. Lancelot argues for 'free love' (1368), love without ties. Arthur answers that love is based upon a recognition of what is best: '"Free love, so bound, were freëst," said the King. "Let love be free; free love is for the best"' (1369–70). When Lancelot refuses to cleave to what is best, the best, as symbolized by Elaine, withers within him.

Lancelot's final soliloquy (1382–1416) brings the patterns of the idyll together, and suggests another dimension of them. John Reed has pointed out that 'the primary concern of the poem is in the contrast between Guinevere and Elaine, and the effect of that contrast upon Lancelot.'[38] From the most obvious point of view, Guinevere is the mistress Lancelot should avoid because their relationship is a sin and has consequences that reach far beyond their two selves; Elaine is the girl he should marry, and together they should have children, 'noble issue, sons / Born to the glory of thy name and fame' (1360–1) as Arthur says. From another more complex point of view, Elaine is the good aspects of Guinevere herself, and so reveals the division in the queen. Her love declines as jealous pride grows; in Lancelot's words, 'May not your crescent fear for name and fame / Speak, as it waxes, of a love that wanes?' (1389–90). Much is made in the idyll of Elaine as not just different from the queen but similar to her, and many details emphasize their parallel situations. Just as Guinevere will eventually fall because of her love for Lancelot, so Elaine gives herself up to 'that love which was her doom' (259). Elaine's dream (210–14) foreshadows Guinevere's throwing of the diamonds into the river. When Sir Torre disparages his sister, Lancelot gallantly defends her by insisting that she is as fit as a queen to wear diamonds. The conversation in which Elaine gives Lancelot the token parallels the earlier conversation with Guinevere. The scene in which Lancelot departs, and Elaine watches him from the casement window, foreshadows the scene in which Arthur departs and Guinevere watches him from the casement of the convent (*Guinevere* 581–601). (It should be noted here that Tennyson had finished *Guinevere* just before writing *Lancelot and Elaine*.) Elaine's instructions for the funeral barge are explicitly royal: 'deck it like the Queen's / For richness, and me also like the Queen' (1111–12). She is given a funeral in Camelot 'like a queen' (1325), and her tomb is like that of royalty. Tennyson thus balances the contrast between Elaine and Guinevere with important similarities, and the balance gives us a fuller portrayal of the queen than we at first seem to have.

The purpose of these links between Elaine and Guinevere becomes apparent when we return to the pattern of waxing and waning that we have already seen in the relations between Elaine and Lancelot. In *Guinevere* (if we look ahead for a moment to that idyll, keeping in mind again the fact that its composition preceded the writing of this one) Tennyson gives us a picture of Guinevere sitting in her garden with Enid and Vivien. The picture suggests the triple role of woman as mother, wife, and destroyer, and though the picture itself is static, the pattern it suggests plays itself out through time. Hence, as Guinevere the faithful wife wanes, Guinevere the destroyer waxes. Tennyson never gives us a dramatic portrayal of this inner process, as Browning would have; instead, he uses techniques of romance, and suggests Guinevere's decline obliquely in the decline of Elaine. Elaine's role is thus a weighty one, and her death symbolizes the death of certain aspects of both Lancelot and Guinevere.

In this idyll, however, it is Lancelot who is the central figure, and the final part of the poem focuses on his experience. He has been concerned throughout with woman as potential wife and woman as destroyer. Now, in his agony, he turns to the third of woman's roles. He only mentions his actual mother, and dwells instead on a far more mysterious figure, the Lady of the Lake. She is woman in all her aspects: the beginning of life, the joy of it, and the end of it. And she is both firmly natural and mysteriously supernatural. Lancelot associates her with his name (Lancelot of the Lake) and hence with the mystery of his individuality. In doing so he reflects a concern of Tennyson himself, who could induce a sense of the spiritual world lying behind the appearances of this world by concentrating intently on his own name.[39] 'Why did the King dwell on my name to me?' (1391), Lancelot asks, and then he himself proceeds to dwell on it,

> As when we dwell upon a word we know,
> Repeating, till the word we know so well
> Becomes a wonder ... (1020–2)

That wonder here is the Lady of the Lake, the mysterious woman who defines Lancelot's individuality by giving him his name ('of the Lake') and yet at the same time links him with the universal, the abiding, and the eternal. In dwelling on his name Lancelot dwells on the total shape of his experience. What he remembers is his childhood; what he desires is his death; and he associates the Lady of the Lake with both morning and evening, life and death. When he speaks of 'my name / Of greatest knight' (1402–3) he means his fame, but that concern is fused with the mystery of his individuality, the unique course of his life. This wonder he can only contemplate rather than understand, but that contemplation is analogous to the kind of insight a tragic hero conventionally comes to. Lancelot's final monologue, then, elevates the end of the idyll, and moves the romance quest, treated ironically throughout, toward tragedy.

In *Lancelot and Elaine* narrative dominates, but the form of *The Holy Grail* is primarily dramatic. The shift is consistent with Tennyson's practice in the 1869 volume of assigning stories of improbable events to a character in them, and the dialogue in this idyll adds a further dimension to that technique. Like Bedivere, Percivale is a keen observer and an honest reporter, but he is more limited in his understanding, and in his capacity for growth, than Bedivere is. His account ends with the line, 'So spake the King: I knew not all he meant' (916). Not knowing all that is meant characterizes Percivale's account of actions, events, and speeches.

Moreover, Percivale is more conscious than Bedivere of his lack of understanding, and he tries to make up for it by consciously shaping the story, selecting and discarding incidents and characters so that his narrative will focus clearly and triumphantly on Galahad's successful quest. But Percivale has a listener, Ambrosius, who is as devoted to human considerations and to the common concerns of earthly life as Percivale is devoted to the pursuit of the vision. Ambrosius constantly prods Percivale to tell of characters and events he leaves out, to go back and round out his narrative with things Percivale initially considered as digressions, to go forward and give a detailed account of his return to Arthur's court. Percivale focuses on the vision of the Grail; Ambrosius focuses on the human context of that vision. The form of the dialogue thus embodies in a precise way the theme of the idyll. Tennyson treats the Grail quest as a foolish endeavour that destroys part of the Round Table and leads to a neglect of the ordinary duties and responsibilities of the knights. In his final speech, Arthur focuses on the ordinary tasks of human life, whose commonplace concerns the Grail quest has failed to serve. It is these concerns that Ambrosius embodies, and his comments and questions throughout the idyll make him a surrogate for Arthur, as Clyde de L. Ryals has pointed out.[40] To examine the course of the dialogue is revealing. For its interest lies not so much in the supernatural events that are described as in the human reactions to them. In spite of the material, then, Tennyson treated the idyll in a realistic way. And though Hallam reports his father as speaking of 'the mystical treatment of every part of his subject,' Mrs Tennyson's journal for 1869 is perhaps more accurate: 'A. read "The Holy Grail" to the Bradleys, explaining the realism and symbolism, and how the natural, if people cared, could always be made to account for the supernatural.'[41] One would like an elaboration of this comment, but one may at least speculate that by 'the natural' Tennyson was referring to the point of view of characters who see what they see because of what they are.

It is not surprising, then, that the idyll should begin with a brief account of Percivale himself. What we learn is that he has forsaken the active life for 'the silent life of prayer, / Praise, fast, and alms' (4–5). The idyll as a whole will condemn the ascetic life, and this brief sketch prepares us for that theme. For it gives us the result of Percivale's quest: a withdrawal from the ordinary concerns of human life. And it establishes Percivale's point of view: a devotion to the contemplation of heavenly things. That point of view shapes his entire narrative. When Ambrosius gets the story going by asking, 'what drove thee from the Table Round, / My brother?

was it earthly passion crost?' (28–9), Percivale replies in a fashion that will be typical of his point of view throughout the idyll:

> 'Nay,' said the knight; 'for no such passion mine.
> But the sweet vision of the Holy Grail
> Drove me from all vainglories, rivalries,
> And earthly heats that spring and sparkle out
> Among us in the jousts, while women watch
> Who wins, who falls; and waste the spiritual strength
> Within us, better offered up to Heaven.'   (30–6)

In the last two lines Percivale sums up the ethos of the ascetic life. It is an important piece of patterning to have the idyll begin with this statement and end with Arthur's correction of it. Arthur affirms in Carlylean fashion that spiritual strength must be offered to the work that lies nearest one. And, since Percivale does not change or grow in the way that Bedivere does, it is not surprising that he should say of Arthur's statement, 'I knew not all he meant' (916).

A narrator who understands imperfectly the events he is recounting creates irony, for the reader is aware of more in the events than the speaker. The irony in this idyll is complicated by the questions and comments of Ambrosius, for Ambrosius seems to know nothing of visions and miracles, and has to ask questions that seem to Percivale impossibly naïve. What is the Grail? 'The phantom of a cup that comes and goes?' (44). Percivale has to explain the legend of Joseph of Arimathea, and Ambrosius knows only that Joseph built a primitive church at Glastonbury: 'For so they say, these books of ours, but seem / Mute of this miracle, far as I have read' (65–6). Ambrosius, in short, is as blind to the nature of visions as Percivale is to the demands of ordinary life. He has no sense of a spiritual world around and about and within 'the little thorpe' (547), the people and things of 'this small world of mine' (559) in which he takes so much delight. It is a world of

> 'gossip and old wives,
> And ills and aches, and teethings, lyings-in,
> And mirthful sayings, children of the place,
> That have no meaning half a league away ...'   (553–6)

When he reads of 'miracles and marvels' (543) in 'ancient books' (541), he does so without profit or understanding, 'Till my head swims' (546). His is, then, a point of view which also is corrected by Arthur's final statement. For Arthur's image of ploughing as a way of explaining his duties as king is the kind of homely image Ambrosius would appreciate, but it is linked with Arthur's account of visions, which, though unsought, constantly remind him of a spiritual world that transcends this one. For Percivale's account of Arthur's words, and indeed for everything that Percivale says in response to Ambrosius' question about the return ('was there sooth in Arthur's prophecy, / Tell me, and what said each, and what the King?' 706–7), Ambrosius has no comments and no further questions. During the last two hundred lines of the idyll he says nothing. It is not just that Arthur has taken over his function of criticizing the Grail quest, as Clyde de L. Ryals has argued in the study I have already referred to. It is that Arthur has a balanced view of the intertwining of the phenomenal and noumenal worlds, and that view is one that Ambrosius is not likely to appreciate. To Percivale's account of miracles and marvels, Ambrosius can react in exactly the same way that he reacts when reading his ancient books: he can turn his attention to the ordinary concerns of earthly life. But that habit is of no help in coping with Arthur's words, which suggest that he see those concerns in a broader spiritual context. His lack of understanding finds eloquent expression in his silence.

The dialogue, then, is a web of ironies, in which two speakers try to cope with events that neither fully understands. It should not be surprising, then, that the story is full of fits and starts; that the line of the narrative is constantly interrupted for backtracking, explanation, and amplification. Such shifts and changes foreshadow the discontinuous technique of Eliot's *The Waste Land*, for in both poems the discontinuity depends upon the limited understanding revealed by the speakers.

The story of the Grail quest gets under way with Ambrosius' question, 'who first saw the holy thing today?' (67), and from that question until line 202 Percivale proceeds with his narrative without interruptions. His shaping of the story is revealing. Ambrosius' question makes him begin with the holy nun, his sister, whose virtue and piety he praises highly, and whose motives for either becoming a nun or being devoted to the Grail he never questions. Yet she became a nun because she was disappointed in love; and though, according to Percivale, she is devoted 'Only to holy things' (76), she is in fact obsessed with 'the scandal of the Court' (78), so that when she does have a vision of the Grail, it is hard to distinguish the

Grail from a phallus and her ecstasy from sexual orgasm. Percivale gives all these details without any sense that they undermine his assertions of his sister's piety or of the validity of her visions. He is caught up by the idea of the vision, and hence it is appropriate that he should give credit to her story because of the look in her eyes:

> 'And when she came to speak, behold her eyes
> Beyond my knowing of them, beautiful,
> Beyond all knowing of them, wonderful,
> Beautiful in the light of holiness.' (102–5)

But this description is preceded by an account of her wasting away by fasting and praying, so that the look may have a natural cause that Percivale, in his concern with the vision, does not even consider.

Galahad is the hero of Percivale's narrative. In Percivale's view, Galahad, rather than the king, sets the standard of conduct, and Percivale is proud of his associations with him. The parenthesis at lines 307–8 is revealing: '(For thus it pleased the King to range me close / After Sir Galahad)'. Nonetheless, Galahad is genuine. He alone of all the knights is suited for the Grail quest, and he alone is successful. It is with considerable skill that Tennyson makes this view of Galahad prevail when his story must be told by a narrator as biased as Percivale. For it is not just that Percivale selects his materials and shapes his story so that Galahad emerges as a hero, but rather that Percivale knows only those things about Galahad that make him appear to be what he in fact is. When Percivale is dealing with his sister, his treatment is full, detailed, and explicit, and he even quotes her exact words. But when he is dealing with Galahad, he gives few details, so that this pure knight remains as mysterious to us as he is wonderful to Percivale. The nun's identity, her reasons for becoming a nun, and her visions, are explicit. Galahad's identity is mysterious:

> 'Sister or brother none had he; but some
> Called him a son of Lancelot, and some said
> Begotten by enchantment ...' (143–5)

Percivale rejects such explanations but gives none of his own. Similarly, when the nun weaves the sword-belt for Galahad, Percivale gives her presentation speech, but of Galahad he simply says, 'he believed in her belief' (165). When Percivale does quote Galahad, he quotes speeches that suggest nothing of the character of an individual man, and that indicate rather the type of the pure knight. So, in the story of the Siege Perilous, Percivale quotes Galahad as saying, 'If I lose myself, I save myself' (178), and the Biblical reference suggests both the mysterious paradox that Galahad fully grasps and the quality that makes him more than an ordinary individual.

Percivale's account of the appearance of the Grail is riddled with irony. He associates it with Galahad's seating of himself in the Siege Perilous, and therefore assumes that the Grail actually appeared. Indeed, he presents the appearance of the Grail as a fact which he does not question, though he himself did not see the Grail. For that reason he vows to undertake the quest. The other knights make the same vow, and it is only later that we learn that none of them has seen the Grail either. Yet this fact, which Percivale is too honest to suppress, does nothing to change the direction of his story or to undermine his belief that the Grail has actually appeared.

At this point Ambrosius asks about Arthur: 'What said the King? Did Arthur take the vow?' (204). The question changes the direction of the narrative, and forces Percivale to give his story a context that he would probably have preferred to leave out, so singleminded is his concern with the Grail. For Arthur was absent from the hall when the Grail appeared, destroying a bandit hold at the request of an 'outraged maiden' (208). This action is a clear example of doing the duty which lies nearest to one, and is the kind of practical task that Arthur refers to in his final speech. Moreover, the marvel that the knights think they have seen Arthur sees as a thunderbolt, and his fear is the practical fear that his hall is on fire. By way of accounting for Arthur's concern, Percivale describes the hall. This description, like the account of Arthur's activities, is an implicit comment on the Grail quest, particularly when Percivale describes the 'four great zones of sculpture':

> 'And four great zones of sculpture, set betwixt
> With many a mystic symbol, gird the hall:
> And in the lowest beasts are slaying men,
> And in the second men are slaying beasts,
> And on the third are warriors, perfect men,
> And on the fourth are men with growing wings,
> And over all one statue in the mould
> Of Arthur, made by Merlin, with a crown,
> And peaked wings pointed to the Northern Star.'   (232–40)

The first zone is a jungle existence; the second is the ordinary, postlapsarian world, while the third is the best world that is humanly possible, and hence the kind of world that is the proper goal of human existence. That this is so is indicated by the phrase 'warriors, perfect men' (236), and perfect means complete so far as this stage of human progress is concerned. The fourth stage goes beyond the ordinary round of human life. It is a stage represented by Galahad, but Galahad, as Percivale's narrative makes clear, is unsuited to ordinary human life. The description is thus an implicit comment on the Grail quest, though Percivale seems unaware of the import of his description. But when the criticism of the quest is explicit, as it is in the dramatic scene in which Arthur questions his knights, Percivale quotes Arthur at length (293–327). For he is an honest and honourable knight, and though he is devoted to the vision he will when pressed give its full context.

It is his very honesty that leads Percivale to reveal unconsciously his state of mind on undertaking the quest, and the effect of the vision on him. If one examines carefully his two descriptions of Camelot (227–31, 339–60), the change in his outlook is apparent. In the first the city, though built long ago, seems as bright and fresh as ever:

> 'And all the dim rich city, roof by roof,
> Tower after tower, spire beyond spire,
> By grove, and garden-lawn, and rushing brook,
> Climbs to the mighty hall that Merlin built.'   (228–31)

In the second, the city is

> 'so old
> The King himself had fears that it would fall,
> So strange, and rich, and dim; for where the roofs
> Tottered toward each other in the sky
> Met foreheads all along the street of those
> Who watched us pass ...'   (340–5)

The groves and lawns have disappeared. In their place are tottering roofs, 'crazy walls' (347), and crowded streets. The sense of a city all askew reflects the unsettling nature of the quest, and foreshadows the destruction it will bring. Moreover, appropriate tasks like Arthur's twelve great battles recede in Percivale's understanding. Here they are 'rendered mystically' (359) on the Gate of the Three Queens; earlier they were blazoned explicitly on the twelve great windows of Arthur's hall.

Percivale's account of the quest itself is conventional in that the outer landscape and events mirror his inner experience. Up to this point he has been acting as a reporter, giving, so far as is possible from his point of view, an accurate account of who said what and who did what. But now his narrative shifts to a mixture of symbolism and allegory. First we have the familiar technique of romance where the landscape appears, not as it actually is, but as the quester sees it. When Percivale is 'lifted up in heart' (361), 'never yet / Had heaven appeared so blue, nor earth so green' (364–5); but when Arthur's warning comes 'like a driving gloom' (370) across his mind, he finds himself in a waste land, 'a land of sand and thorns' (376). His narrative style shifts to include Biblical turns of phrase ('And lifting up mine eyes' 375; 'And I was thirsty even unto death' 377), and the change marks his turning to a different kind of event in his account. For he presents a series of allegorical scenes in which the events have the logic of dreams or nightmares rather than that of ordinary waking life. Each scene presents a tableau representing something that is the object of human desires – a pastoral landscape, family life, wealth, and fame – and each tableau crumbles into dust. The idea is clear enough: the Grail quest has made Percivale discontented with the ordinary pursuits of human life. Percivale himself interprets the allegory in a slightly different way. The scenes were evoked by Arthur's warning, and Percivale sees each scene as prophetic of his ultimate failure in the Grail quest. And he assumes that such scenes indicate some sin, as yet unrecognized, within himself. The recognition apparently comes with his meeting with the hermit, who lectures him on the virtue of humility. Clearly this is the kind of instruction Percivale wants to receive, for the hermit holds up Galahad as the standard of true humility: 'Thou hast not lost thyself to save thyself / As Galahad' (456–7). At this point Galahad himself appears, and the rest of Percivale's account of the quest focuses on him: the celebration of the Mass, when Galahad has yet another vision of the Grail; the great storm; Galahad's rush toward the sea and his apotheosis; and Percivale's vision of the Grail and then of the New Jerusalem. The pattern of the entire narrative is revealing: Percivale undertakes the quest, learns the virtue of humility, and is rewarded with a vision of the Grail; his account is pervaded with a sense of failure and of his own unworthiness, and that sense, coupled with humility, leads him to concentrate on the one knight who is both worthy and successful. In short, Percivale is still judging himself by the impossible standard of Galahad rather than by the entirely possible ideals of Arthur.

For Percivale at this point the story of the Grail quest has been told, and his brief account of his return to Arthur's court (534–9) has the tone of an ending. But Percivale has said little of the things of most interest to Ambrosius, who here tells him about the homely folk and events of his 'little thorpe' (547), and asks, 'Came ye on none but phantoms in your quest, / No man, no woman?' (562–3). Percivale's response to this question indicates clearly that he has not told everything, that he has described the quest only as he would like it to have been:

> 'O, my brother,
> Why wilt thou shame me to confess to thee
> How far I faltered from my quest and vow?' (565–7)

The question introduces a note quite different from his triumphant account of his association with Galahad and from his joy at the climax of his own quest, his vision of the Grail. The sense of failure underlying that account now becomes explicit, for Percivale tells Ambrosius of his meeting with a Princess who loved him and would have married him. Percivale did not entirely omit this incident from his earlier account, for if we look carefully at the four allegorical scenes, we begin to realize that they refer obliquely to various aspects of life with the Princess. The pastoral landscape, with its brook and apple-trees, is related to the orchard and stream beneath her castle walls; the 'woman at a door / Spinning' (391–2) is the Princess herself, who offers marriage and a warm domestic life; the Princess is wealthy, and her people acknowledge Percivale's fame. Percivale's suppression of this part of his quest indicates his nagging sense of opportunity missed, of failure to do the work that lay nearest him, work that promised the best of earthly rewards. But the old pattern of his thought prevails: 'Then after I was joined with Galahad / Cared not for her, nor anything upon earth' (610–11). Tennyson's theme is clear: marriage and the responsibilities that go with it are truly heroic, while the Grail quest, which seems so heroic, is foolish and destructive.

Ambrosius, of course, would have chosen marriage, and his next question is not so much an attempt to get Percivale to reveal more as it is an attempt to avoid sweet dreams of marriage that he speaks of 'too earthly-wise' (626): 'Saw ye none beside, / None of your knights?' (630–1). Percivale responds with the story of Bors: his coming among the Druids, his incarceration (a symbolic death), his miraculous release (a symbolic rebirth), and his vision of the Grail. The story of Bors' quest is one that Percivale can tell readily and without a sense of guilt. It serves to release tension before Ambrosius' final question:

> 'But when ye reached
> The city, found ye all your knights returned,
> Or was there sooth in Arthur's prophecy,
> Tell me, and what said each, and what the King?' (704–7)

Again, these are matters that Percivale would just as soon avoid. He had already referred, without elaboration, to his return to court, largely because he wanted to focus attention on Galahad. But he is also an honest narrator, and he responds willingly to Ambrosius' question. His willingness is based upon the chief flaw in his character: an admiration for heroism in others (a flaw that leads him to try to imitate others rather than to make the most of his own abilities). It is the 'living words' (709) of Lancelot and Arthur that he is eager to recount, and since these words 'Pass not from door to door and out again, / But sit within the house' (711–12), one might expect that Percivale has absorbed the wisdom of what was said. But at the end he confesses to a partial lack of understanding, and it is clear that the words are living because he has a retentive memory for preserving the records of heroism, rather than the insight to develop from the words a truth by which he might live.

The account of the return takes up the final two hundred lines of the idyll, an extended account that undermines the narrative with which Percivale would have ended. For though the Grail quest began as a seeking for renewal, the goal quickly shifted to the visions themselves. For the kingdom, then, there has been no renewal, but rather deterioration. In treating the quest in this way Tennyson is simply reversing the traditional direction of the Grail story. The successful quest should restore to health and vitality both the Fisher King and his land; this quest contributes to the downfall of Arthur's society. When the knights return, they find 'heaps of ruin' (714) throughout Camelot. Those who return are 'but a tithe of them' (720) that set out, and they are 'Wasted and worn' (720). The final scene is not a celebration of a renewal but a lament over a decline. Arthur's questioning of each of the knights in turn is a chastening experience for his Order. Percivale himself Arthur does not comment on, and the king turns sharply away from him. Nor does he comment on the statements of Gawain and Bors. Lancelot gives in detail his story of the quest (763–849); he has seen the Grail in its legendary home, the castle at

Carbonek, but the sight may be no more than what he thought he ought to see 'for all my madness and my sin' (846). Again here, as throughout this idyll, the supernatural can be accounted for by the natural, the nature of the vision by the condition of the person seeing it. Arthur's final speech (865–915) directs us to a balanced view of all that has happened. He focuses his attention not on the extremes, Galahad and Gawain, but on those in the middle:

> 'But if indeed there came a sign from heaven,
> Blessèd are Bors, Lancelot and Percivale,
> For these have seen according to their sight.' (869–71)

The statement is more far-reaching than would at first appear. To begin with, the 'if' clause is crucial. Arthur does not deny the possibility of a sign, but he does not affirm that a sign was actually given during the Grail quest. And where the questing knights all focused their attention on the sign itself, Arthur focuses his on the individual response to the sign. For in the long run, it matters little whether any of the questing knights has actually seen the Grail. What does matter is the human response to the vision. The idyll as a whole totally rejects the traditional efficacy of the Grail, and exalts human agency. What each knight discovers in the Grail is himself and, in all cases except Galahad's, a self that needs nurturing and development. Hence Arthur's response to Lancelot is central to the meaning of the idyll. Lancelot had spoken of sin and virtue growing together in him, and of the sin as dominant:

> 'all of pure,
> Noble, and knightly in me twined and clung
> Round that one sin ...' (770–2)

Arthur denies that sin can govern everything in a man:

> 'but apart there grew,
> Save that he were the swine thou spakest of,
> Some root of knighthood and pure nobleness;
> Whereto see thou, that it may bear its flower.' (880–3)

'Whereto see thou ...' The advice is crucial. For the duty that lies nearest one is often not an outward task or struggle, but the nurturing of the best in oneself. Arthur's image of cultivation appropriately sums up both the outer and inner responsibilities of an individual.

Tennyson's treatment of the Grail quest is thus determinedly realistic. And his statement that 'I have expressed there [ie, in this idyll] my strong feeling as to the Reality of the Unseen'[42] is misleading in its emphasis. For the idyll undermines not so much the validity as the efficacy of visions. Tennyson's statement properly refers only to the last part of Arthur's speech and to 'the (spiritually) central lines of the Idylls'[43] – lines 912–14. Percivale might indeed understand these lines, but he is unlikely to understand the relation between visions and ordinary life. And that failure is the basis of Tennyson's ironic treatment of the story.

Although *Pelleas and Ettarre* was published alongside *The Coming of Arthur*, *The Passing of Arthur*, and *The Holy Grail*, Tennyson chose for this idyll the same kind of material that he chose for the idylls published in 1859: it is a story without wonders or marvels, and it is told by an anonymous narrator. The chief wonder in Malory's telling of the tale is the intervention of Nimuë, the Lady of the Lake, who by enchantment causes an ironic reversal in the roles of the lovers: Ettard is smitten with love for Pelleas who can no longer stand the sight of her. Tennyson makes no reference whatsoever to enchantment; and he makes only a passing reference to Ettarre's change of attitude, attributing it to him 'that tells the tale' (482). For Tennyson, as always, was less interested in marvels than in human responses to them, and changes of attitude, such as those which Pelleas and Ettarre both undergo, clearly had to be explained in psychological terms.

The idyll focuses on the experience of Pelleas. The central event is his discovery of Ettarre's falseness, and the central moral concern of the idyll is bound up with his response to that discovery. It is not just that Pelleas is inexperienced; Gareth, after all, was equally inexperienced. But Pelleas' response to experience indicates little capacity for growth. When he discovers the world is not what he imagines it to be, he is not sadder and wiser, but as ready as ever to assume that he knows everything about it (just as he was ready to boast to Arthur at the beginning of the idyll that he knew all about knighthood). His lack of capacity for growth manifests itself in a devotion to extremes. At the beginning he assumes that all the world is good; at the end he assumes all the world is false, and he becomes the Red Knight of the demonic Round Table in *The Last Tournament*. The point is that Pelleas' apparently dramatic reversal of attitude is really no change at all. Experience for him is only a succession of events, and not a matter of incremental growth and the integration of disparate experiences.

Tennyson embodies these psychological and moral concerns in a familiar pattern: the knight undertakes a quest, of which the chief event is the approach to a maiden in a forbidden castle; there is a crucial struggle, which takes place over a period of three days, and which culminates at midnight in a forbidden garden; and there is a discovery, which would ordinarily be a symbolic rebirth following a symbolic death. But the conventional conjunction of the outer and inner events is broken in this idyll. The pattern implies inner development, but Pelleas simply flips from one extreme to another. His response to events indicates a deterioration in the ideal of 'use' or service. 'Use' is closely linked with the kind of growth which produces 'warriors, perfect men' (*The Holy Grail* 236), but in this idyll it gives way to the ideal of courtly love, which is essentially static. For the courtly lover traditionally finds his satisfaction in the devoted service of a lady who is distant and disdainful. Marriage and children, the growth of a relationship and of a family, are all foreign to courtly love, which focuses on a single unchanging situation. The active ideals of knighthood give way to the passive ideals of the lover, and an inspiring king gives way to a sovereign mistress. Similarly, the familiar romance pattern of the idyll is fused with some of the conventional situations of courtly love: the first sight of the lady, her scorn of the lover, his trials and his desperate situation, his faithful service and devotion. It is an elaborate ritual, and it comes to an end only when Pelleas discovers that the lady, who he thought was being disdainful in the conventional way, is in fact refusing to play the game at all. Pelleas then discards all patterns and formulations, though in doing so he thinks, ironically, that he is professing what others practise. Such a profession is no more than the demonic side of courtly love.

The entire narrative is pervaded with the conventional situations of courtly love, modified by Tennyson for the purposes of his romance. The first sight of the beloved, for instance, is conventionally described as a vision of a goddess. That convention informs Pelleas' first sight of Ettarre, which also seems like a medieval dream vision. He retires to a grove, sleeps, and dreams of love; he awakens and sees Ettarre and her damsels. The simile draws the conventional analogy with the vision, for the damsels are 'Strange as to some old prophet might have seemed / A vision hovering on a sea of fire' (50). Accompanying the vision is the conventional blazon or catalogue of the lady's attributes (67–73). Equally conventional are 'those large eyes, the haunts of scorn' (71), for the lady is usually cold and distant, and scorns her lover's attentions. Pelleas sees what he expects to see, but the narrator corrects the reader's attitude by defining Pelleas' error explicitly: 'The beauty of her flesh abashed the boy, / As though it were the beauty of her soul' (74–5).

This comment of the narrator is an example of a recurring feature of his story-telling: he appeals to the reader to recognize Pelleas' blindness and hence creates the common kind of irony where the reader knows more than the character he is reading about. Such irony constantly modifies Tennyson's use of the courtly love tradition. For instance, the lover is conventionally pictured as struck dumb by the sight of the lady. And indeed, Pelleas 'Stammered, and could not make her a reply' (81). But the lines that follow undercut the convention. Pelleas is a raw country youth, the narrator tells us, who doesn't know how to address a creature like Ettarre. Similarly, the lady is conventionally portrayed as proud and aloof, but the narrator presents Ettarre's pride with bitter irony: 'she was a great lady in her land' (94), a line echoed later in 'she was a great lady' (118). For it soon becomes apparent that Ettarre's is not just the conventional pride that manifests itself primarily in scorning a lover. Hers is a far more pervasive pride that warps her character and manifests itself in her willingness to use Pelleas to become Queen of Beauty. It is appropriate that, when Pelleas wins, she crowns herself.

It is conventional for a lover to serve his mistress faithfully, even though she remains cool to his attentions. In the courtly love tradition, this service falls into an elaborate but essentially static pattern of approach and retreat. That pattern informs the action of the central part of the idyll, where it is fused with the romance pattern that Tennyson uses so often: the questing knight's approach to a lady in a forbidden place. And, as one would expect in romance, the action of approach and retreat falls into a pattern of threes. Three times Pelleas overthrows three knights. Three times he appears before Ettarre. And the sequence of events is amplified by patterns of threes, each of the three stages in the sequence being marked by the moment when Pelleas and Ettarre confront each other face to face. In the initial stage, Pelleas first overthrows three knights whom Ettarre sends out in anger, then overthrows three knights whom she sends out in hatred, and finally allows himself to be bound and taken in to her. Here Pelleas is clearly acting out the paradoxes of the lover's situation. Strong to overthrow, he is himself overthrown by his mistress:

> Then when he came before Ettarre, the sight
> Of her rich beauty made him at one glance
> More bondsman in his heart than in his bonds.   (229–31)

In the second stage, Pelleas again overthrows three knights, and again allows himself to be bound and taken before Ettarre. He still remains her devoted lover, but he is willing now to obey her, even though obedience means that he must see her no more. The tone of this second stage is subtly different. There is a wistful quality to Pelleas' speech (288–96), a sense of genuine feeling in spite of the conventional protestations of love. Moreover, the narrator forces a shift in our attitude toward Ettarre by giving her an interior monologue (299–305). Hitherto, his portrayal of her has been entirely unsympathetic, and he has shown her to us only from the outside. Now we see Ettarre realizing, dimly, that she hates Pelleas because she senses that 'something – was it nobler than myself? – / Seemed my reproach' (302–3). And we note, in retrospect, that she berates the three knights as 'scarce ... fit to touch' Pelleas (284). Ettarre does not change, for she concludes that Pelleas 'is not of my kind' (303), but we do sense that she is not a totally unmixed character. Thus Tennyson prepares us for Ettarre's change of heart, even though this change is on the periphery of his narrative. For Pelleas is his main concern.

The third stage of Pelleas' quest is the crucial one, and it takes place over a period of three days. It is designed both as the climactic stage, and as a contrast to the preceding stages. The chief difference is that Pelleas agrees to a surrogate wooer in the person of Gawain. And his antagonists are no longer the three knights, solid creatures he knows how to deal with, but his own doubts. The struggle, in short, is now an internal one, and there Pelleas (who has never examined himself or his motives) is on unfamiliar ground:

> So those three days, aimless about the land,
> Lost in a doubt, Pelleas wandering
> Waited ...   (382–4)

The doubt arises from Gawain's reputation as a 'light-of-love' (353) – the very opposite of the faithful lover who is conventional in the courtly love tradition – and is symbolized by the worm which mars the rose, the flower which is often the central symbol of courtly love. The climax of the crucial struggle comes at midnight, the lowest point in the cycle of the day (the two earlier stages took place in daylight). Earlier, Pelleas had twice entered the castle only when he was bound; now he enters freely. And he finds himself not in a hall but in a

> garden, all
> Of roses white and red, and brambles mixt
> And overgrowing them ...   (412–14)

The scene suggests Sleeping Beauty's bower, and indeed the states of sleeping and waking are important to the action. Here, in contrast to the first two stages, Ettarre is asleep, and remains asleep; it is Pelleas who experiences an awakening, but it is no more fruitful for him than Ettarre's subsequent awakening and change of heart. What we have, in short, is an ironic version of the Sleeping Beauty story, for the moment of discovery represents not a release of vitality and fertility, but a descent into an underworld. The bower, the secret place protecting the seeds of new life, has become the dark hole that is traditionally the entrance to hell. And the fruitful kiss is replaced by the divisive sword.

What might have been renewal after a crucial struggle, then, is instead a spiritual death. The turning point is Pelleas' soliloquy (452–76). When he placed his sword across the lovers' throats, he was still conscious of his vows (439–40), and those vows kept him from slaying a fellow knight. Now he rejects them completely: 'the King / Hath made us fools and liars' (469–70). His soliloquy proceeds through a series of images: an earthquake destroying a castle, a harlot becoming a skeleton, men becoming animals. Pelleas himself reverses the progress symbolized by the four zones of sculpture in Arthur's hall, and affirms that his animal nature is only real: 'I never loved her, I but lusted for her' (475).

Pelleas' spiritual death takes a conventional form: a journey through a waste land (487–509):

> But he by wild and way, for half the night,
> And over hard and soft, striking the sod
> From out the soft, the spark from off the hard,
> Rode ...   (487–90)

As one would expect, the outward circumstances are closely connected with Pelleas' inner state, and the narrator makes the connection explicit by saying, 'hard his eyes; harder his heart / Seemed' (502–3). It is in this context that he meets Percivale and asks the crucial question about the queen's purity. Percivale does not reply, and Pelleas (without any evidence) assumes the worst. It is an indication of his fallen state that his assumption has the force of certainty based on indisputable evidence.

At this moment Pelleas' personal history, in one important sense, comes to an end. He sees his own role as that of a 'scourge' (553) of the Round Table, and in the rash and intemperate actions in which he becomes involved, he refuses to give his name. In *The Last Tournament*, as the Red Knight, he becomes indeed the scourge of the Round Table, and his personal identity is submerged, not just by his own efforts, but in the minds of others as well (Arthur, for instance, recognizes Pelleas' voice, but 'the name / Went wandering somewhere darkling in his mind' *The Last Tournament* 455–6). Pelleas' transformation into a destructive force represents more than the history of an individual who turns out badly. For the narrator identifies him with the forces about to destroy the Round Table by constantly associating him with darkness. He rides in darkness away from Ettarre's castle, and the dawn brings only a dream of destruction. He and Lancelot fight on a 'dark field' (563), and when he leaves the hall for the last time, he springs out 'into the dark' (591). When he rides wildly away after the revelation of Guinevere's falseness, he rides

> till the gloom,
> That follows on the turning of the world,
> Darkened the common path ...   (537–9)

The periphrasis is an important one. It links Pelleas with universal dissolution, but also forces us to see the dissolution and darkness as only part of a cycle which is as orderly as the calm tone of the phrase 'the turning of the world' suggests. But in spite of the comprehensive view which such phrases imply, the narrator's chief attention is focused on Pelleas himself. In other chapters we have seen that a major aspect of the ideal associated with the pastoral and the domestic (an ideal given in heroic terms in the *Idylls*) is the recognition of individuality. And the vows that are the basis of the Order of the Round Table foster the perfection of the individual. When Pelleas denies those vows, he loses his individuality. Instead of finding himself on his quest, as Geraint, for instance, did, he has lost himself. His repeated assertion that 'I have no sword' is a confession of his loss of identity as a knight. From Arthur's point of view, the history of Pelleas has come to an end.

The Last Tournament is much more complex in structure than *Pelleas and Ettarre*, and it is a telling commentary on the idyll and on its place in the whole poem that much of the modern critical debate about it has centred on the question of its unity.[44] In the writing of this idyll Tennyson was facing a particularly difficult artistic problem: he had to give a picture of social disintegration, and he had to choose a structure which would suggest that break-up without falling apart itself. How well he succeeded is open to question, but there are some considerations which suggest that he solved the problem rather well. In the first place, there are two narrative lines here: Arthur's quest against the Red Knight and Tristram's quest for Isolt. The two quests are very different, and yet the fact that they are described concurrently suggests that we are to see parallels between them. Like the two quests in *Balin and Balan*, these are given unequal portions of the idyll, but here there is more jerkiness in moving from one to the other, more lurching from scene to scene. That kind of roughness in the narrative is appropriate to an account of the disintegration and fragmentation of society, and it contrasts strongly with the single narrative line of *Pelleas and Ettarre*, a line which is appropriate to the simplicity of extremes. Here, too, the characters are less sure of themselves, and more confused about what they want and about what they must do.

The mythic dimensions of this confusion of values are suggested in two details, one from each quest. Both present us with the idea of a hanged man; they occur close together, and close to the centre of the idyll. First, Arthur and his knights discover one of their fellows before the Red Knight's castle:

> 'Lo there,' said one of Arthur's youth, for there,
> High on a grim dead tree before the tower,
> A goodly brother of the Table Round
> Swung by the neck ...   (428–31)

Then Tristram, riding through the forest, comes upon 'one lone woman, weeping near a cross' (492) because 'my man / Hath left me or is dead' (493–4). The figure of the hanged man is absent here, but the suggestion is the same as in the first quotation. In terms of myth, the time of this idyll corresponds to the death or absence of the god: the second day of the fertility rites, after the god has been slain and before his rebirth is celebrated; the second day of the Passion, after the crucifixion and before the resurrection. It is a time when the old order is dead and the new is not yet born. Its chief features are confusion and fragmentation, mingled with memory and desire. Memory looks back to the old order which has disappeared; desire looks forward to the re-creating of it. This mixture of memory and desire is the basis of most of the characterization in the idyll. Most of the characters, including Tristram, are conscious of the gap between the vows and the way in which they are acted upon. Many, including Tristram, would like a better time, and partly recognize that adherence to the vows might bring it about. The two quests embody this confusion precisely. In both actions the questers reach their goals, but their successes are marred or obliterated by deeds characterized by violence and amorality. Yet these deeds are done in the name of vows: chivalric vows in the case of Arthur's knights, marriage vows in the case of Mark.

The mixture of memory and desire is suggested at the beginning of the idyll, in the account of finding the 'maiden babe' (21) in the eagle's nest, Guinevere's caring for it, and its death. In one sense, it is the child that Arthur and Guinevere never had. For them, there is no specific biological link with future man – an important omission that indicates that Tennyson's concept of the Arthurian story is a tragic one. In another sense, the child is the promise of renewal, a Persephone whose time has not yet come. The renewal is specifically the renewal of civilization, and hence there is much about the child to suggest that she is both a reborn Merlin (she is rescued from 'A stump of oak half-dead, / From roots like some black coil of carven snakes' 12–13, and those lines contain some central images from the *Merlin and Vivien* idyll) and a reborn Arthur (the nest is another form of the dragon-winged ship that brought the infant Arthur to Merlin, and the fact that this nest is an eagle's may suggest the words of the psalmist, 'Thy youth is renewed like the eagle's,' Psalm 103:5). The child's death is a symptom of the present state of Arthur's kingdom, which will be brought down by a failure to realize his vows and the ideals they bear witness to. The Tournament of Dead Innocence commemorates the child in a complex way. It is named 'By these in earnest those in mockery' (135), a line that indicates a double attitude. Some take the tournament at face value, as a commemoration of what might have been; others take it ironically as an indication of what is. The ironic view implies the recognition of a gap between the ideal and the real, and acquiescence to this situation rather than an attempt to change it.

The two narrative lines begin with Arthur's decision to destroy the Red Knight. He undertakes the quest himself and leaves Lancelot to chair the tournament. That arrangement suggests a distinction between the two men that we are already familiar with: Arthur is first in battle, Lancelot first in tournaments. Here their primacy collapses. Lancelot is not only a participant in the tournament, but, as 'their great umpire' (159), 'He saw the laws that ruled the tournament / Broken, but spake not' (160–1). He is described as weary, 'as one / Who sits and gazes on a faded fire' (156–7), and this relaxation of will and purpose might be compared with the Christmas Eve setting in *The Epic* and the reference there to the dying fire. Similarly, Arthur watches his knights act like savages in the massacre of the Red Knight's followers, and he is powerless to do anything about it. But where Lancelot gives himself up to languor, Arthur feels pain.

The account of Arthur's quest against the Red Knight (419–85) is given in the context of a dream of Tristram, a dream that mingles memories of Isolt of Brittany with desire for Isolt of Cornwall. Moreover, the quest is framed by two parallel actions of Tristram: his entry into the rustic lodge ('A lodge of intertwisted beechen-boughs / Furze-crammed, and bracken-rooft' 375–6) and his entry into Isolt's room in the tower at Tintagil. The parallelism suggests that we are to see a further parallel with Arthur's quest, though at first glance the two quests seem to have little in common. Both, however, are pervaded with the consequences of vows imperfectly held. The consequences are seen most clearly in the Red Knight, Pelleas, himself, for when Arthur finally confronts him, he 'deigned not use of word or sword' (457) and lets Pelleas fall of his own weight. Pelleas' philosophy is clearly self-destructive; he is the extreme form of the denial which we see in a more mixed form in Tristram, who does not reject the vows altogether, but 'sware but by the shell' (270). Moreover, Tristram's emotions lead him to be loyal in love, even though that love is adulterous, and the interior monologue that the narrator gives him (391–404) forces the reader to have mixed feelings for him. The Red Knight is absolutely sure of himself and absolutely consistent in his actions. Tristram, for all his self-assurance in the dialogue with Dagonet, is much less certain about his own desires and course of action: 'I know not what I would' (497).

Tristram's feelings point to the dominant motif in his story. It is primarily a story of lovers who are separated, and hence the recurring situation is one of waiting with a mixture of memory and desire. This motif is, as we have seen, particularly appropriate to this stage of the *Idylls*, and Tennyson makes the most of it in the lengthy dialogue between Tristram and Isolt that brings the idyll to a climax. Though the lovers are reunited, the forces that dominated their thoughts when they were apart are still very much in evidence. This is no ecstatic reunion of carefree lovers. 'How ye greet me – fear / And fault and doubt' (573–4), Tristram complains. And indeed Isolt begins by expressing her hatred for Mark and her fear of his furtive, spying ways. The distrust extends to Tristram:

'What dame or damsel have ye kneeled to last?' (548). Tristram tries to deal with the situation by flattering Isolt (549–53), a solution that is typically expedient. But Isolt already knows of Isolt of Brittany, and she focuses on Tristram's faithlessness, not in marrying the other Isolt, but in abandoning her: 'her too hast thou left / To pine and waste in those sweet memories' (592–3). Again Tristram tries to deal with the situation by flattery. The turning point comes with Tristram's prayer for Isolt's old age (624–5). It angers Isolt, who accuses Tristram of failing in the courtesy of a lover. And she draws an explicit parallel between lovers' vows and knightly vows. At this point Tristram abandons the expedient of flattery and the pose of light-heartedness, and gives voice to the thoughts that have been growing within him.

He begins with a statement which, we recognize, allies him philosophically with Pelleas:

> 'The vow that binds too strictly snaps itself –
> My knighthood taught me this – ay, being snapt –
> We run more counter to the soul thereof
> Than had we never sworn.'
>
> (652–5)

That in effect is his conclusion, which he proceeds to illustrate with a history of his relations with Arthur. At first he spontaneously believed in Arthur as more than man, and his sense of an unquestioning response to a mystery he conveys in the verb 'amazed,' which he uses twice (666, 669). Then came a pragmatic acceptance of Arthur's vows because they worked:

> 'They served their use, their time; for every knight
> Believed himself a greater than himself
> And every follower eyed him as a God;
> Till he, being lifted up beyond himself,
> Did mightier deeds than elsewise he had done,
> And so the realm was made ...'
>
> (671–6)

Finally came the questioning of Arthur's authority: what claim had he to be king? What right had he to bind the knights to himself 'by inviolable vows, / Which flesh and blood perforce would violate' (683–4)? The history of Tristram's relations with Arthur falls into a pattern which contrasts with the experience of Leodogran and Bedivere. Both these figures advanced from a questioning of Arthur's authority to an acceptance of him. Tristram moves in just the opposite direction, and keeps his eye not on goals but on origins. 'Worldling of the world am I' (691), he says; 'we are not angels here / Nor shall be' (693–4). He realizes how this view undermines his vows as a knight. What he does not yet realize is how it undermines his vows as a lover. But Isolt has already drawn a parallel between the two kinds of vows, and she presses it by pointing out that Tristram's belief in free love frees her to love Lancelot. For that Tristram threatens to strangle her, and his threat suggests, in a perverse way, his lingering desire for vows that mean something. The gap between his actions and his desires is embodied dramatically in the conclusion of the idyll. The narrator tells us that 'both were brought to full accord' (716) (though the divisions evident in the dialogue suggest that the statement is ironic) – and then Mark does what Tristram threatened to do, and presumably for the same reasons.

All of these complex concerns of the two quests of the idyll are framed by the account of Dagonet, the fool, who both sums up the main motif of the idyll – the mixture of memory and desire – and, in his dialogue with Tristram, defines the central irony. The conversation (240–358) turns on the distinction between a wise man and a fool, a distinction that shifts and changes as the conversation proceeds. But it rests upon the fact that the fool remains loyal to Arthur while Tristram looks out for himself, and this fact is the basis of the central paradox. From Tristram's point of view, the fool is a fool twice over for remaining loyal to Arthur when the majority are falling away from him, and Tristram himself is the wise man who turns the trend to his own advantage; but from Dagonet's point of view, Tristram is the fool whose self-regard will eventually destroy him, while Dagonet himself is wise in adhering to ideals that are independent of changing situations. His wisdom manifests itself in the shifting meanings of the adjectives 'wise' and 'foolish.'

The fool traditionally displays his wit for the amusement of others, but Dagonet insists he is 'the wisest knight of all' (248) because he remains silent; 'too much wit / Makes the world rotten' (246–7). The fool's wit is traditionally directed at the world as it is, and though Dagonet is agonizingly conscious of reality, he is devoted to the world as it ought to be. Tristram is not. His wisdom is the worldly wisdom by which he accommodates himself to political and social realities: 'Fool, I came late, the heathen wars were o'er, / The life had flown, we sware but by the shell' (269–70). The nature of wisdom and folly depends on how a man reacts to the world he finds himself in, and hence the centre of this conversation is 'The dirty nurse, Experience' (317) rather than 'poor Innocence the babe' (292).

The lesson Tristram has learned from experience is the value of expediency; the lesson Dagonet has learned is that of an ideal realizing itself in a fuller and fuller way. Experience from his point of view is essentially purgation: 'I wallowed, then I washed' (318). As a result of this experience, he assumes the title 'King Arthur's fool' (320). And he applies the title fool in a different sense to Tristram:

> 'when the land
> Was freed, and the Queen false, ye set yourself
> To babble about him, all to show your wit –
> And whether he were King by courtesy,
> Or King by right – and so went harping down
> The black king's highway, got so far, and grew
> So witty that ye played at ducks and drakes
> With Arthur's vows on the great lake of fire.'   (338–45)

Dagonet thus identifies folly with doubts about Arthur's kingship, and wisdom (which he ironically calls folly) with insight into the ideals Arthur serves. The conversation ends when Dagonet identifies Arthur as his brother and elevates him as 'the king of fools' (354):

> 'Conceits himself as God that he can make
> Figs out of thistles, silk from bristles, milk
> From burning spurge, honey from hornet-combs,
> And men from beasts – Long live the king of fools!'   (355–8)

It is a telling indication of the decline of Arthur's civilization that his ideals must be referred to in such an ironic way.

When we look back over these four idylls, we can see that parody is one of Tennyson's main techniques. Men and women are still attracted to each other; the Order of the Round Table still exists; and quests are still undertaken. But the character of all these has dwindled from the original, or become an inversion of it. If James R. Kincaid is right in arguing that *Gareth and Lynette* provides 'the standard against which all else is measured'[45] – and I think he is – then we can see these four idylls as parodies of that one. And although *Gareth and Lynette* was written after all four idylls, in the final form of the poem it precedes them, and thus provides the pattern we are to measure them against. That pattern is a quest in which the quester must lose himself to find himself; his loss of self is symbolized

by anonymity or namelessness, and the quester's companion in the descent which accompanies such a loss is a scornful woman; his recovery of
self takes place in a cave or dark enclosure, from which he emerges with
name and bride. In *Lancelot and Elaine* and in *Pelleas and Ettarre* we can see
the parody of that pattern clearly. Lancelot fights in disguise, and his
namelessness is the cause of his downfall rather than of his renewal; he
descends into a cave to heal himself, and takes up his old name and his old
nature; the woman who accompanies him is not scornful but loving, and
he rejects her, rather than the other way around. Pelleas' disguise takes
the form of a surrogate lover, whom he delegates to approach a woman as
scornful as Lynette; when Pelleas enters the dark place, he loses his name
instead of finding it. *The Holy Grail* and *The Last Tournament* are less
obviously parodies of *Gareth and Lynette*, but one can see that, of all the
knights seeking the Grail, only Galahad finds himself by losing himself.
The renewal and the integration brought about by the quests in *Gareth and
Lynette* are replaced here by decline and dissolution, just as they are
replaced by decay and death in *The Last Tournament*. In addition, the
nameless Red Knight and his establishment are parodies of Arthur and
Camelot (see in particular lines 77 to 88), and the fall of the Red Knight is
like the fall of Noonday Sun in *Gareth and Lynette*. Finally, if we look ahead
to *Guinevere*, we can see that the Tristram-Isolt-Mark love triangle parallels the Lancelot-Guinevere-Arthur triangle. In fact, the latter triangle
sets a standard which is parodied in the former; in *The Last Tournament*, a
husband confronts his erring wife and kills her lover – 'Mark's way' (748) –
but in *Guinevere* the king confronts his erring queen and brings about a
renewal in her   Arthur's way. So much has been said about Arthur's
failure in marriage, however, that we must examine the *Guinevere* idyll
closely to see how Tennyson is in fact treating his central figures.

TRAGEDY: *GUINEVERE* AND *THE PASSING OF ARTHUR*

Idylls of the King is, like *Paradise Lost*, about a fall, and hence it is a tragedy.
But, as in Milton's epic, the reader is constantly encouraged to see the
tragic events of the poem in a context ordered and sustained by Providence. One must not confuse the collapse of one man or one civilization
with the collapse of divine purpose. That is the fault of many people in
Pelleas and Ettarre and in *The Last Tournament*. But others, like Bedivere at
the end of *The Passing of Arthur*, recognize a renewal, and the central
figures' understanding is still more complex. The tragic hero convention-

ally comes, as a result of his suffering, to recognize a more comprehensive order than the one that has failed in his own endeavours. Arthur, as we shall see, gains such insight in *The Passing of Arthur*, and Guinevere does so in her idyll. But whereas Arthur's insight is concerned with the cycle of generations and civilizations, Guinevere focuses on the change of heart within the individual. The *Guinevere* idyll, then, balances the concern with a change of heart in such figures as Lynette, Edyrn, and Geraint, while Arthur's insight expands the understanding that Leodogran comes to in *The Coming of Arthur*.

The central movement in *Guinevere* is a familiar one: an approach to a lady in an enclosed space. There are in fact two such movements here, and they are introduced by a third, demonic version of the same movement, Modred's spying on the queen in the garden. The two movements, Lancelot's approach to the queen in the tower and Arthur's approach to the queen in the nunnery, present, with the usual Tennysonian precision, both likenesses and differences. Both end in separation, isolation, and loneliness. Relations are broken up rather than established. There is no release of joy or celebration of vitality, for the adulterous relationship is sterile, and the married relationship is childless. In spite of all these parallels, the chief difference between the two movements is crucial. Guinevere's last meeting with Lancelot confirms an established pattern; her last meeting with Arthur leads to repentance, insight, and renewal. The one suggests a spiritual death or (to be more precise) a dormant spirit; the other results in a spiritual rebirth. The second meeting is the more important one, and it is the chief action of this idyll. The first is included as a flashback. Once again Tennyson makes use of his characteristic narrative structure, for he begins with the queen at Almesbury, goes back to the story of how she came there, and then goes forward to the final meeting with Arthur. And once again he develops all the parallels and contrasts that such a structure makes possible.

Within this general structure are a number of flashbacks, rather like the many stories included in *Merlin and Vivien*. There is the little novice's account of 'signs / And wonders ere the coming of the Queen' (230–1); there is the queen's memory of her journey with Lancelot to Arthur's court; and there is Arthur's review of his entire career. In all of these flashbacks the remembrance of things past is particularly acute, and the sense that time has swept all these things away gives them poignancy. It is not for nothing that the nucleus of the poem is a parting, specifically the parting of Arthur and Guinevere in the lines of the poem that Tennyson composed first:

'But hither shall I never come again,
Never lie by thy side; see thee no more –
Farewell!'   (575–7)

In this expression of loss, the motif of *The Last Tournament* – the mixture of memory and desire – is repeated. This motif is given a Biblical context by the song which the little novice sings.

'Too late, too late! ye cannot enter now' (171) – that is the refrain of the song which is based, as Ricks points out in his notes (p 1729), on the parable of the virgins, Matthew 25: 1–13. The parable distinguishes between wise and foolish virgins. The wise prepare their lamps with oil for the coming of the bridegroom; the foolish do not. When the bridegroom arrives unexpectedly at midnight, the wise go in to the marriage, but the foolish are too late, and find the door shut. The theme of the parable is preparedness for the second coming of Christ. As far as the little novice is concerned, the song is designed to remind the nuns of their duty, and of the tragic results of failing in it. Through dramatic irony, Tennyson has the song apply to Guinevere in much the same way. But the critic must define that way carefully. The parable does not present a simple distinction between good and evil, as one might uncritically assume at first reading. All the virgins await the bridegroom and desire his coming, and all have lamps. But only half are ready. The key is preparedness. The parable expands our understanding of the Sleeping Beauty pattern which is so pervasive in the *Idylls* by indicating that the maiden who is to be the bride has some responsibilities as well. Guinevere is not unworthy of Arthur, but she is unprepared for him. Her tragedy has as its basic cause a sin of omission, based upon her assumption (never carefully explored) that Arthur's ideals are humanly impossible.

In other idylls the flashbacks might suggest that the central character is reliving the chief events of his or her inner life, but the flashbacks do not serve such a function here, largely because Guinevere's inner life has been, for the most part, dormant. The first genuine crisis she experiences is the discovery of her guilty love and the parting from Arthur, and it is a crisis because it raises, for the first time, questions about the direction and purpose of her life. Because these questions come so late, the flashbacks tell us relatively little about Guinevere, or give us little more than an account of her from the outside. Nonetheless, they are arranged in a particular sequence leading to Guinevere's inner awakening.

The first flashback, the account of Modred spying on the queen by climbing to 'the high top of the garden-wall' (25) is proleptic, especially since Modred's action suggests Satan's spying on Adam and Eve in the garden of Eden in book IV of *Paradise Lost*. But the queen's garden, one of the most important settings in the *Idylls*, is not, in spite of appearances, a world of paradisal innocence. Tennyson elsewhere describes its characteristics in terms of opposites: roses and lilies, red and white, walks crossing one another at right angles. These opposites suggest that the garden is really the battleground on which the soul struggles, particularly in making the all-important choice between good and evil. The queen, however, has never made a clear choice. She allows contrasting or incompatible things to lie side by side in her garden as in herself. For her there has been no weeding of either garden or heart. Her failure to shape both is indicated here by the scene Modred sees when he peeps over the wall:

> the Queen who sat betwixt her best
> Enid, and lissome Vivien, of her court
> The wiliest and the worst ... (27–9)

The scene is an emblem of Guinevere's unpreparedness.

The meeting between Guinevere and Lancelot is to be the last because of the queen's fear of their being discovered. A more melodramatic treatment of this scene might have made it a scene of passion enhanced by the sense that it must be the last of a torrid affair. But Tennyson treats the scene quite differently. It is remarkable for its lack of activity:

> Hands in hands, and eye to eye,
> Low on the border of her couch they sat
> Stammering and staring. (99–101)

It is as if the affair has somehow numbed them both, so that they cannot act or make the choices that must be made. In sharp contrast to this inactivity are Guinevere's inner turmoil preceding the meeting and the fight with Modred that interrupts it. Both the inner and the outer actions are the first steps of Guinevere's awakening.

The next step is the long scene with the 'little maid,' the novice who rambles on 'with a babbling heedlessness' (149). As John R. Reed has pointed out in his analysis of the idyll, 'there remains now the confrontation with the self, and sequestration in the convent represents that confrontation.' For Guinevere the novice 'serves as an articulate conscience.'[46] Her symbolic function is made possible by the dramatic irony of the scene, since Guinevere does not reveal her identity. But if the novice is Guinevere's conscience, she torments the queen in unexpected ways. She focuses, not upon the actual affair with Lancelot, but on the state of the kingdom before the coming of the queen, and on its state after her flight. In short, she gives the queen's sin an historical context, and that is something that Guinevere herself has failed to do until now. Another way of defining her dormant moral state is to say that she has never really considered the effects and consequences of her actions, just as she has never really shared in the vitality of the kingdom to which her marriage has brought her. Now she is made to realize that her actions cannot remain detached and isolated. The novice tells her first about the war between Lancelot and the king, and then about the land as 'full of signs / And wonders ere the coming of the Queen' (230–1). These wonders ended with her coming, and society descended into ordinary existence where miracles do not happen. Conventionally, Guinevere's marriage should have represented a great release of vitality. Instead, it marked a time when that vitality and all the imaginative forms of it became dormant. Thus we begin to sense the inversion of a familiar pattern in this idyll. The marriage which usually marked the end of the Sleeping Beauty story here marks its beginning. And only now, at the time of separation, does the queen begin to wake.

The inversion is apparent in other ways as well. Following the conversation with the novice, the queen remembers how she was first escorted to Arthur's court by Lancelot (375–404), 'the golden days / In which she saw him first' (377–8). Arthur did not come to her, as the Prince did in the Sleeping Beauty story. Rather, she journeyed to him. Consequently she responded to Lancelot, but there was no awakening to Arthur and all that he represented. It is significant that the queen rehearses this memory 'from old habit of the mind' (376) and that she is described as 'immersed in ... a trance' (398). In effect, this trance is one she has never awakened from. It is also significant that at this very moment Arthur should arrive at the nunnery. Like the prince in the Sleeping Beauty story, he will be the agent of Guinevere's waking, but it is a moment marked not by a marriage but by a parting. The moment makes clear the nature of this idyll: it is the treatment of the Sleeping Beauty story as tragedy.

The tragedy has a medieval shape in that it deals with the fall of a person of high estate, but it also has the classical shape where the fall comes about through the interweaving of circumstances with the central figure's purposes and actions, and where his sense of his responsibility for his fate is ultimately linked with his insight into the nature of the human condition. Before the appearance of Arthur, Guinevere is agonizingly conscious of the fact of the fall and its consequences. And she has some sense of her responsibility for what has happened, as her response to the novice's song and its theme of preparedness indicates. But Arthur is the agent of a more comprehensive understanding. The long speech (419–523) in which he reviews his entire career is spoken for the moral education of Guinevere: 'Bear with me for the last time while I show, / Even for thy sake, the sin which thou hast sinned' (451–2).

This climactic scene between Arthur and Guinevere has been regularly condemned by readers and critics alike. It seems to take us into the world of Victorian melodrama: a sinning wife, confronted by a husband who now knows all, grovelling on the floor at his feet; a parting in which the wife leans in despair from a window to catch a last glimpse of her husband's face. To modern readers, Arthur seems cold and priggish, and Guinevere improbably submissive and remorseful. But if we can get beyond these superficial difficulties, and see the scene as the playing out of a serious moral drama, we shall be much closer to Tennyson's concept of the action.

The kind of moral drama we are dealing with can perhaps be understood better if we compare this scene with a similar scene in book IX of *Paradise Lost*, where, as here, a husband confronts a sinning wife. However great our sympathy with Adam's unwillingness to abandon Eve to her fate, the poem condemns that sympathy as misplaced, and suggests that Adam's duty was to instruct Eve – in fact, to damn her – and thus bring her to a conviction of sin. But Adam fails in his duty, and becomes just as responsible as Eve for the Fall. Arthur, by way of contrast, does not fail. Although he is as much in love with his wife as Adam was with Eve (see lines 505–7), he does not allow that bond to hinder his better judgment; he acts correctly by condemning his wife's sin, and by bringing about repentance in her.

To act correctly in a situation like this is not likely to gain much sympathy, because Arthur must bring Guinevere to a conviction of sin, and he can do that only by using the vows of knighthood and marriage to accuse her, and by showing her that the consequences of her sin cannot be confined to her alone. Hence he deals with the establishment of the Order of the Round Table, and gives us the fullest account of the vows of knighthood that we have had so far in the poem (lines 464 to 480). To those who have upheld the ideals of the Order, the vows (like the Ten Commandments) are a revealing and liberating force; to those who have fallen away from these ideals, the vows are an accusation. Indeed, moral law is fulfilling its proper function in a fallen world when it is an accuser, and Arthur, as the embodiment of such law, is playing his proper role here. Moreover, as he quite rightly insists, this law is the basis of society as well as of individual relationships, and marriage is its highest expression. Arthur thus firmly links the domestic and the heroic. From his point of view – and indeed from Tennyson's, as the shape of the whole *Idylls* indicates – the central action is his marriage, and on that marriage the fate of a civilization depends. The link between an individual and the state is thus much more than just an analogy. Domestic life is the type of civilization, its essence, its informing vitality. And when it fails, civilization decays. We come back again to Hallam Tennyson's statement about his father: 'Upon the sacredness of home life he would maintain that the stability and greatness of a nation largely depend.'[47] This archetypally Victorian view of domestic life informs the treatment of the *Idylls*, and of this idyll in particular. As a result, more conventional epic actions, such as Arthur's 'twelve great battles' (which he mentions at line 429), are pushed into the background, and the central action, a marriage, though unheroic from a more conventional point of view, is made the event upon which everything else depends.

To modern ears, Arthur's accusations, and his forgiveness of Guinevere, seem wrong. 'It's all your fault,' he seems to be saying – 'thou hast spoilt the purpose of my life' (450) – '[but] I forgive thee, as Eternal God / Forgives' (541–2). Nonetheless, Arthur is acting correctly, as Guinevere's response (which is crucial) indicates. In the same passage in which Arthur forgives Guinevere, he says, 'do thou for thine own soul the rest' (542), for he has acted as he ought to have, and it is up to Guinevere to respond. The strength and worth of her character are confirmed in her response, which falls into the familiar pattern of regeneration and repentance. The stages in this pattern – Milton defines them in *The Christian Doctrine* as 'conviction of sin, contrition, confession, departure from evil, conversion to good' (I, xix) – are clear in the responses of Adam and Eve in book x of *Paradise Lost*, and are clear in Guinevere's response as well. Conviction of sin is apparent in her first words after Arthur's departure: 'Gone – my lord! / Gone through my sin to slay and to be slain!' (607–8). She is contrite in mind and heart. 'The King,' she says, 'Called me polluted' (614–15), and she is afflicted with the truth of that statement: 'mine will ever be a name of scorn' (622). She confesses her sin by praising Arthur,

> 'To whom my false voluptuous pride, that took
> Full easily all impressions from below,
> Would not look up, or half-despised the height
> To which I would not or I could not climb ...'　　　　　(636–9)

She accepts Arthur as 'the highest and most human too' (644), and recognizes that it was her duty to love the highest:

> 'It surely was my profit had I known:
> It would have been my pleasure had I seen.
> We needs must love the highest when we see it,
> Not Lancelot, nor another.'   (653–6)

The idea is the same as that which Arthur expresses to Lancelot at the end of *Lancelot and Elaine*: 'Free love is for the best' (1370). In recognizing and accepting the truth of these words, Guinevere has at last weeded her heart.

This inner action of regeneration and repentance is the highest form of the quest, and the success of that quest here tempers our sense of the tragedy which is playing itself out. Moreover, if one stands back from Guinevere's experience, it is possible to see that the quest falls into a familiar pattern. It begins with her flight to Almesbury, a journey in which she (like many knights before her) hides her name. Her anonymity indicates that she is losing herself to find herself. Her crucial struggle – the first genuine crisis she has faced in her life – takes place in an enclosed space, and the success of that struggle is indicated when she recognizes her role as it ought to have been, and when she is in turn recognized by the nuns (663–4). In reassuming her name, she assumes her true identity, and thereafter is admired

> for her good deeds and her pure life,
> And for the power of ministration in her,
> And likewise for the high rank she had borne ...   (687–9)

In spite of Guinevere's conversion, we leave the idyll with a sense of tragedy, a sense which is evoked mainly by the parable of the wise and foolish virgins. In that parable, as was mentioned above, the tragedy comes about, not because the foolish virgins do not desire the bridegroom, but because they are too late for the wedding feast. We remember how often, in fairy tales and romances, it is important that deeds be done at the right time; in *The Tempest*, for instance, Prospero's timing is crucial, and even he cannot stay the passage of time, as he indicates in the epilogue when he turns the responsibility for renewal over to us. So, too, Arthur must come to terms with time. Guinevere's conversion is real, but it is too late to save the civilization which has been realized in the Round Table.

And Arthur has the difficult problem of understanding why his best efforts, and his constant purpose to make the most of the circumstances in which he has been placed, have nonetheless led to his defeat. It is easy enough to explain a tragedy in terms of a flaw in the central character; but it is difficult to explain it in terms of that character's virtues and ideals. This is the problem that Arthur focuses on, and the final idyll, *The Passing of Arthur*, traces the stages by which his understanding grows.

Arthur's state of mind just before his last great battle is apparent in the soliloquy which Bedivere overhears (9–28). There seem to be two Arthurs: the Arthur who confesses to utter confusion and desolation ('My God, thou hast forgotten me in my death' 27) and the Arthur who is aware of the total pattern of his life ('Nay – God my Christ – I pass but shall not die' 28). The quotations are the last two lines of Arthur's soliloquy, and they define two points of view that Arthur states here but does not attempt to reconcile. The first is the point of view appropriate to the winter solstice, 'that day when the great light of heaven / Burned at his lowest in the rolling year' (90–1); the second is appropriate to the sunrise with which the idyll ends. The idyll explores the meeting point of the old year and the new by exploring the links between Arthur's two attitudes. The initial gap between those two attitudes is presented in another way in the soliloquy: Arthur says that he has found God in nature, 'But in His ways with men I find Him not' (11). His whole life's work has come to nothing:

> 'For I, being simple, thought to work His will,
> And have stricken with the sword in vain;
> And all whereon I leaned in wife and friend
> Is traitor to my peace, and all my realm
> Reels back into the beast, and is no more.'   (22–6)

This is the view of human action that Arthur starts with. It is a view which apparently denies the value of human endeavour, and it is a view that must be corrected in the course of the idyll.

The first step is Arthur's dream of Gawain. In Malory, and in Tennyson's early version (quoted by Ricks, p 586), the dream is a warning: Gawain tells Arthur not to fight the next day. Tennyson retains that warning in Gawain's prophecy ('tomorrow thou shalt pass away' 34) but changes the main emphasis of the dream to Gawain's view of earthly life and all its delights as hollow. This view is appropriate to Arthur's state of mind, but the fact that it is advanced by Gawain discredits it. It is in fact a brilliant stroke on Tennyson's part to give this view to one of the least satisfactory of Arthur's knights. Gawain had no sense of high purpose, and his courtesy was too shallow to mask his lack of moral sense. He was easily deflected from his responsibilities by an attractive female, as he was by Elaine in his quest for Lancelot, and by the 'merry maidens' in the silk pavilion in his quest for the Grail. Gawain's character undermines his generalization about the hollowness of life, as Bedivere is quick to point out: 'Light was Gawain in life, and light in death / Is Gawain, for the ghost is as the man' (56–7). Bedivere holds to the old view, that ideals are eternal:

> 'thy name and glory cling
> To all high places like a golden cloud
> For ever ...'   (53–5)

Thus Bedivere, the first of the warriors to be knighted by Arthur, becomes the last of those holding to the old ideals of the Round Table. There is a considerable distance between his view of human endeavour and Gawain's, and Arthur must qualify the views of both: Bedivere is too optimistic ('Arise, go forth and conquer as of old' 64) and Gawain is too despairing. Arthur presents a third and more balanced point of view when he attempts to define his tragedy. His sense of the tragic course of his life will ultimately fuse the two attitudes: his very ideals have brought about his defeat, but such failure does not undermine the validity of the ideals.

Arthur's progress is marked by the statements in which he defines the nature of the tragedy. There are three such statements, and each draws attention to the dissolution of the kingdom and to Arthur's sense that he is responsible for the catastrophe. But each statement has a different context, and these contexts make clear considerable progress in Arthur's understanding of his situation.

The first statement appears at line 72 and suggests the disharmony and the disunity that one associates with the catastrophe: 'The king who fights his people fights himself.' The statement comes in the midst of Arthur's description of the difference between his other battles, which were against his enemies, and this one 'against my people and my knights' (71). This distinction is in fact a confession of confusion, which finds its image in the 'blind haze' (76) which he has seen ever since he left Guinevere at Almesbury. This confusion is reinforced by the desolation of the last battle: 'For friend and foe were shadows in the mist, / And friend slew friend not knowing whom he slew' (100–1). Moreover the battle is pervaded by a 'deathwhite mist' (95). 'Even on Arthur fell / Confusion' (98–9), Bedivere tells us, and he quotes Arthur as saying:

> 'O Bedivere, for on my heart hath fallen
> Confusion, till I know not what I am,
> Nor whence I am, nor whether I be King.'   (143–5)

This confusion coincides with the winter solstice, the lowest point in the cycle of the year, and with a low point in the cycle of the day, 'when the dolorous day / Grew drearier toward twilight falling' (122–3).

The second statement appears at line 154: 'My house hath been my doom.' Arthur makes this statement in response to Bedivere's information that Modred still lives. But he is careful to define 'my house' as 'they who sware my vows' (157). It is well known that Tennyson rejects Malory's story of Modred as Arthur's illegitimate son by an incestuous union with his sister. In *To the Queen* he refers obliquely to Malory's account of Arthur's downfall as 'the adulterous finger of a time / That hovered between war and wantonness' (43–4). Rather, Arthur's statement suggests that the knightly vows, good in themselves, have ironically been the cause of his downfall. The statement is thus an advance over the confusion of his first statement, and the advance is marked by an affirmation quite different from his doubts about himself: 'King am I, whatsoever be their cry' (162). And this affirmation of his kingship is confirmed when he slays Modred in single combat.

The third statement appears at line 190: 'I perish by this people which I made.' This statement is near the beginning of the section that was the original *Morte d'Arthur* of 1842, but in the complete idyll Tennyson makes it part of a continuous development in Arthur. The statement is linked with Merlin's prophecy that Arthur will come again (191–2), and with Arthur's own resignation to the course of events: 'let what will be, be' (192). But the context of the statement is a state of being more closely associated with the domestic idyls:

> 'I think that we
> Shall never more, at any future time,
> Delight our souls with talk of knightly deeds,
> Walking about the gardens and the halls
> Of Camelot, as in the days that were.'   (185–9)

The state Arthur describes is a period of 'fallow leisure,' a period after his major battles had been fought and won, when life at court was characterized by the rest and contentment usually associated with the domestic (and, in earlier ages, with the pastoral). This is, in fact, the time in which the central idylls are set. Arthur's tone in describing it is elegiac, and when this tone is fused with the tragic tone of line 190 we have a sense of tragic inevitability. Even the best state of being has within it the seeds of its own destruction. For here it is not the 'house' and the breaking of vows that Arthur associates with his fate, but rather the highest stage of the civilization he has created. In associating the best and the worst equally with the tragedy, Arthur shows that he is gaining a far more comprehensive view of his fate than he had before.

The stage that Arthur has reached may be defined in other ways. In terms of physical and outward things, Arthur has become less and less. In the great battle, he loses his entire army, and sees all his enemies but one disappear. In single combat he slays Modred but suffers a fatal wound. Finally, he disposes of Excalibur. But as Arthur is increasingly isolated and stripped of physical powers, he is more and more aware of the spiritual context of his earthly endeavours. In the last great battle, he is a defeated man, old, weary, and confused; in single combat with Modred, he is a king affirming the heroic ideal to which he has adhered throughout his life; and in his instructions for the disposal of Excalibur, he is almost a mage or high priest with insight into magic and mysterious powers. As such, he presides over Bedivere's testing and initiation. Once an old man much in need of Bedivere's words of encouragement, he is now a wise man instructing Bedivere in the things of the spirit.

The final stage is Arthur's famous speech:

> 'The old order changeth, yielding place to new,
> And God fulfils himself in many ways,
> Lest one good custom should corrupt the world.'　　　　(408–10)

This speech is the central piece of this idyll, and everything leads to it. For Bedivere, it represents instruction in the mysteries that he has confronted but not penetrated; for Arthur, it represents the culmination of his development from a defeated man to a hero wise in the ways in which ideals manifest themselves. The three lines quoted above are Arthur's final formulation of the tragic sense that he has been struggling to understand throughout the idyll. It is a long way from 'The king who fights his people fights himself' (72). He affirms that spiritual ideals are constantly realizing themselves in many ways, and that change characterizes God's guidance of earthly affairs. When he advises Bedivere to pray, he is not advising him to give up the life of action in favour of the life of contemplation, but rather advising him to have faith in human action as part of God's plan for the world, and in prayer as the essence of all such action. Arthur began the idyll by asserting that 'in His ways with men I find Him not' (11). He ends by asserting just the opposite.

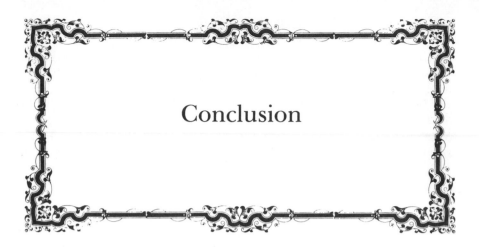

Conclusion

If we turn back to the questions raised in the introduction to this book, we can now perhaps begin to understand how to answer them. These were the questions: Why does Tennyson use domestic themes and images? What is their significance? To what literary styles and kinds do they lend themselves? Why does Tennyson use the idyl(l) so frequently when he is dealing with domestic matters?

The answers to the first two questions are simple enough. Tennyson shared the popular view of the home and of family life as an ideal existence. In his view, and in the views of his contemporaries, the home was a place to which one could retreat from the confusing struggles and confused striving of modern life, a place which preserved all those things that made life worth living. If it was a retreat, it was also a place in which to prepare to return to the wider world. For the ideals and values of family life were meant to permeate society, and the family was both the model of social order, and a civilizing influence on the nation. The Royal Family set the pattern, as indicated by the praise throughout the period of the strength of the queen's domestic affections. And every other family was, in aspiration if not always in fact, a type of this ideal.

When these ideals are seen in literary terms, the tradition to which they are closest is the pastoral. But pastoral conventions were difficult to use in a fresh way in the nineteenth century, and bore the stigma of artificiality. They were no longer as immediate and appealing as they had once been. Hence, when Tennyson set about writing an elegy in which he faced the problem of fusing his deepest feelings with a literary form and literary conventions that would make such feelings typical and universal, he replaced the pastoral with the domestic. The result was *In Memoriam*, a poem that was immensely effective, for the domestic references both appealed to the ideals of the age, and universalized the emotion by making it seem common and familiar. Hence, though the elegy moves in the conventional way from grief to consolation, its character is defined by the three Christmases. Christmas was the chief family celebration of Victorian England, and the Christmas spirit one which many wished prevailed all year round. For it was a time when human relations were governed by sympathy and love rather than by selfishness and the cash nexus. Three times the elegy returns to the Christmas season, and the variations and differences in treatment of the parallel occasions define the main movement of the poem. Moreover, Christmas is the celebration of a myth which here has a Christian form. That myth is the story of the birth of a child who will usher in a new golden age. The home is where the hero is nurtured, and hence we see the link between the domestic and the heroic that parallels the older link between the pastoral and the heroic. The classical figure of Paris and the Biblical figure of David embody this link. In *In Memoriam*, the link is embodied in Hallam (who becomes the type of the greater man), in the child who is conceived at the end of the poem, and in every individual who struggles to bring mankind closer to 'the crowning race.' By thus focusing on aspects of *In Memoriam* with which the twentieth century has had little sympathy, we begin to understand the dominant character of the poem, and to respond to it more as its original readers may have.

If Tennyson replaced the pastoral with the domestic in *In Memoriam*, one might expect him to do the same in using other genres. And indeed he does, especially with the idyl. The very word suggested the idyllic, and evoked ideas of a rural landscape, a simple life, and a contented state of mind. Tennyson often retained the rural setting, but he shifted the centre of interest to family relations, especially in idyls like *Dora*, *The Miller's Daughter*, *The Gardener's Daughter*, and *The Brook*. There was a corresponding shift in some of the central figures and typical actions. The shepherd swain, for instance, was replaced by modern youths of varying occupations; the singing match and rural festivals gave way to a quest-like approach to a maiden in an enclosed space; and the maiden herself was no blushing shepherdess, but a mysterious figure bearing within herself the vital forces of both nature and civilization, and the seeds of future generations. Her type in pagan myth is Demeter, in Biblical stories, Ruth, and in fairy tales, Sleeping Beauty. Tennyson explored these archetypal figures and actions in *Dora*, *Demeter and Persephone* and *The Day-Dream*, and he was to use them in a variety of ways in many other poems.

For this variety, the idyl was a particularly suitable genre. From earliest times it had been defined as a mixed form, the mixture usually consisting of drama, narrative, and description. The mixture of forms made possible a mixture of effects within a relatively brief genre, and Tennyson, who was attracted by both comprehensiveness and concentration, made brilliant use of this mixture in the idyl and in a closely related form, the epyllion. In *Œnone*, for instance, he treated the Judgment of Paris in such a way as to suggest the encyclopedic range of the *Iliad*. In *Edwin Morris* he gave ironic and melodramatic treatment to the story of an approach to the forbidden maiden, and he treated the same action as tragedy in *Aylmer's Field*.

The tragedy is enhanced in *Aylmer's Field* by the satiric treatment of the heroine's parents, who represent 'marriage-hindering Mammon,' the chief obstacle in the approach of the questing lover to his beloved. Tennyson regularly attacked those who were devoted to Mammon – the parents in *Aylmer's Field*, for instance – and he sometimes portrayed such figures satirically. But he distrusted satire, not because it was wrong in what it attacked, but because it revealed a temper of mind that tended to reduce and abstract, to see the type rather than the individual. This fault is the main concern of *Walking to the Mail*, and the fault is corrected dramatically in the change of heart of the husband in *Sea Dreams*, and of Averill in *Aylmer's Field*. Deformity of mind characterized the satirist, in Tennyson's view, and it is significant that in *Idylls of the King* scorn is allowed as part of the defect of men who are 'halt or hunched' (*Guinevere* 41), while Arthur 'never mocks, / For mockery is the fume of little hearts' (*Guinevere* 627–8).

If the satirist reduces and simplifies, it is the romancer who expands and reveals the complex relatedness of all things. The central action of the earlier idyls – the approach to a maiden in a secret or forbidden place – is, as I have already said, a version of the romance quest, and it was a version that Tennyson found particularly fruitful. The heroic dimensions of the quest Tennyson suggests in the epic and romance styles by which he describes the walk into the country in *Audley Court*, while in *The Princess* he uses a medley of styles to explore the various aspects of the central action.

It is characteristic of Tennyson that when he moves toward romance, he renews the form by modifying it with realism. Romance was popularly associated with the improbable, the exotic, and the imaginative, but the fashion of the day was increasingly the realism which readers expected in literature. It would be surprising if a writer as sensitive to the temper of his times as Tennyson ignored such expectations, and indeed he does not. Frequently he solves the problem by using a frame. The Sleeping Beauty fairy tale is given an ironic modern context in *The Day-Dream*, and *The*

Princess has a modern frame that is related in complex ways to the romance. The most important frame of all is *The Epic*. Though not a part of the final form of *Idylls of the King*, it defines the nature of Tennyson's treatment of romance in that poem. Sir Walter Scott had said at the beginning of the century that if we are to allow the romancer the improbable events and wonderful actions that are the chief mark of romance, then we should expect the human responses to them to be probable and psychologically realistic. Improbable events and characters; probable responses – that is Scott's idea, and it is one that Tennyson puts to good use (though we cannot know whether or not he was familiar with Scott's formula). For he assumes an ideal king, and then shows probable responses to him.

Throughout *Idylls of the King*, these responses are closely related to marriage, or to the relations between man and woman, so that the domestic themes which I explored in the earlier poems are central to Tennyson's major work. In older romances, the chief actions were martial and chivalric in character. These actions Tennyson did not wholly reject, but he subordinated them to an action which was, in his view, both common and crucial: a marriage. The shift in focus parallels the shift to which Milton draws our attention in his epic treatment of the fall of man, from the battles and physical prowess celebrated in the pagan epics to Christian heroism, manifested in obedience to God and expressed in the commonest human actions. In Tennyson's work, such a shift is apparent when he recounts Arthur's twelve great battles briefly but explores at length Arthur's society in its time of 'fallow leisure.' Actions remain, for there are tournaments and journeys and encounters of various sorts, but the crucial events take place within each character, and are summed up in the metaphor of weeding one's heart. The choice involved in separating good and evil within the self is best expressed in marriage, for marriage was, in Tennyson's view, a response to what was best and most human too. Hence he has the fate of Arthur's civilization depend, not on quests and battles, but on the failure of a marriage, an event as common and (from an older point of view) as unheroic as a woman eating an apple. The model for Arthur's society is his marriage to Guinevere, and the actions in the ten central idylls are all, in one way or another, responses to that marriage. In each there is a quest to a secret or forbidden place; in the early idylls there is a release of fertility and vitality, symbolized by fruitful marriages; in the later idylls the quest is a failure, and adulterous or treacherous liaisons replace marriage. In the early idylls, the vitality of Arthur's society is summed up in words – both the marriage vows and the vows the knights take on being admitted to the Order of the Round Table – while the decline of Camelot is linked with slander and with words as hollow and worn-out symbols. In thus shifting the attention of his romance from the more conventionally heroic to the domestic, and from the battle against others to the battle within the self, Tennyson met the standards he set for himself in *The Epic*, and recreated the Arthurian material 'in the fashion of the day.'

That fashion is an increasingly acceptable one for twentieth-century readers, and we are learning to value it more and more. The reaction against Tennyson is now long past, and the critical indifference which succeeded that reaction has passed as well. We have moved beyond those studies that valued only a part of Tennyson's achievement: the symbolist poetry, for instance (poetry which, in Yeats' view, was always being undermined by ideas and moral concerns), or the lyric outpourings of the melancholy Lincolnshire mystic (outpourings which, in Nicolson's view, could not be reconciled with the verses of the well-to-do and popular poet laureate). The idea of two Tennysons no longer fits either our critical preoccupations or our tastes. Perhaps we are ready now to accept Tennyson not only as a modern poet (as Carr argued in 1950) but as the Victorian poet he was; maybe we can now value Tennyson, not in spite of the fact that he was a Victorian, but because of it.

To focus on domestic themes and images, and on the forms of idyl(l) and romance, as I have done, takes us to the centre of Tennyson's art as a Victorian poet. Such concerns will, I hope, seem inevitable when one considers recent studies: by Fredeman and Timko, for instance, on the domestic themes of the *English Idyls* and other poems; by McLuhan, Timko, Hunt, and Culler, on the idyl form itself; by Kincaid, on the comic and ironic patterns and the technique of parody, in the major poems; by Joseph, Johnson, and Killham, on Tennyson's ideas of love, marriage, and the relations between man and woman; and by Frye, on the nature of romance (though he is not specifically concerned with Tennyson). Priestley, Shaw, and Sinfield have done a great deal to help us see Tennyson whole by exploring in him the union of style and subject, of sound and sense, just as Buckley and Culler have helped us to see him whole by exploring the entire canon. The fine studies of *Idylls of the King* by Ryals, Reed, Eggers, and Rosenberg (as well as Gray's work on sources and analogues) have led, gradually but inevitably, to the view that the poem is a major achievement. Culler's work in particular anticipates some of my central concerns. He discusses the sources of spiritual authority in Arthur's society; he sees the first and last idylls as a frame, 'establishing the authority of Arthur as a spiritual absolute';[1] he discusses the implications of the fact that most of the events in the poem take place late in Arthur's reign; he comments on Tennyson's avoidance of magic and the supernatural; and he treats the *Idylls* as a logocentric work.*

To see Tennyson as a Victorian poet is, paradoxically, to understand him as a modern poet. Rosenberg begins his excellent study of the *Idylls* by discussing T.S. Eliot's 'obvious and overriding indebtedness to Tennyson,'[2] and that indebtedness includes, I suspect, not just symbolist techniques, but the idyl and epyllion forms as well. (Is *The Waste Land*, for instance, an epyllion?) One would like to bring the keen ears of Douglas Bush and Paul Turner to the exploration of these forms, for they often depend upon echo and allusion, and echo and allusion are central devices in Eliot's poetry.

Whatever the links with our own age, however, one returns, finally, to Tennyson the Victorian; to *In Memoriam*, not just as an elegy which sums up many of the ideas of the age, but as a domestic elegy which embodies its very character; to the idyls, with all those approaches to maidens in enclosed gardens, a myth so suggestive for Tennyson that his exploration of it demanded a form which was encyclopedic as well as concentrated; and to the *Idylls*, where Tennyson reshaped romance to suit the age's increasing taste for realism, especially of a psychological kind. If this study has any worth, it is in the exploration of these particular themes and patterns and forms, 'So wrought they will not fail.'

---

* Two excellent studies of Tennyson appeared while this book was in the process of being published: Robert Pattison's *Tennyson and Tradition* (Cambridge, Mass.: Harvard University Press 1979) and Henry Kozicki's *Tennyson and Clio: History in the Major Poems* (Baltimore: Johns Hopkins University Press 1979). Pattison's account of the idyl(l) is the fullest and best description that we have yet had of a genre difficult to define precisely; and Kozicki's study of the poems in the context of Niebuhr, Carlyle, Hegel, and others is illuminating, especially in providing one answer to the question that every reader of the *Idylls* must face: why did Camelot fail?

Notes

All quotations of Tennyson's poetry are from the text edited by Christopher Ricks (London: Longmans, Green and Co. Ltd. 1969).

INTRODUCTION

1 *Language and Structure in Tennyson's Poetry* 169
2 *Sesame and Lilies*; *The Two Paths*; *The King of the Golden River* 59
3 Houghton *The Victorian Frame of Mind, 1830–1870* 344. The whole section which Houghton calls 'Home, Sweet Home' is valuable and suggestive. Also very good is Jenni Calder's *The Victorian Home*, especially the first chapter, which she calls 'The Place of Peace.' Her *The Victorian and Edwardian Home from Old Photographs* is an interesting visual record.
4 James R. Kincaid (*Tennyson's Major Poems. The Comic and Ironic Patterns* 96–8), K.W. Gransden (*Tennyson: In Memoriam* 14–15), and others have pointed out how pervasive are the references to home and family in the poem. A. Dwight Culler's comments on Tennyson's avoidance of the pastoral elegy provide a different view of the material I am dealing with (*The Poetry of Tennyson* 149–51).

CHAPTER 1

1 The phrases are from *The Morning Post* (31 August 1850) 2, and *The Spectator* 23 (8 June 1850) 546, respectively.
2 NS 6 (July 1850) 439
3 Vol 12 (August 1850) 120
4 NS 28 (September 1850) 330–41

5 Vol 54 (October 1850) 92. The reference is to Mary in the story of Lazarus. The *Wellesley Index* identifies the reviewer, who signs himself Is. Is., only as Adams.

6 *The Inquirer* 9 (22 June 1850) 389

7 G.C., 'Modern and Recent Poetry. II – Recent' *The Edinburgh News and Literary Chronicle* (25 May 1850) 8

8 Vol 25 (15 June 1850) 379

9 Vol 1 (22 June 1850) 303

10 'The Poetry of Sorrow' (28 November 1851) 8. The evidence that the review may have been written by Manley Hopkins is given by Humphrey House in 'The Hopkinses' *Times Literary Supplement* 48 (4 November 1949) 715.

11 Quoted by Hallam Tennyson in *Alfred Lord Tennyson. A Memoir* I, 304. Hereafter referred to as *Memoir*.

12 Ibid. I, 305

13 *Language and Structure in Tennyson's Poetry* 120

14 *Memoir* I, 304

15 *Language and Structure in Tennyson's Poetry* 120

16 No 2210 (8 June 1850) 357

17 *The Language of Tennyson's 'In Memoriam'* 85

18 *A Commentary on Tennyson's 'In Memoriam'* 201

19 *Tennyson and 'The Princess.' Reflections of an Age* 263

20 NS 28 (September 1850) 335

21 *The Language of Tennyson's 'In Memoriam'* 125, 126

22 Valerie Pitt has already pointed out that the domestic analogies universalize the emotion, in *Tennyson Laureate* 116–17.

23 See Wendell Stacy Johnson's sensible treatment of the marriage metaphor in *Sex and Marriage in Victorian Poetry* 135–43.

24 *A Commentary on Tennyson's 'In Memoriam'* 99; *The Language of Tennyson's 'In Memoriam'* 96

25 *Memoir* I, 369

26 *Elizabethan Poetry. A Study in Conventions, Meaning, and Expression* 2, 9

27 *Memoir* I, 44

28 *The Language of Tennyson's 'In Memoriam'* 130, 131

29 As Sinfield has pointed out, 'Matter-moulded Forms of Speech: Tennyson's Use of Language in *In Memoriam*' in *The Major Victorian Poets: Reconsiderations* 62

30 Sinfield 'Matter-moulded Forms of Speech' 65, 66

31 Priestley *Language and Structure in Tennyson's Poetry* 161

32 'Time, the Timeless, and the Timely: Notes on a Victorian Poem' *Transactions of the Royal Society of Canada* (fourth series) 9 (1971) 223
33 *The Language of Tennyson's 'In Memoriam'* 55
34 *Memoir* I, 304
35 Quoted by James Knowles 'Aspects of Tennyson. II (A Personal Reminiscence)' *The Nineteenth Century* 33 (January 1893) 182

CHAPTER 2

1 Quoted by Philip Henderson *Tennyson: Poet and Prophet* 193
2 *Memoir* I 506–7
3 *Memoir* II, 506
4 'Preface to an Uncollected Anthology' in *Contexts of Canadian Criticism* 196
5 See Hallett Smith *Elizabethan Poetry* 3–9
6 *Memoir* I, 196
7 *The Works of Mary Russell Mitford* 209
8 *Memoir* I, 213
9 P 222
10 Tennyson himself apparently regarded it as such. F.T. Palgrave records that he once asked Tennyson, 'Why do you not write an Idyll upon the story of Ruth?' Tennyson answered, 'Do you think I could make it more poetical?' (*Memoir* II, 500).
11 I, 189
12 II, 364
13 II, 364
14 See, for instance, G. Robert Stange 'Tennyson's Mythology: A Study of *Demeter and Persephone*' in *Critical Essays on the Poetry of Tennyson* 148; and James Kissane 'Victorian Mythology' *Victorian Studies* 6 (September 1962) 27. Kissane points out that the passage is really the expression of Tennyson's evolutionism, and that the poem as a whole is concerned with the totality of human experience.
15 As Kissane points out, p 28
16 'Tennyson's mythology' 149
17 See Richard Stingle 'William Morris' *Association of Canadian University Teachers of English Report* (1960) 5.
18 As F.E.L. Priestley argues; see 'Tennyson' *University of Toronto Quarterly* 32 (October 1962) 105; and *Language and Structure in Tennyson's Poetry* 112–13.
19 *Memoir* I, 166
20 Ibid II, 230

21 *Theocritus' Coan Pastorals* 2
22 'Preliminary Remarks on the Life and Writings of Theocritus' in *The Idylls and Epigrams [of] Theocritus* xiii
23 *Memoir* I, 117
24 Ibid. I, 197
25 *Tennyson's 'Idylls of the King' and Arthurian Story from the XVIth Century* 308
26 *Memoir* I, 383; II, 495
27 P xxi
28 *The Epyllion from Theocritus to Ovid* 22, 24
29 'Some Ancient Light on Tennyson's *Œnone*' *Journal of English and Germanic Philology* 61 (1962) 71
30 As Ricks points out in his note on *Ilion, Ilion* 258
31 'Some Ancient Light on Tennyson's *Œnone*' 57
32 Ibid. 64–5
33 Ibid. 65
34 *Quarterly Review* 70 (September 1842) 393
35 *Theocritus' Coan Pastorals* 42
36 This analysis of *Walking to the Mail* is not new. For similar accounts, see Culler *The Poetry of Tennyson* 123–5; Kincaid *Tennyson's Major Poems: The Comic and Ironic Patterns* 225–6; and Turner *Tennyson* 83–4. It seems to me helpful, however, to see the poem as part of Tennyson's attack on the temper of mind of the satirist.
37 *Language and Structure in Tennyson's Poetry* 94–5
38 Ibid. 102
39 Ibid. 103
40 Ibid. 104
41 *Tennyson* 179
42 *Language and Structure in Tennyson's Poetry* 79
43 'A Study of Myth and Archetype in "Enoch Arden"' *Tennyson Research Bulletin* 2 (November 1974) 106
44 *Language and Structure in Tennyson's Poetry* 78
45 *Theocritus' Coan Pastorals* 5, 12
46 Ibid. 3
47 *Tennyson: The Growth of a Poet* 80

CHAPTER 3

1 Northrop Frye defines the three main stages of the quest thus in *Anatomy of Criticism* 187. I am deeply indebted to the section on romance in the *Anatomy* (pp 186–206), and to *The Secular Scripture*. Frye's work enables us to see how

good were some of the nineteenth-century critics of this form. See in particular Scott's *Essay on Romance* and the first chapter of *Waverley*.

2 *Tennyson and 'The Princess.' Reflections of an Age* 186, 188
3 *Memoir* I, 251
4 *Language and Structure in Tennyson's Poetry* 80
5 Ibid. 81
6 See also Joseph's statement: 'Psyche and Blanche are extensions of Ida, two contending sides of herself who are jealous of each other and bicker throughout the narrative' (*Tennysonian Love. The Strange Diagonal* 87).
7 Davies *The Mythology and Rites of the British Druids* 224–5
8 *Memoir* I, 254
9 *A Study: with Critical and Explanatory Notes of Lord Tennyson's Poem 'The Princess'* 35
10 Ibid. 35
11 Ibid. 35–7
12 Ibid. viii
13 Ibid. 29
14 Ibid. 30
15 Ibid. 30–1
16 Ibid. 31
17 Ibid. viii–ix
18 '*The Princess*: The Education of the Prince' *Victorian Poetry* 11 (Winter 1973) 285–94
19 *Memoir* I, 253

CHAPTER 4

1 I cannot agree with Kincaid's statement that 'Tennyson was perhaps least in sympathy with the genre of romance,' nor can I agree with him that comedy, tragedy, and romance appear in the poem 'only in parody' (*Tennyson's Major Poems. The Comic and Ironic Patterns* 151). These forms and the parodies of them are both present in this work. Rosenberg's comments on romance, particularly in relation to symbolist poetry, are illuminating (*The Fall of Camelot. A Study of Tennyson's 'Idylls of the King'* 103 and passim).
2 *Memoir* I, 194
3 *Progress of Romance* 14
4 *Essays on Chivalry, Romance, and the Drama* 92
5 'Remarks on *Frankenstein*' *Blackwood's Edinburgh Magazine* 2 (March 1818) 614
6 *Perception and Design in Tennyson's 'Idylls of the King'* 150. See also Cullen's

argument that 'Arthur is the great spiritual authority that dominates the poem' (*The Poetry of Tennyson* 217).

7 There is, however, much in the theme and style of *Idylls of the King* that suggests the classical epic. See Turner *Tennyson* 163–4.

8 *Works* v, 450

9 *A Variorum Edition of Tennyson's 'Idylls of the King'* 30

10 Culler comments that 'Tennyson has written an entire poem on King Arthur and his knights without one single instance of magic or the supernatural offered on the poet's own authority' (*The Poetry of Tennyson* 225) and goes on to talk about Tennyson's practice in an illuminating way (pp 225–36). Shaw (*Tennyson's Style* 202) and Rosenberg (*The Fall of Camelot. A Study of Tennyson's 'Idylls of the King'* 58) also deal with this method of presenting the story.

11 *Man and Myth in Victorian England: Tennyson's 'The Coming of Arthur'* 5

12 Ibid. 6

13 Rosenberg has commented on the 'ever-foreshortening time-scale' of the *Idylls* (*The Fall of Camelot. A Study of Tennyson's 'Idylls of the King'* 56), and Culler is good in discussing the fact that Tennyson has chosen to describe events that occur late in Arthur's reign (*The Poetry of Tennyson* 219–20).

14 Quoted by Sir Charles Tennyson in *Alfred Tennyson* 491

15 'The power of the word is central in the *Idylls*,' argues Culler (*The Poetry of Tennyson* 236).

16 'Under the Microscope' in *The Complete Works of Algernon Charles Swinburne* VI, 405

17 *Memoir* II, 133

18 *Tennyson in Lincoln. A Catalogue of the Collections in the Research Centre* volume I, item #836

19 *A New System, or, an Analysis of Ancient Mythology* I, xiii

20 *The Origin of Pagan Idolatry* I, 21

21 *Memoir* I, 20

22 See also the discussion of the sea imagery by Ryals in *From the Great Deep. Essays on 'Idylls of the King'* 57–68.

23 Tom Peete Cross 'Alfred Tennyson as a Celticist' *Modern Philology* 18 (January 1921) 485–92; Gerhard Joseph *Tennysonian Love. The Strange Diagonal* 167–9.

24 *Memoir* II, 123

25 'Tennyson's "Gareth and Lynette"' *Texas Studies in Literature and Language* 13 (Winter 1972) 664

26 *Memoir* II, 127

27 Herbert G. Wright 'Tennyson and Wales' *Essays and Studies* 14 (1929) 71–103; J. Philip Eggers 'The Weeding of the Garden: Tennyson's Geraint Idylls and *The Mabinogion*' *Victorian Poetry* 4 (Winter 1966) 45–51

28 Eggers 46
29 Quotations from *Geraint the Son of Erbin* are from Lady Charlotte Guest's translation of *The Mabinogion*. Page references will be inserted in the text.
30 'Introduction' to Tennyson *The Marriage of Geraint. Geraint and Enid* xlv
31 'Aspects of Tennyson. II (A Personal Reminiscence)' *The Nineteenth Century* 33 (January 1893) 165
32 'The Argument of the Geraint-Enid Books in *Idylls of the King*' *Victorian Poetry* 2 (Autumn 1964) 273
33 'Source and Symbol in "Geraint and Enid": Tennyson's Doorm and Limours' *Victorian Poetry* 4 (Spring 1966) 132
34 Poston 270
35 *Tennyson's Doppelgänger: Balin and Balan* 9
36 *Memoir* I, 449
37 *Perception and Design in Tennyson's 'Idylls of the King'* 81
38 Ibid. 78
39 *Memoir* I, 320; II, 473–4
40 'Percivale, Ambrosius, and the Method of Narration in "The Holy Grail"' *Die Neueren Sprachen* 12 (1963) 533–43
41 *Memoir* II, 63
42 Ibid. II, 90
43 Ibid. II, 90
44 See, for instance, Boyd Litzinger 'The Structure of Tennyson's "The Last Tournament"' *Victorian Poetry* 1 (January 1963) 53–60; and Masao Miyoshi 'Narrative Sequence and the Moral System: Three Tristram Poems' *Victorian Newsletter* no 35 (Spring 1969) 5–10.
45 'Tennyson's "Gareth and Lynette"' *Texas Studies in Literature and Language* 13 (Winter 1972) 664
46 *Perception and Design in Tennyson's 'Idylls of the King'* 72
47 *Memoir* I, 189

CONCLUSION

1 *The Poetry of Tennyson* 217
2 *The Fall of Camelot* 2

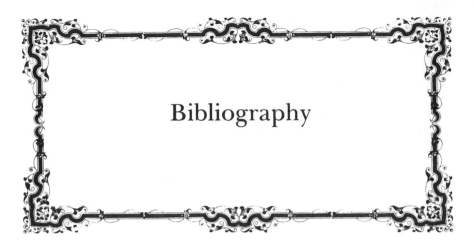

Bibliography

[Adams] Review of *In Memoriam*. *Westminster and Foreign Quarterly Review* 54 (October 1850) 85–103

Adler, Thomas P. 'The Uses of Knowledge in Tennyson's *Merlin and Vivien*' *Texas Studies in Literature and Language* 11 (Winter 1970) 1397–1403

Anonymous Review of *In Memoriam*. *The Atlas* 25 (15 June 1850) 379; (29 June 1850) 411

– Review of *In Memoriam*. *The Christian Reformer* NS 6 (July 1850) 439–41

– Review of *In Memoriam*. *Eclectic Review* NS 28 (September 1850) 330–41

– Review of *In Memoriam*. *The Inquirer* 9 (22 June 1850) 389–90

– Review of *In Memoriam*. *The Morning Post* (31 August 1850) 2

– Review of *In Memoriam*. *Sharpe's London Journal* 12 (August 1850) 119–21

– Review of *In Memoriam*. *The Spectator* 23 (8 June 1850) 546

– *Treatise on the Progress of Literature, and its Effects on Society; including a Sketch of the Progress of English and Scottish Literature* Edinburgh: Adam and Charles Black 1834

Beattie, James 'On Fable and Romance' in *Dissertations Moral and Critical* Philadelphia: Hopkins and Earle 1809, III, 1–113

Bible *The Interpreter's Bible* 12 vols. New York and Nashville: Abingdon Press 1953

Bradley, A.C. *A Commentary on Tennyson's 'In Memoriam'* third edition, revised. London: Macmillan 1915

Bryant, Jacob *A New System, or, an Analysis of Ancient Mythology* 3 vols. London 1774–6

Buckley, Jerome Hamilton *Tennyson. The Growth of a Poet* Cambridge, Mass.: Harvard University Press 1961

Burstein, Janet 'Victorian Mythography and the Progress of the Intellect' *Victorian Studies* 18 (March 1975) 309–24

Bush, Douglas *Mythology and the Romantic Tradition in English Poetry* Cambridge, Mass: Harvard University Press 1937

Calder, Jenni *The Victorian and Edwardian Home from Old Photographs* London: Batsford 1979

– *The Victorian Home* London: Batsford 1977

Campbell, Nancie, compiler *Tennyson in Lincoln. A Catalogue of the Collections in the Research Centre* vol I. Lincoln: Tennyson Society 1971

Claudian *Claudian* with an English translation by Maurice Platnauer. 2 vols. Loeb Classical Library. London: William Heinemann; Cambridge, Mass.: Harvard University Press 1956

Collins, Winston 'The Princess. The Education of the Prince' *Victorian Poetry* 11 (Winter 1973) 285–94

Cross, Tom Peete 'Alfred Tennyson as a Celticist' *Modern Philology* 18 (January 1921) 485–92

Crump, M. Marjorie *The Epyllion from Theocritus to Ovid* Oxford: Basil Blackwell 1931

Culler, A. Dwight *The Poetry of Tennyson* New Haven: Yale University Press 1977

Davies, Edward *The Mythology and Rites of the British Druids* London: J. Booth 1809

Dawson, S.E. *A Study; with Critical and Explanatory Notes, of Lord Tennyson's Poem 'The Princess'* Montreal: Dawson Brothers 1882; second edition 1884

Dunlop, John Colin *History of Prose Fiction* 2 vols. New York: AMS Press 1969 (first published as *The History of Fiction* London 1814)

Edmonds, J.M., translator *The Greek Bucolic Poets* Loeb Classical Library. London: William Heinemann; New York: Macmillan 1912

Eggers, J. Philip *King Arthur's Laureate. A Study of Tennyson's 'Idylls of the King'* New York: New York University Press 1971

– 'The Weeding of the Garden: Tennyson's Geraint Idylls and *The Mabinogion*' *Victorian Poetry* 4 (Winter 1966) 45–51

Faber, George Stanley *The Origin of Pagan Idolatry ascertained from Historical Testimony and Circumstantial Evidence* 3 vols. London: F. and C. Rivingtons 1816

[Forster, John] Review of *In Memoriam. The Examiner* no 2210 (8 June 1850) 356–7

Fredeman, William E. '"The Sphere of Common Duties": The Domestic Solution in Tennyson's Poetry' *Bulletin of the John Rylands Library* 54 (Spring 1972) 357–83

Fricke, Douglas C. 'A Study of Myth and Archetype in "Enoch Arden"' *Tennyson Research Bulletin* 2 (November 1974) 106–15

Frye, Northrop *Anatomy of Criticism: Four Essays* Princeton: Princeton University Press 1957

– 'Preface to an Uncollected Anthology' *Contexts of Canadian Criticism* ed Eli Mandel. Chicago: University of Chicago Press 1971, pp. 181–97

- *The Secular Scripture. A Study of the Structure of Romance* Cambridge, Mass.: Harvard University Press 1976
G.C. 'Recent Poetry. IV. – Tennyson' *The Edinburgh News and Literary Chronicle* (24 August 1850) 8; (14 September 1850) 8
- 'Modern and Recent Poetry. II. – Recent' *The Edinburgh News and Literary Chronicle* (25 May 1850) 8
Gilfillan, George *A Second Gallery of Literary Portraits* Edinburgh: James Hogg 1850
Gransden, K.W. *Tennyson: In Memoriam* Studies in English Literature, no 22. London: Edward Arnold 1964
Gray, J.M. *Man and Myth in Victorian England: Tennyson's 'The Coming of Arthur'* Lincoln: Tennyson Society 1969
- 'Source and Symbol in "Geraint and Enid": Tennyson's Doorm and Limours' *Victorian Poetry* 4 (Spring 1966) 131–2
- *Tennyson's Doppelgänger: Balin and Balan* Lincoln: Tennyson Society 1971
- 'Two Transcendental Ladies of Tennyson's *Idylls*: The Lady of the Lake and Vivien' *Tennyson Research Bulletin* 1 (November 1970) 104–5
Grube, G.M.A. *The Greek and Roman Critics* Toronto: University of Toronto Press 1965
Guest, Charlotte, translator *The Mabinogion, from the Llyfr Coch o Hergest, and other Ancient Welsh Manuscripts* 3 vols. London: Longman, Brown, Green, and Longmans; Llandovery: W. Rees 1849
Henderson, Philip *Tennyson: Poet and Prophet.* London: Routledge & Kegan Paul 1978
[Hopkins, Manley?] 'The Poetry of Sorrow' *The Times* (28 November 1851) 8
Houghton, Walter E. *The Victorian Frame of Mind 1830–1870* New Haven: Yale University Press 1957
Hunt, John Dixon 'The Poetry of Distance: Tennyson's "Idylls of the King"' *Victorian Poetry* ed Malcolm Bradbury and David Palmer. Stratford-upon-Avon Studies, no 15. London: Edward Arnold 1972, pp. 88–121
- '"Story Painters and Picture Writers": Tennyson's Idylls and Victorian Painting' *Tennyson* ed D.J. Palmer. Writers and Their Background. London: G. Bell 1973, pp 180–202
–, ed *Tennyson. In Memoriam. A Casebook.* London: Macmillan 1970
Johnson, E.D.H. 'The Lily and the Rose: Symbolic Meaning in Tennyson's *Maud*' *Publications of the Modern Language Association* 64 (December 1949) 1222–7
Johnson, Wendell Stacy *Sex and Marriage in Victorian Poetry* Ithaca: Cornell University Press 1975
Joseph, Gerhard *Tennysonian Love. The Strange Diagonal* Minneapolis: University of Minnesota Press 1969

Jump, John D., ed *Tennyson. The Critical Heritage* London: Routledge & Kegan Paul; New York: Barnes & Noble 1967

Kennedy, Ian H.C. *'In Memoriam* and the Tradition of Pastoral Elegy' *Victorian Poetry* 15 (Winter 1977) 351–66

Killham, John, ed *Critical Essays on the Poetry of Tennyson* London: Routledge & Kegan Paul 1960

– *Tennyson and 'The Princess.' Reflections of an Age* London: Athlone Press 1958

Kincaid, James R. 'Tennyson's "Gareth and Lynette"' *Texas Studies in Literature and Language* 13 (Winter 1972) 663–71

– *Tennyson's Major Poems. The Comic and Ironic Patterns* New Haven: Yale University Press 1975

Kissane, James 'Victorian Mythology' *Victorian Studies* 6 (September 1962) 5–28

Knowles, James 'Aspects of Tennyson. II. (A Personal Reminiscence)' *The Nineteenth Century* 33 (January 1893) 164–88

Lawall, Gilbert *Theocritus' Coan Pastorals. A Poetry Book* Washington, D.C.: The Center for Hellenic Studies 1967

Lawry, J.S. 'Tennyson's "The Epic": A Gesture of Recovered Faith' *Modern Language Notes* 74 (May 1959) 400–3

[Lewes, George Henry] Review of *In Memoriam. The Leader* 1 (22 June 1850) 303–4

Litzinger, Boyd 'The Structure of Tennyson's "The Last Tournament"' *Victorian Poetry* 1 (January 1963) 53–60

[Lushington, Franklin] Review of *In Memoriam. Tait's Edinburgh Magazine* 17 (August 1850) 499–505

Macaulay, G.C., ed Tennyson *The Marriage of Geraint. Geraint and Enid* London: Macmillan 1892

MacCallum, Mungo W. *Tennyson's 'Idylls of the King' and Arthurian Story from the XVIth Century* Freeport, N.Y.: Books for Libraries Press 1971 (first published in 1894)

Marinelli, Peter V. *Pastoral* The Critical Idiom, ed John D. Jump. London: Methuen 1971

Mayor, Joseph B.; Fowler, W. Warde; Conway, R.S. *Virgil's Messianic Eclogue. Its Meaning, Occasion, & Sources. Three Studies* London: John Murray 1907

McLuhan, Marshall 'Introduction' to *Alfred Lord Tennyson. Selected Poetry* New York: Holt, Rinehart and Winston 1956

– 'Tennyson and Picturesque Poetry' and 'Tennyson and the Romantic Epic' in *Critical Essays on the Poetry of Tennyson* ed John Killham (London: Routledge & Kegan Paul 1960) 67–95

Mitford, Mary Russell *The Works of Mary Russell Mitford, Prose and Verse* Philadelphia: Crissy & Markley n.d. [1846?]

Miyoshi, Masao 'Narrative Sequence and the Moral System: Three Tristram Poems' *Victorian Newsletter* no 35 (Spring 1969) 5–10

Paden, W.D. *Tennyson in Egypt. A Study of the Imagery in his Earlier Work* University of Kansas Publications, Humanistic Studies, no 27 (Lawrence, Kansas: University of Kansas 1942) 75–88

Pater, Walter 'The Myth of Demeter and Persephone' in *Greek Studies. A Series of Essays* (London: Macmillan 1910) 81–151

Perrault, Charles *Contes* Paris: Éditions Garnier Frères 1967

– *Perrault's Popular Tales* ed Andrew Lang. Oxford: Clarendon Press 1888

Pettigrew, John *Tennyson: The Early Poems* Studies in English Literature, no 41. London: Edward Arnold 1970

Pfordresher, John 'A Bibliographic History of Alfred Tennyson's *Idylls of the King*' *Studies in Bibliography* 26 (1973) 193–218

– *A Variorum Edition of Tennyson's 'Idylls of the King'* New York: Columbia University Press 1973

Pitt, Valerie *Tennyson Laureate* Toronto: University of Toronto Press 1962

Poston, Lawrence, III 'The Argument of the Geraint-Enid Books in *Idylls of the King*' *Victorian Poetry* 2 (Autumn 1964) 269–75

Priestley, F.E.L. 'Control of Tone in Tennyson's *The Princess*' *Transactions of the Royal Society of Canada* (fourth series) 1 (June 1963) 295–304

– *Language and Structure in Tennyson's Poetry* The Language Library, ed Eric Partridge and Simeon Potter. London: André Deutsch 1973

– 'Tennyson' [Review of Buckley, *Tennyson. The Growth of a Poet*] *University of Toronto Quarterly* 32 (October 1962) 102–6

– 'Tennyson's *Idylls*' *University of Toronto Quarterly* 19 (October 1949) 35–49

Reed, John R. *Perception and Design in Tennyson's 'Idylls of the King'* Athens, Ohio: Ohio University Press 1969

Reeve, Clara *The Progress of Romance and the History of Charoba, Queen of Aegypt* New York: The Facsimile Text Society 1930

Rosenberg, John D. *The Fall of Camelot. A Study of Tennyson's 'Idylls of the King'* Cambridge, Mass.: Belknap Press 1973

Rosenmeyer, Thomas G. *The Green Cabinet. Theocritus and the European Pastoral Lyric* Berkeley and Los Angeles: University of California Press 1969

Ross, Malcolm 'Time, The Timeless, and The Timely: Notes on a Victorian Poem' *Transactions of the Royal Society of Canada* (fourth series) 9 (1971) 219–34

Ruskin, John *Sesame and Lilies; The Two Paths; The King of the Golden River* Everyman's Library. London: Dent 1907

Ryals, Clyde de L. *From the Great Deep. Essays on 'Idylls of the King'* Athens, Ohio: Ohio University Press 1967

- 'Percivale, Ambrosius, and the Method of Narration in "The Holy Grail"' *Die Neueren Sprachen* 12 (1963) 533-43
Scott, P.G. *Tennyson's 'Enoch Arden': A Victorian Best-Seller* Lincoln: Tennyson Society 1970
Scott, Sir Walter *Essays on Chivalry, Romance, and the Drama* The Chandos Classics. London: Frederick Warne and Co. [1868]
- 'Remarks on *Frankenstein*' *Blackwood's Edinburgh Magazine* 2 (March 1818) 613-20
- *Waverley* London: T. Nelson and Sons n.d.
Sendry, Joseph '*In Memoriam* and *Lycidas*' *Publications of the Modern Language Association* 82 (October 1967) 437-43
Shannon, Edgar Finley, Jr *Tennyson and the Reviewers. A Study of his Literary Reputation and of the Influence of the Critics upon his Poetry 1827-1851* Hamden, Connecticut: Archon Books 1967 (first published 1952)
Shaw, W. David *Tennyson's Style* Ithaca: Cornell University Press 1976
Sinfield, Alan *The Language of Tennyson's 'In Memoriam'* Oxford: Basil Blackwell 1971
- 'Matter-moulded Forms of Speech: Tennyson's Use of Language in *In Memoriam*' in *The Major Victorian Poets: Reconsiderations* ed. Isobel Armstrong (London: Routledge & Kegan Paul 1969) 51-67
Smith, Hallett *Elizabethan Poetry. A Study in Conventions, Meaning, and Expression* Cambridge, Mass.: Harvard University Press 1952
[Spedding, James] Review of Tennyson's *Poems. Edinburgh Review* 77 (April 1843) 373-91
Stange, G. Robert 'Tennyson's Mythology: A Study of *Demeter and Persephone*' in *Critical Essays on the Poetry of Tennyson* ed John Killham (London: Routledge & Kegan Paul 1960) pp 137-50
[Sterling, John] Review of *Poems* by Alfred Tennyson. *Quarterly Review* 70 (September 1842) 385-416
Stingle, Richard 'William Morris' *Association of Canadian University Teachers of English Report* 1960
Swinburne, Algernon Charles 'Under the Microscope' in *The Complete Works of Algernon Charles Swinburne* ed Sir Edmund Gosse and T.J. Wise. The Bonchurch Edition (New York: Russell and Russell 1968) VI, 375-444
Taylor, Edgar, ed *German Popular Stories* A New Edition, with introduction by John Ruskin. London: John Camden Hotten 1869
Tennyson, Alfred *Works* annotated by Alfred Lord Tennyson; edited by Hallam, Lord Tennyson. The Eversley Edition, 9 vols. New York: AMS Press 1970 (reprinted from the London edition of 1907-8)

— *The Poems of Tennyson* ed Christopher Ricks. Longmans' Annotated English Poets. London: Longmans 1969

Tennyson, Charles *Alfred Tennyson* London: Macmillan 1949

— 'The Idylls of the King' *The Twentieth Century* 161 (March 1957) 277–86

[Tennyson, Hallam] *Alfred Lord Tennyson. A Memoir by his Son* 2 vols. London: Macmillan 1897.

Theocritus *The Idylls and Epigrams commonly attributed to Theocritus* with English notes by Herbert Snow. Oxford: Clarendon Press 1869; second edition 1873

Tillotson, Kathleen 'Tennyson's Serial Poem' in *Mid-Victorian Studies* by Geoffrey and Kathleen Tillotson (London: Athlone Press 1965) 80–109

Timko, Michael '"The Central Wish": Human Passion and Cosmic Love in Tennyson's Idyls' *Victorian Poetry* 16 (Spring-Summer 1978) 1–15

— 'Arnold, Tennyson, and the English Idyl: Ancient Criticism and Modern Poetry' *Texas Studies in Literature and Language* 16 (Spring 1974) 135–46

Turner, Paul 'Some Ancient Light on Tennyson's *Œnone*' *Journal of English and Germanic Philology* 61 (1962) 57–72

— *Tennyson* Routledge Author Guides. London: Routledge & Kegan Paul 1976

Wendel, Charles, ed *Scholia in Theocritum Vetera* Stuttgart: B.G. Teubner 1967

Wright, Herbert G. 'Tennyson and Wales' *Essays and Studies* 14 (1929) 71–103

Zuckermann, Joanne P. 'Tennyson's *In Memoriam* as Love Poetry' *Dalhousie Review* 51 (Summer 1971) 202–17

Index